UNIVERSITY OF NORTH CAROLINA AT CHAPEL HILL
DEPARTMENT OF ROMANCE LANGUAGES

NORTH CAROLINA STUDIES
IN THE ROMANCE LANGUAGES AND LITERATURES

Founder: URBAN TIGNER HOLMES

Editor: CAROL L. SHERMAN

Distributed by:

UNIVERSITY OF NORTH CAROLINA PRESS

CHAPEL HILL
North Carolina 27515-2288
U.S.A.

NORTH CAROLINA STUDIES IN THE
ROMANCE LANGUAGES AND LITERATURES
Number 260

GALDÓS'S *SEGUNDA MANERA*

GALDÓS'S
SEGUNDA MANERA
Rhetorical Strategies and
Affective Response

BY

LINDA M. WILLEM

CHAPEL HILL

NORTH CAROLINA STUDIES IN THE ROMANCE
LANGUAGES AND LITERATURES
U.N.C. DEPARTMENT OF ROMANCE LANGUAGES

1998

863
P438 /x wu

Library of Congress Cataloging-in-Publication Data

Willem, Linda M.
    Galdós's segunda manera: rhetorical strategies and affective response / by Linda M. Willem.
    p. – cm. – (North Carolina studies in the Romance languages & literatures; no. 260).
    Includes bibliographical references.
    ISBN 0-8078-9264-5 (pbk.)
    1. Pérez Galdós, Benito, 1843-1920 – Technique. 2. Narration (Rhetoric) I. Title.
II. Series.

PQ6555.Z5W55   1999   98-33882
863'.5 – dc21   CIP

Publication-support granted by the Program for Cultural Cooperation between Spain's Ministry of Education and Culture and United States' Universities.

Cover: Narciso Méndez Bringa, *Madrid – Una tarde de Semana Santa en Las Cuatro Calles*. From *La Ilustración Española y Americana*, April 22, 1895.

Cover design: Shelley Gruendler

ISBN 0-8078-9264-5

IMPRESO EN ESPAÑA

PRINTED IN SPAIN

DEPÓSITO LEGAL: V. 816 - 1999

ARTES GRÁFICAS SOLER, S. L. - LA OLIVERETA, 28 - 46018 VALENCIA

AE)-0044

TABLE OF CONTENTS

ACKNOWLEDGMENTS

One becomes indebted to many people over the course of a project such as this, and mentioning them on an acknowledgments page seems far too little payment for what has been received. Nevertheless, it is my hope that all who have contributed to the making of this book will sense the depth of gratitude behind these few words. Above all, I would like to thank Geoffrey Ribbans, Harriet Turner, Vernon Chamberlin, and James Phelan for reading portions of this manuscript. Their comments were often insightful, always useful, and occasionally quite challenging. I sincerely appreciate the time that went into them. I am further grateful to James Phelan for including me in his 1995 NEH Seminar entitled Issues in the Rhetorical Theory of Narrative: Form, Ideology, Ethics, and Audiences. Many of the ideas in this book took shape as a result of the readings that were assigned and discussions that took place during those eight weeks of blazing hot summer at Ohio State. Jim's support and expertise, along with the lively after-hours conversations among the participants, made that seminar one of the most professionally rewarding experiences of my career. I also wish to thank Butler University for the travel grants they provided which allowed me to examine Galdós's manuscripts and galleys at the Casa-Museo Pérez Galdós in Las Palmas and the Biblioteca Nacional in Madrid. The director of Galdós's archives in the Canary Islands, Rosa María Quintana Domínguez, was particularly helpful in meeting my research needs. Finally, I would like express my appreciation to Rubén Benítez, whose graduate class on Galdós at UCLA inspired me to specialize in nineteenth-century Spanish literature. As a result, I have had the good fortune to spend the last decade among

Galdosian colleagues who are the very essence of professionalism and congeniality.

Parts of chapters two and three first appeared, in substantially the same form, as the following articles: "The Narrative Voice Presentation of Rosalía de Bringas in Two Galdosian Novels," *Crítica Hispánica* 12 (1990): 75-87 and "The Narrative Premise of Galdós's *Lo prohibido*," *Romance Quarterly* 38 (1991): 189-96. I extend my thanks to the editors of these journals for giving their permission to reproduce this material.

On a more personal note, I cannot conclude these remarks without mentioning the encouragement, patience, and much-needed sense of humor of my husband, Stephen Asunto.

INTRODUCTION

> Authors play games with readers,
> and the text is the playground.
>
> Wolfgang Iser

My three-pronged approach to Galdós's *segunda manera* is summarized in the few words that make up the epigram above. [1] The game-playing relationship which Iser indicates between the author and the reader implies the use of strategies and a reliance on agreed-upon rules. These strategies and rules correspond, respectively, to the rhetorical and reader-response aspects of my analysis. In addition, the image of a playground suggests not only a field to play *on* but also the presence of apparatus to play *with*. That apparatus is taken into account by the narratological facet of my examination. Throughout this book, then, I will employ a pluralistic approach which combines narratology with both rhetorical and reader response criticism. The narratological terminology will allow me to identify and analyze the various aspects of Galdós's narrative presentation, while rhetorical and reader response theories will allow me to place his new mode of presentation within the context of its role in the communication between the author and the reader. Thus, I will focus on narrative technique, but I will emphasize the affective quality of the text, thereby examining the ways that technique influences the reading experience.

---

[1] Wolfgang Iser, *Prospecting: From Reader Response to Literary Anthropology* (Baltimore: Johns Hopkins UP, 1989) 250.

11

The subject of my study is Galdós's *segunda manera*, so called because of the now-famous letter which Galdós wrote to D. Francisco Giner. In it Galdós stated: "Efectivamente, yo he querido en esta obra entrar por nuevo camino o inaugurar mi *segunda* o tercera *manera*, como se dice de los pintores (Galdós's emphasis)." [2] That novel, of course, was *La desheredada*, and with it Galdós truly did mark the beginning of a new phase in his literary production. After his break with "La Guirnalda" editorial house in 1897, Galdós formalized the distinction between his early and later work by separating his novels into three categories – *Episodios Nacionales, Novelas de la Primera Época* (*La Fontana de Oro* through *La familia de León Roch*), and *Novelas Españolas Contemporáneas* – thereby distinguishing the novels of this "nuevo camino" from the historical and thesis novels that preceded them.

As can be imagined, Galdós's shift toward a different kind of writing has occasioned a great deal of critical interest. Discussion of what constitutes Galdós's new *manera* in *La desheredada* has largely centered on the issue of Naturalism, and has generated a lively debate concerning the degree to which Galdós follows Zola's theory of the novel. In related discussions, scholars have noted the less overtly political and religious nature of the novels following Galdós's *primera época*. These concerns have served as a backdrop to the multitude of articles and books which examine the themes, characterizations, structures, and politics of the various contemporary novels.

Overall, critical work on Galdós's *segunda manera* has tended to concentrate on the content of his novels, with surprisingly little attention given to the way in which Galdós conveys that content to the reader. While it is true that underlying many of these studies is the tacit assumption that the reader's appreciation of the content is influenced by how the story is told, few critics specifically address the issue of Galdós's narrative technique. Yet when the early contemporary novels are examined in light of the narrative devices they contain, it becomes clear that the change in Galdós's writing is not confined to content alone. Indeed, *La desheredada* marks the beginning of a more sophisticated and varied mode of narrative presentation in Galdós's novels. In this book I will examine that complexity

---

[2] See Manuel Bartolomé Cossío, "In Memorium: Galdós y Giner: Una carta de Galdós," *Boletín de la Institución Libre de Enseñanza* 44 (1920): 62.

and show how Galdós's narrative technique contributes toward the development of the characters and the ideological concerns of the novels in which they are found. That is, rather than simply providing a narratological description of the features which characterize the narrative presentation of Galdós's *segunda manera*, I will use that description as a point of departure to explore how those features function rhetorically within the individual novels. In so doing I will show how the affective response associated with particular narrative devices plays a role in influencing the reader's reception of the characters and the social, political, religious, or ethical attitudes they display. Thus, I will not be limited to the structuralist concerns of "pure" narratology. Rather, my narratological treatment will link Galdós's use of narrative devices to the rhetorical, ideological, and affective aspects of his *segunda manera* novels. "Critical narratology" is the term given to this type of endeavor by Ingeborg Hoesterey because it mingles "impulses from critical theory and narratology proper into a hybrid form of critical discourse."[3] Such discourse has at its base the close reading of texts and the attention to narrative devices which characterizes narratology, but this methodology is placed within a broader theoretical framework that can draw on any of the post-structuralist perspectives. The various dimensions of my own approach will be addressed in this introduction.

NARRATOLOGICAL DIMENSION

In *Story and Discourse* and its sequel *Coming to Terms*, Seymour Chatman draws on a wide variety of Anglo-American, Russian, and French theorists to define the various features of a narrative text.[4] The foundation of his theory rests on the structuralist distinction between the basic components of narrative: the content plane (including the characters, setting, and chain of events) and the expression plane through which the content is transmitted. Chatman refers to these as the "story" and the "discourse," respectively. The

---

[3] Ingeborg Hoesterey, introduction, *Neverending Stories: Toward a Critical Narratology*, eds. Ann Fehn, Ingeborg Hoesterey, and Maria Tatar (Princeton: Princeton UP, 1992) 4.

[4] Seymour Chatman, *Story and Discourse: Narrative Structure in Fiction and Film* (Ithaca: Cornell UP, 1978) and *Coming to Terms: The Rhetoric of Narrative in Fiction and Film* (Ithaca: Cornell UP, 1990).

story concerns the *what* of the narrative while the discourse deals with the *how* (SD 19-26). Based on this duality Chatman is able to clearly define a number of problematic concepts. Of particular importance to my study of Galdós's works is Chatman's distinction between two terms that often are used interchangeably in literary discussions: point of view and narrative voice.[5]

Point of view concerns the concept of perspective, which can have any of three different orientations: perceptual (through one's physical senses); conceptual (through one's attitudes/world view); and interested (through the personal stake one has in the situation) (SD 151-58). Since perspective can pertain either to a character or to the narrator, Chatman designates the agent involved by referring to the "filter" of a character and the "slant" of the narrator (CT 143-44). Certain perspectives reside in the story and others in the discourse. Since characters exist within the realm of the story, their perspectives similarly are part of that domain. The narrator's point of view, however, is more complex. The perspective of the heterodiegetic narrator belongs entirely to the discourse.[6] In contrast, the ho-

---

[5] The problems associated with the concept of "focalization" – both in its original formulation by Genette and in the modifications introduced by Bal – are avoided through Chatman's distinction between narrative voice and point of view, as well as through his classification of point of view according to orientation and agency. William Nelles also has attempted to clarify the issue by modifying Genette's theory yet another time, and most recently, Manfred Jahn has provided the framework for a new "revitalized" theory of focalization by deconstructing Genette's text-centered theory to include a place for the reader in the transaction. Despite all of these refinements, I agree with Chatman that the term "focalization" has become too controversial and it should be replaced by more precise terminology. See Gérard Genette, *Narrative Discourse: An Essay in Method* (Ithaca: Cornell UP, 1980) 185-94 and *Narrative Discourse Revisited* (Ithaca: Cornell UP, 1988) 72-78; Mieke Bal, *Narratology: Introduction to the Theory of Narrative*, trans. Christine van Boheemen (Toronto: U of Toronto P, 1985) 100-18; William Nelles, "Getting Focalization into Focus," *Poetics Today* 11 (1990): 365-82; and Manfred Jahn, "Windows of Focalization: Deconstructing and Reconstructing a Narratological Concept," *Style* 30 (1996): 241-67.

[6] Gérard Genette's definition of narrators is based on two separate types of attributes. One of these attributes pertains to narrative level: the extradiegetic narrator narrates the primary narrative; the intradiegetic narrator narrates a secondary narrative embedded in the first; and the metadiegetic narrator narrates a tertiary narrative embedded in the secondary one. The other attribute pertains to the narrator's relationship to the story: a homodiegetic narrator is a character in the story, while a heterodiegetic narrator is not (when the homodiegetic narrator is the protagonist, he or she may be referred to as autodiegetic). Consequently, any given narrator can be described by two attributes, one identifying the level and the other stating the function. See *Narrative Discourse* 243-48 and *Narrative Discourse Revisited* 84-87.

modiegetic narrator has two perspectives, one as a character within the story, and one as the narrator within the discourse. Thus we can speak of the perceptual, conceptual, or interest filter of the narrator-as-character, but we should speak of his slant when he is functioning in the discourse.[7] Often these perspectives are identical, but they need not be so, as will be seen in my discussion of *El amigo Manso*.

Narrative voice is the means by which the various points of view are conveyed to the reader. As such, it pertains to the realm of the discourse and encompasses all of the narrative devices available to an author. Chatman lists these in the order of ascending degree of narratorhood, from total narrator effacement to the maximum amount of narrator presence (SD 166-253). For my purposes, however, I will divide these devices into two broad categories based on the concept of interior vs. exterior views. Interior views grant the reader access to the mental workings of a character (thoughts, impressions, etc.) while exterior views do not. Exterior views of a character are achieved through:

1. Narrative statement: commentary, summary, or description by the narrator concerning the characters.

2. Direct speech: record of the words spoken between the characters (including dialogue and dramatic monologue).

3. Indirect speech.

4. Free indirect speech.

Interior views of characters are achieved through:

1. Direct thought: record of a character's thoughts.

2. Indirect thought.

3. Free indirect thought.

Some of these terms may need clarification. Direct speech or thought records can either be *tagged* or *free*. Tagged refers to the use of introductory clauses (such as *he said* or *she thought*) to explicitly note the spoken words or thoughts. These indicators are absent in free (also referred to as untagged) statements. Both forms, however, record the exact words of a character, with or without quotation marks. As such, these records have a first-person refer-

---

[7] This distinction for the homodiegetic narrator is not explicitly stated by Chatman, but is implied in his argument. Since events and settings can be filtered through any of the characters in the story, they also can be filtered through the narrator when he or she is functioning as one of the characters in the story.

ence and a present tense orientation (with memories in the preterite or imperfect tenses and plans in the future tense). Direct speech and thought differ from their indirect counterparts in that direct statements are actual quotes while indirect statements are reports of quotes. For indirect speech and thought the tag becomes an introductory clause (such as *he said that* or *she thought that*), the reference is in the third-person, and the tense system "back-shifts" to a past tense orientation (with memories in the past perfect and plans in the conditional). In free indirect speech and thought the introductory clause is omitted, thereby blurring the difference between the two. Chatman illustrates these various forms in the following chart (SD 201):

	TAGGED	FREE
Direct:		
Speech	"I have to go" she said	I have to go
Thought	"I have to go" she thought	I have to go
Indirect:		
Speech	She said that she had to go	She had to go
Thought	She thought that she had to go	She had to go

Free indirect speech and thought are sub-categories of free indirect style, a technique that has been the subject of numerous studies aimed at isolating its characteristics and delineating its effects. Of particular importance to nineteenth-century studies are Stephen Ullmann's study of its development in Flaubert's novels, and Roy Pascal's extensive examination dealing with its variations in four national languages: English, French, German, and Russian. [8] Other scholars have proposed alternative ways of referring to free indirect style (the English translation of Charles Bally's term *style indirect libre*) based on its properties. [9] For example, Graham Hough considers it a concentrated form of what he calls "coloured narrative"; Gérard Genette classifies it as a variant form of "transposed speech"; Dorrit Cohn gives free indirect thought its own designation of "narrated monologue" to distinguish it from free indirect

[8] Stephen Ullmann, *Style in the French Novel* (New York: Barnes & Noble, 1964) 94-120; and Roy Pascal, *The Dual Voice* (Manchester: Manchester UP, 1977).
[9] Charles Bally, "Le style indirect libre en français moderne," *Germanisch-Romanisch Monsatsschrift* 4 (1912): 549-56 and 597-606.

speech; Paul Hernadi's term "substitutionary narration" accounts for perception as well as thought; and for Ann Banfield these are "narratorless sentences of non-reflective consciousness." [10] Throughout my study of Galdós, however, I will use the terms "free indirect speech" and "free indirect thought" because they clearly describe their relationship to both the tagged and the indirect forms; and because they indicate the difference between speech and thought which is vital to my discussion of exterior and interior views.

The range of discoursive devices permitted in any particular text is determined by the status of the narrator. [11] Norman Friedman's classic study of narrator typology provides some useful descriptions. The protagonist-narrator is "limited almost entirely to his own thoughts, feelings, and perceptions." [12] The omniscient narrator, on the other hand, can enter the minds of the characters at will. The latter type of narrator can provide interior views of any character in the text, but the former type only can give interior views of himself. That is, omniscient narration can use direct, indirect, and free indirect thought to reveal the motivations of its various characters, but this option is not available for protagonist-narrated texts. With the exception of the protagonist-narrators in *El amigo Manso* and *Lo prohibido*, all of the narrators in the contemporary novels I will discuss are omniscient. They do, however, masquerade as "witness-narrators." [13] That is, they purport to interact with the characters on a personal level. They play the role of a chronicler, citing informants or documents as sources for their information. Nevertheless, these chroniclers do not display the limitations appropriate to witness narration. Not only do they have the

---

[10] Graham Hough, "Narrative and Dialog in Jane Austen," *The Critical Quarterly* 12 (1970): 205; Gérard Genette, *Narrative Discourse* 171-72; Dorrit Cohn, *Transparent Minds: Narrative Modes for Presenting Consciousness in Fiction* (Princeton: Princeton UP, 1978) 99-140; Paul Hernadi, "Dual Perspective: Free Indirect Discourse and Related Techniques," *Comparative Literature* 24 (1972): 38; and Ann Banfield, *Unspeakable sentences: Narration and representation in the language of fiction* (Boston: Routledge and Kegan Paul, 1982) 183-223.

[11] Throughout my study I will not use the standard spelling of *discursive* due to the numerous definitions associated with that word. Rather, I will use *discoursive* and *discoursively* as the adjectival and adverbial forms, respectively, of the noun *discourse* in order to make clear that I am using these terms in reference to Chatman's specific use of the term *discourse*.

[12] Norman Friedman, "Point of View in Fiction: The Development of a Critical Concept," *PMLA* 70 (1955): 1176.

[13] To use Genette's terminology, they are extra-homodiegetic.

capacity to reveal the thoughts of the characters, but they also are at liberty to shift spatially between locations and temporally between moments. That is, they are both omniscient and omnipresent. The concept of "privilege" is useful for understanding Galdós's typical chronicler-narrator. Although he uses the "yo" form when addressing the reader, he is not bound by the restrictions of first-person narration because he is "privileged to know what could not be learned by strictly natural means or limited to realistic vision or inference." [14] Yet Galdós preserves the illusion of limited narration by occasionally suspending the narrator's privilege concerning minor facts. For example, the narrator may not be aware of the exact date of an occurrence, or he may be unclear about the order of certain events, or he may be unsure if one of the characters acted in a particular way, or he may not know which characters were present at a certain function. But these lapses into ignorance are only temporary and do not affect the narrator's "godlike vantage point beyond time and place," which characterizes what Friedman calls "editorial omniscience" (1171).

RHETORICAL DIMENSION

As James Phelan states, "[t]he rhetorical approach is rooted in the relation between narrative strategies and the activities of readers in the way that what occurs on the levels of both story and discourse influences what readers know, believe, think, judge, and feel." [15] In my analysis of Galdós's *segunda manera*, I will focus primarily on the discursive level of Galdós's novels in order to show how the various devices making up that discourse can influence the reader's affective response toward the characters, and in turn, toward their social, political, and ethical positions.

All of the discursive devices listed above are available for use in omnisciently-narrated texts, but their combination, frequency, and duration vary from text to text at the discretion of the author. What is it that prompts an author to use certain devices over others

---

[14] Wayne C. Booth, *The Rhetoric of Fiction*, 2nd ed. (1961; Chicago: U of Chicago P, 1983) 160.

[15] James Phelan, "*Self-Help* for Narratee and Narrative Audience: How 'I' – and 'You'? – Read 'How'," *Style* 28 (1994): 354.

in any given narrative? Jonathan Culler states that "choices between words, between sentences, between different modes of presentation, will be made on the basis of their effects; and the notion of effect presupposes modes of reading which are not random or haphazard. Even if the author does not think of readers, he is himself a reader of his own work and will not be satisfied with it unless he can read it as producing effects." [16] Applying Culler's concept of effect-related choices to Galdós's novels, I will show how the interpretive behavior of the reader can be affected by the discoursive devices used to depict characters. According to Chatman, each individual character is a paradigm of traits which exist on the story level and are communicated to the reader through the discourse (SD 119-28). Thus, the discoursive manner in which these traits are conveyed has a bearing on the way each character is perceived by the reader.

Characters who are presented solely through exterior views are received differently by the reader than those who are allowed to unfold through their thoughts as well as their words. Chatman notes that access to a character's consciousness insures an intimate connection between the reader and that character (SD 157). Similarly, Wayne Booth states that the sustained use of a sympathetic inside view to depict a character is one of the most successful means of inducing a parallel response in the reader, and therefore it is a particularly effective way to reduce the emotional distance between the reader and a morally deficient character (243-49). In *Reading with Feeling* Susan L. Feagin directly addresses this issue of the reader's affective response to fictional characters. [17] She focuses on two basic types of response: empathy and sympathy. Empathy involves the reader's simulation of the mental activity and processes of a particular character. This simulation allows the reader to understand, affectively, how the character feels. Feagin also states that "[a]n author is more likely to induce a simulation of an emotion or other affect felt by a character by 'showing' rather than 'telling' " (106). Thus, interior views facilitate the process of empathizing with characters, and discoursive devices which directly represent the mind

[16] Jonathan Culler, *Structuralist Poetics: Structuralism, Linguistics, and the Study of Literature* (Ithaca: Cornell UP, 1975) 116.

[17] Susan L. Feagin, *Reading with Feeling: The Aesthetics of Appreciation* (Ithaca: Cornell UP, 1996).

are especially effective. The *content* of these interior views, however, also is important because it contributes toward the amount of sympathy elicited in the reader for a character. Sympathy, according to Feagin, involves the reader's concern for the welfare of a particular character. When responding sympathetically, the reader has feelings or emotions that are in concert with the interests and desires of the character, and the reader wishes to see those interests and desires fulfilled (114-20). Thus, interiorizations which reveal lying schemes, selfish motives, or cruel intentions do not elicit a sympathetic response. In the absence of such negative elements, however, interior views do render the reader sympathetically disposed toward a character thus depicted because of the intimacy resulting from the act of empathizing. That sympathetic response increases when the interiorizations show a character engaged in the process of self-discovery, self-analysis, or self-debate. Carol Hanbery Mac-Kay calls this type of internalization the soliloquy.[18] Since her designation is based on content – self-awareness through confronting one's own limitations – it cuts across narrative forms. Whether expressed in direct, indirect, or free indirect thought, these soliloquies feature characters questioning themselves and their situations. These generally are emotionally charged segments that occur at pivotal points in a character's development. Because they portray moments of anguish and vulnerability, they arouse compassion in the reader for the character undergoing the experience. This is the very essence of the sympathetic inside view. Of course, the sympathy can be undercut in a variety of ways (by the character's actions, the narrator's comments, etc.), but nevertheless, some measure of sympathy for the character will remain in the reader as a consequence of the intimacy established by the prolonged exposure to that character's mind. Conversely, an exclusively external presentation of a character can produce a sense of emotional distance in the reader, and with it, a reluctance to excuse that character's faults.

In the chapters that follow I will show how Galdós skillfully uses interiorizations as an empathy creating strategy – granting inside views to some characters and withholding them from others – to influence the reader's feelings in favor or against the individual characters in these novels. But this narrative strategy does not mere-

---

[18] Carol Hanbery MacKay, *Soliloquy in Nineteenth-Century Fiction* (MacMillan P, 1987) 7-33.

ly serve as a characterization technique. Rather, it is rhetorically motivated. Through his use of discursive devices Galdós influences
how the reader responds to the various characters, and consequently, that response disposes the reader in favor of certain world views.
As Mikhail Bakhtin has noted, "[t]he activity of a character is always ideologically demarcated" because "he has his own perception
of the world that is incarnated in his actions and in his discourse."
Thus, "[t]he speaking person in the novel is always, to one degree
or another, an *ideologue*, and his words are always *ideologemes*." In
addition, "the person in a novel may *act* – but such action is always
highlighted by ideology, is always harnessed to the character's discourse . . . and occupies a definite ideological position." [19] Because
characters become associated with their opinions, when the reader
is discoursively guided toward the acceptance of certain characters
and the rejection of others, the reader also is disposed toward the
acceptance of certain sets of values over others. Thus, interiorizations become a subtle but powerful tool of rhetorical persuasion.

In addition, the reader's affective response to the characters
serves as a powerful counterbalance to the authority of the narrator.
As a result of the text's distribution of interior and exterior views,
the reader develops a degree of intimacy or distance with each of
the characters. These feelings allow the reader to assess the validity
of the comments which the narrator makes concerning the various
characters. Thus, the effects produced by interiorization and exteriorization devices can support, modify, or even contradict the opinions offered by the narrator. Indeed, Galdós's *segunda manera*
novels frequently play on the tension between the narrator's overt
judgment concerning certain characters and the reader's emotional
response to those characters.

READER RESPONSE DIMENSION

The various characters' perspectives, whether conveyed through
interior or exterior views, hold a fundamental position in the theories of Wolfgang Iser, as stated in *The Implied Reader* and *The Act*

---

[19] M. M. Bakhtin, "Discourse in the Novel," *The Dialogic Imagination*, trans.
Michael Holquist, ed. Caryl Emerson and Michael Holquist (Austin: U of Texas P,
1981) 333-35.

of Reading.[20] They, along with the perspective of the narrator and the actions of the plot, form the "written" portion of the text, which is the raw material upon which the reader's mind works. As the various perspectives and actions interact with one another, the "unwritten" portion of the text emerges, which consists of the connections that the reader must make to link the written portions together. For example, the actions of a character in the story, as well as his or her reactions to the events, setting, and other characters in the story allow the reader to draw conclusions and infer character traits which are not explicitly stated by the narrator. These inferences arise from the "blanks" or "gaps" present in the text whenever perspectives or actions are juxtaposed without narrative explanation. For Iser the literary work is a virtual entity which comes into existence through the convergence of the text and the reader. This is a dynamic and interactive process in which the text engages the imagination of the reader, who in turn actualizes the potential meanings in the text. The blanks are important because they stimulate the reader's active participation in this endeavor. The reader must establish connections by filling in the gaps left by the text. Furthermore, the links supplied by the reader to contend with these empty spaces also influence the reader's response to the written parts of the text. Throughout the process the reader repeatedly anticipates what is to come and reevaluates what has occurred. By assuming a "wandering viewpoint" the reader constantly shifts among the various textual perspectives, making the necessary connections and drawing inferences which are either reinforced or amended by each new development in the text (AR 96-114). Although this process allows the reader a certain latitude, the reader's role is tied to the text, as Iser explains:

> The impressions that arise as a result of this process will vary from individual to individual, but only within the limits imposed by the written as opposed to the unwritten text. In the same way, two people gazing at the night sky may both be looking at the

---

[20] Wolfgang Iser, *The Implied Reader: Patterns of Communication in Prose Fiction from Bunyan to Beckett* (Baltimore: Johns Hopkins UP, 1974); and *The Act of Reading: A Theory of Aesthetic Response* (Baltimore: Johns Hopkins UP, 1978). In the last chapter of *The Implied Reader*, "The Reading Process: A Phenomenological Approach," Iser outlines the theory which he later explains in detail in *The Act of Reading*.

same collection of stars, but one will see the image of a plough, and the other will make out a dipper. The 'stars' in a literary text are fixed; the lines that join them are variable. The author of the text may, of course, exert plenty of influence on the reader's imagination – he has the whole panoply of narrative techniques at his disposal . . . (IR 282)

It is these narrative techniques and their effects which is the subject of my discussion of Galdós's novels: how the written portions, communicated through both the discourse and the story, not only influence the reader's reaction toward the characters, but also regulate the reader's appreciation of what Iser calls the configurative meaning of the text. This term refers to the unformulated intention of the text that is uncovered through the process of reading.

The organizing principle of that intention is what Wayne Booth calls the implied author – the guiding hand which controls "every detail, every quality, that is found in the work or implied by its silences" (429). [21] This agency establishes the overall design of the text and defines the norms and values implied within it. These norms and values represent the implied author's social, political, religious, and ethical attitudes and assumptions. Since the implied author cannot speak directly to the reader, these attitudes must be *inferred* from the story elements and discursive devices in the text. The implied author is a textual construct separate from both the real author and the narrator, but its relationship to the narrator is highly important. The narrator who upholds the attitudes and assumptions of the implied author is reliable, the narrator who does not is unreliable. The degree of narrator reliability is a fundamental element in the narrative transaction which must be ascertained by the reader. In so doing, however, it is important to keep in mind that reliability depends on the relationship between the implied author and the narrator rather than between the narrator and the reader. As Elizabeth Preston has noted, this "keeps readers – who

---

[21] In response to Booth's tendency to use descriptive terms which anthropomorphize the implied author, Chatman stresses the need to use terminology that identifies the implied author as a textual construct. Therefore, he refers to the implied author as the text's "inscribed principle of invention and intent" and "[t]he source of a narrative text's whole structure of being – not only of its assertions and denotations but also of its implications, connotations, and ideological nexus." (CT 75 & 83).

are exceedingly different from one another – from simply indicting any narrator who doesn't share their norms as unreliable." [22] In my analysis of Galdós's *segunda manera* I will refer frequently to narrator reliability or unreliability in order to show how it can alter the effects produced by the interplay of interior and exterior views in individual novels.

The counterpart of the implied author is Iser's implied reader, which is the role inscribed within the text for its audience (AR 34-38). This role involves the active participation of the real reader in discovering and understanding the attitudes and assumptions of the implied author. How does this process of discovery take place? As Jonathan Culler has indicated, the real reader must possess the requisite knowledge of how to assume the implied reader's role – a literary competence – based on a familiarity with the literary conventions used by authors (113-30). Peter Rabinowitz elaborates on this concept by stressing the social dimension of these conventions. [23] Rather than fixed, universal norms, these literary conventions are tied to cultural communities who collectively agree to their validity. As members of a particular cultural community, real authors and real readers share expectations about the literary use of characters, plotting devices, themes, symbols, etc. Thus, these conventions become the basis for both the writing and the reading of texts.

Rabinowitz's study of the reading process also is useful because it stresses the social and ideological dimension of the relationship between the real reader and the implied reader, an issue which Iser doesn't deal with sufficiently. Although Iser acknowledges the importance of the norms and values of the author and the implied author, he discounts the importance of the norms and values held by the reader and the implied reader. Specifically, Rabinowitz challenges Iser's view of the implied reader as a "pure" reader, devoid of any social, political, religious, or ethical attitudes and assumptions (26). Rabinowitz addresses this situation by reformulating the reader's reception of the text in terms of three audiences. The first is the "actual audience," which consists of the flesh-and-blood peo-

---

[22] Elizabeth Preston, "Implying Authors in *The Great Gatsby,*" *Narrative* 5 (1997): 151.
[23] Peter J. Rabinowitz, *Before Reading: Narrative Conventions and the Politics of Interpretation* (Ithaca: Cornell UP, 1987).

ple who read the novel. The other two audiences, "authorial" and "narrative," are functions which the real reader carries out during the act of reading. Rabinowitz explains that due to the wide variety of possible real readers of a novel – all of whom can differ in terms of race, class, gender, education, religion, political affiliation, and historical situation – the real author must design his or her book rhetorically for some more or less specific hypothetical audience of ideal readers (20-23). Rabinowitz calls these ideal readers the "authorial audience." The author's artistic choices are then based upon social and ideological assumptions – conscious or unconscious – about that audience. Thus, although the authorial audience is a fictional construct, it is tied to the social, political, religious and ethical realm of the extra-textual world. Since the novel is designed for the author's ideal readers, the real reader must take on the values and beliefs of the authorial audience in order to understand the text. Included among the authorial audience's beliefs is an acceptance of the fictional status of the characters and events occurring in the novel, despite any similarity they may have to the real world. In contrast, the "narrative audience" exists totally in terms of the world of the text. It is related to Coleridge's concept of a "willing suspension of disbelief" in that the narrative audience reacts to the novelistic world as if it were real. That is, it treats the characters as real beings and accepts their actions as actually happening. Thus, it is through the real reader's joining of the narrative audience that he or she can affectively respond to the novel and experience its emotional impact. Rabinowitz stresses that real readers carry out the functions of the authorial and narrative audiences simultaneously, thereby allowing themselves to become emotionally engaged with the characters and events while also keeping a critical distance.

Rabinowitz's clarification of the dual nature of the implied reader – as part of both the authorial and narrative audiences – enriches Iser's original conception of the term by foregrounding the ideological and affective functions which the implied author routinely asks the implied reader to perform over the course of the text. In general, the reading process can be described as a collaborative effort between the real author and the real reader who, sharing a knowledge of literary conventions, enter into a tacit contract in which the real author creates an implied author who communicates through the story and the discourse to the implied reader, thereby allowing the real reader to actualize one of the numerous potential interpretations in the text. As Iser, Booth, and Rabinowitz all stress, however, the communication between the implied author and the implied reader is predicated on the willingness of the real reader to allow his or her own beliefs and values to recede into the background while assuming the social, political, religious, and ethical attitudes and assumptions of the implied author for the duration of the reading process. But what happens when the real reader is unwilling to do so? Such is the case with what Judith Fetterley calls the "Resisting Reader." [24] Although Fetterley's aim is to have feminist critics expose the misogynistic assumptions that underlie American literature, the term itself can be used to refer to the activities of any real reader who takes exception to any of the authorial audience's attitudes which are promoted or taken for granted in a text. Lou Charnon-Deutsch and Catherine Jagoe follow this path of resistance by showing how bourgeois patriarchal constructions of gender – particularly those pertaining to the domestic ideal of womanhood – are regarded as the natural order of things in nineteenth-century Spanish novels. [25] But both Charnon-Deutsch and Jagoe also stress that many of Galdós's novels, including the ones I will deal with in the following chapters, contain female protagonists who transgress the boundaries of their gender roles, and succeed in gaining some degree of self-determination in the process. Jagoe shows how Fortunata subversively redefines the *ángel del hogar* ideal to conform to her rebellion, while Charnon-Deutsch cites Rosalía de Bringas's victorious struggle for domestic power. Nevertheless, Jagoe and Charnon-Deutsch point out that the nonconformity of these and other Galdosian heroines inevitably ends in their death or dishonor. The resulting tension between these characters' rejection of socially acceptable behavior on one hand, and society's unyielding response on the other creates an ambiguity with regard to gender issues. Jagoe's exploration of that ambiguity as it operates in what she calls the middle period of Galdós's production – from *La desheredada* through *Fortunata y Jacinta* – reveals how it tacitly calls into question the norms and values of patriarchal bourgeois

---

[24] Judith Fetterley, *The Resisting Reader: A Feminist Approach to American Fiction* (Bloomington: Indiana UP, 1978) xxii.

[25] Lou Charnon-Deutsch, *Gender and Representation: Women in Spanish Realist Fiction*, Purdue U Monographs in Romance Languages 32 (Amsterdam: John Benjamins, 1990) and Catherine Jagoe, *Ambiguous Angels: Gender in the Novels of Galdós* (Berkeley: U of California P, 1994).

society. Jagoe does not credit Galdós with any overtly feminist agenda in these novels (178), but she does state that these novels can be said to have a "feminist impulse" because they "contribute to the denaturalizing of the culture's feminine ideal" by having the text implicitly criticize its own ideology (9-10).

Although Iser discourages real readers from allowing their own ideological beliefs to "taint" the reading process, recent strides in cultural studies and feminist criticism have shown the importance of reading resistantly in order to foreground the norms and values which are taken for granted in a text. In the following chapters I will mention conclusions drawn by resisting readers of Galdós's *segunda manera* novels. However, my own focus differs from their enterprise. Rather than offering resistance to these novels, I will show how *the novels themselves* endeavor to challenge the norms and values of *assenting* readers. That is, I will discuss how an acceptance of the invitation to become the implied reader of a *segunda manera* novel compelled Galdós's contemporary reader to examine the middle-class attitudes and assumptions that informed the nineteenth-century society in which he or she lived. As Jagoe has shown in the case of gender roles, the ambiguous stance of Galdós's implied authors does not represent an unequivocal endorsement of the patriarchal values which the contemporary readers of Galdós's texts would have held. Indeed, in my own study I will show how various social attitudes prevalent in Galdós's time and presumably accepted by his nineteenth-century readers are strongly criticized by the implied author.

My approach to the real readers of Galdós's novels recognizes what Elizabeth Preston calls their "historical situatedness" (154). Today's readers, especially those of academia, are historically situated in a critical environment which trains them to scrutinize texts for processes of race, class, gender, and sexuality, as well as the myriad of power relations underlying society – all of which may not have even been noticed by Galdós or his contemporary readers. But it is from those contemporary readers – historically situated in Spain of the 1880's – that Galdós drew his original audience. Thus, the issues he raises, albeit implicitly, are directly related to what he considered important to that historical period. Clearly some of those issues continue to hold significance in the 1990's, but it is Galdós's contemporary reader, not our own, to whom he directs his texts and to whom he issues his challenges. How can we characterize this contemporary reader? In the case of the *segunda manera* novels Galdós's audience can be described as middle class and higher, predominantly male, largely urban, familiar with literary conventions and genres, knowledgeable about current and historical events, and aware of behavior deemed acceptable or unacceptable according to gender and class lines.[26] He or she also formed part of a society undergoing major social, economic, and political changes due to the rise of the middle class. Galdós's novels reflect these changes through the attitudes and assumptions held by the various characters. Part of the implied reader's role in a *segunda manera* text involves detecting when certain attitudes and assumptions of the characters are not in accord with those of the implied author. In so doing the real reader focuses attention on these attitudes and assumptions, causing him or her to judge their validity not only within the realm of the novel, but also within the extra-textual world of the reader. Thus, the reader's active assessment of the various characters' beliefs subtly obliges him or her to extend that assessment process into his or her own life as well. In particular, Galdós asked his nineteenth-century readers to examine some of the negative traits of society which they themselves may have exhibited.

In short, throughout my analysis of Galdós's novels, when I refer to "the reader" or "us" or "we," I am speaking of the collective roles performed by the actual audience, the authorial audience,

---

[26] The class, gender, and geographic characteristics of this readership are based on literacy rates. According to Ángel Bahamonde and Jesús A. Martínez, *Historia de España: Siglo XIX* (Madrid: Cátedra, 1994) 486, in 1857 the literacy rate in Spain was only 25 % (3,129,921 adults). By the end of the century it had risen to 36 %, which in real numbers represented an increase to 6 million adults due to the overall increase in the Spanish population during the nineteenth century. Germán Rueda, *Historia de España: El reinado de Isabel II* (Madrid: Temas de Hoy, 1996) 44, notes that throughout the century literacy rates were higher for men than for women. Approximately 22 % more males than females were literate in 1860, but that percentage had narrowed to approximately 20% by 1877 due to the larger number of women who learned to read and write. He cites that for every 77 men who become literate from 1860 to 1877, 100 women did so. Stephanie Sieburth, *Inventing High and Low: Literature, Mass Culture, and Uneven Modernity in Spain* (Durham: Duke UP, 1994) 31, states that literacy rates were higher in urban centers, especially for women. In 1860 37% of women in Madrid were literate, and the rate increased to 47 % by 1877. Bahamonde and Martínez do not credit the public school system with the increased literacy of Spaniards (484-85). Rather, they show that the lack of government financing for primary education meant that basic literacy remained within the reach of only those who could afford to pay for private schooling.

and the narrative audience. That is, I am referring to a reader in the process of assenting to the social, political, religious, and ethical attitudes and assumptions of the implied author, while also responding affectively to the characters as if they were real. By focusing on the rhetorical strategies aimed at influencing this implied reader, I will show how Galdós asks his real readers to question some of the behavior commonly associated with the upwardly mobile middle class.

GALDOS'S *SEGUNDA MANERA*

I propose that the ideological thrust of these novels centers on the role of the middle class as the dynamic force within nineteenth century society. In his 1870 essay "Observaciones sobre la novela contemporánea en España," Galdós stresses the dominant position of the middle class in modern life. [27] "Esa clase" writes Galdós "es la que determina el movimiento político, la que administra, la que enseña, la que discute." In addition, "ella determina el movimiento comercial, una de las grandes manifestaciones de nuestro siglo, y la que posee la clave de los intereses, elemento poderoso de la vida actual." In short, "ella asume por su iniciativa y por su inteligencia la soberanía de las naciones." As "la base del orden social," the middle class is what Galdós calls "la fuente inagotable" from which the modern novel should draw: "La novela contemporánea de costumbres ha de ser la expresión de cuanto bueno y malo existe en el fondo de esa clase." Thus, this literary picture of "el hombre del siglo XIX con sus virtudes y sus vicios" should recognize that the middle class is made up not only of "los grandes innovadores" but also of "los grandes libertinos." Galdós specifically notes the presence in middle class society of "ciertos males que turban las familias," citing religious fanaticism and adultery as particularly destructive to domestic life. [28] In addition, Galdós acknowledges that the "inmenso bien" that has been realized through the middle class's

---

[27] Benito Pérez Galdós, "Observaciones sobre la novela contemporánea en España," *Ensayos de crítica literaria*, ed. Laureano Bonet (Barcelona: Península, 1990) 105-20.

[28] I see no indication in the text to support Catherine Jagoe's contention that Galdós's reference to adultery is confined to female infidelity alone. See *Ambiguous Angels* 53.

recent involvement in politics and commerce has produced some unfortunate side effects: unbridled ambition, positivism, and vanity. Galdós goes on to define the role of the writer in exposing these evils: "Sabemos que no es el novelista el que ha de decidir directamente estas graves cuestiones, pero sí tiene la misión de reflejar esta turbación honda. . . Si nos corregimos, bien; si no, el arte ha cumplido su misión, y siempre tendremos delante aquel espejo eterno reflejador y guardador de nuestra fealdad." Indeed, in my analysis of Galdós's first seven *segunda manera* novels, I will show how the interplay of each text's story and discourse requires the middle-class audience to confront these "graves cuestiones" and acknowledge its "fealdad."

Whereas Galdós's *primera época* novels primarily address the issue of religious fanaticism, Galdós broadens his scope in the *segunda manera* novels to depict the wider array of societal ills mentioned in his essay. Adultery, for example, is directly dealt with in *Fortunata y Jacinta*, *El amigo Manso*, *La de Bringas*, and *La desheredada*, and adulterous minor characters are commonplace in Galdós's other novels as well. But above all, the *segunda manera* novels explore the myriad of problems resulting from what Galdós cites as the most prevalent of all social vices: vanity. "Somos muy vanidosos" states Galdós "todos queremos ser algo superior a los demás, distinguirnos de cualquier modo. Si no podemos hacerlo con buenas y grandes acciones, lo hacemos con un título, con un nombre, con una cinta u otra fórmula convencional." The *segunda manera* novels are a catalog of characters engaged in just such attempts. Some are social climbers, others are political opportunists, several are dishonest, many live beyond their means to affect false appearances, and most are hypocrites. Only a few display the "buenas y grandes acciones" of which they are capable. Through the interaction of these characters, the distribution of interior or exterior views used to portray them, and the degree of reliability afforded the narrator of each *segunda manera* novel, Galdós requires the reader to identify those aspects of modern society which are detrimental to the social, political, and ethical enterprise undertaken by the middle class. As Catherine Jagoe has aptly stated, Galdós regarded the modern realist novel as "the epic of the middle class" (54). But merely being a member of the middle class does not guarantee a character sympathetic treatment by Galdós. Rather, the determining factor is how well each character fulfills his or her role honestly within society. Implied through both the story and the discourse of these novels is a view of what the middle class should be – a meritocracy based on personal commitment, responsibility, integrity, generosity, tolerance, moderation, hard work, and gradual progress. Characters who display these qualities, regardless of their social class, are treated sympathetically in Galdós's novels.

In keeping with Galdós's preoccupation with the Spanish middle class and with his desire to create a novelistic medium to chronicle its daily life, Galdós also used his "Observaciones" essay to level criticism at existing literary forms which ignored the middle class (e.g. the regional novel), or which imitated the plots of French models (e.g. the serialized "novela de impresiones y movimiento"), or which did both (e.g. the salon novel). In their place Galdós proposed the need for "la gran novela de costumbres" which would further cultivate the realistic portrayals of everyday life seen in *cuadros de costumbres*. But rather than simply presenting static and isolated sketches of individual characters, the realist novel would bring them together to "formar un cuerpo multiforme y vario, pero completo, organizado y uno, como la misma sociedad." Galdós explicitly set up a distinction between this preferred form of the novel (which he himself would help to develop), and the non-realist novel then existing in Spain (which was "destinada sólo a la distracción y deleite de cierta clase de personas"). Catherine Jagoe points out that Galdós's direct attack on idealist novels also constituted an indirect attack on their writers (many of whom were women) and their readers (who were primarily petty bourgeois and often were women), and that this critique was implicitly continued in his fictional works. [29] Indeed, in Galdós's *segunda manera* novels both the writers (Ido del Sagrario and Alejandro Miquis) and the consumers (Isidora Rufete) of non-realistic literature are presented as suffering from over-stimulated imaginations which render them incapable of functioning productively within their middle-class environment. The idealist novels associated with these characters therefore acquire the connotation for being laughable at best and dangerous at worst.

Although characters in the *segunda manera* novels are the agents for raising certain ideological issues, Galdós does not reduce them

---

[29] Catherine Jagoe, "Disinheriting the Feminine: Galdós and the Rise of the Realist Novel in Spain," *Revista de Estudios Hispánicos* 27 (1993): 225-48.

to mere vehicles for expressing his own beliefs. Rather, they function in what Bakhtin calls a polyphonic relationship with each
other, the narrator, and the author.[30] The "defining structural feature" of such a relationship is based on the author's willingness to
cede ultimate control over his or her characters, thereby allowing
them to operate within the novelistic world with as much autonomy
as the author. In such a relationship, the author, the narrator, and
the characters all have an equal voice, and all participate in an interactive dialogue which permits their voices to coexist without being
merged. The key to achieving this simultaneity of independent voices is to treat "[s]elf consciousness as the artistic dominant governing the creation of a character," particularly with regard to the hero
(50). What is important is not how the hero appears in the world,
but "how the world appears to [the] hero, and how the hero appears to himself" (47). Thus, the hero represents "*a particular point
of view on the world and on oneself*, as the position enabling a person to interpret and evaluate his own self and his surrounding reality" (47). Bakhtin frequently laments that critics tend to focus on
novelistic content independent of form, thus failing to appreciate
the artistic principle governing polyphony: the plurality of independent and unmerged consciousness. Bakhtin also points out that particular formal devices pertaining to narrative voice can function as
"tools" in the realization of "polyphonic artistic design" because of
their ability to convey character consciousness (57). Indeed, such is
the case in Galdós's *segunda manera* novels, which communicate
the characters' perspectives to the reader through a wide range of
interiorization devices. Like Dostoevsky, whom Bakhtin considers
the founder of the polyphonic novel, Galdós frequently shows his
characters on the threshold of a final decision or at a moment of
crisis, with their consciousness revealing an internally dialogic
struggle to escape the finalizing definitions placed on them by other
characters. Fortunata is but the most obvious example of a character whose dialogic relationship with herself produces a "pícara
idea" that challenges society's view of her. That idea, when placed
within dialogue with the other characters and with the narrator, retains it validity despite their efforts to negate it.

---

[30] Mikhail Bakhtin, *Problems of Dostoevsky's Poetics*, trans. and ed. Caryl Emerson, Theory and History of Literature 8 (Minneapolis: U of Minnesota P, 1984)
5-100.

In Bakhtin's concept of the polyphonic novel, then, each character's consciousness consists of a point of view which represents a personalized truth about the world, and each of these truths is given as much autonomy as the truth held by the narrator and the author. This organizational principle strengthens the role of the characters, but it does not eliminate the author. "At issue here is not the absence of, but a *radical change in, the author's position*" (67). Bakhtin emphasizes "the positive and active quality of the new authorial position in the polyphonic novel," going on to state that "[t]he author of a polyphonic novel is not required to renounce himself or his own consciousness, but he must to an extraordinary extent broaden, deepen, and rearrange this consciousness (to be sure in a specific direction) in order to accommodate the autonomous consciousnesses of others" (67-68). Although the author's truth holds an equal status along side the truths of the characters, Bakhtin stresses that this "polyphonic approach has nothing in common with relativism" which excludes "all authentic dialogue" (69). Rather, it is precisely the interactive dialogue among independent truths which creates the concept of a "unified truth," which "is born at a point of contact among various consciousnesses" (81). In Booth and Iser's terminology, it is at this point of contact that the *implied author's* position resides, and it is this unified truth which the implied reader is asked to discern.

Galdós's *segunda manera* novels are polyphonic in that they reveal the social, political, religious, and ethical attitudes and assumptions of the implied author indirectly, through an interplay of various voices. The reader must piece together the unified truth (what Iser calls the configurative meaning of the text) through a continual process of evaluation and reassessment of textual evidence. By assuming a "wandering viewpoint" the reader constantly shifts among the various perspectives, drawing inferences from what the characters do, say, and think. Through the interaction of the characters' voices and consciousnesses within these novels, an interaction of ideas and values occurs as well. But no one character is privileged as the authoritative voice of the text. Each character holds attitudes and assumptions which interact with those of other characters and those of the narrator, creating a dialogic exchange that requires the reader's active participation in formulating the range of ideas and values that make up the position of the implied author on a variety of issues. Since this position must be inferred through a composite of the various characters' perspectives, the *segunda manera* novels provide the reader ample access to the characters' own views. In general, these novels display an overall tendency toward self-revelation by the characters rather than through narrative summary or commentary. The narrator of a *segunda manera* novel often remains silent as the reader listens to the characters' spoken words and unspoken thoughts. The heroes, in particular, receive extensive internal portrayals through a variety of discursive devices which open their minds to the reader. Indeed, as I will show in the following chapters, the revelation of character consciousnesses are one of the narratological hallmarks of Galdós's *segunda manera*.

Although this discursive dimension of Galdós's *segunda manera* has not received the critical attention it deserves, it has not been entirely neglected. The most extensive examination to date is found in Kay Engler's *The Structure of Realism: The Novelas Contemporáneas of Benito Pérez Galdós.*[31] Engler's focus is on the narrator as the primary center of consciousness in the novel, and consequently, the mediator of novelistic reality for the reader. In that capacity the narrator can enter into a shared consciousness with the characters to a greater or lesser extent throughout the narrative. The degree to which the characters' consciousnesses are revealed depends on the narrative devices present in the text. The purpose of Engler's study is to establish a theory that will structurally define all of nineteenth-century realism as based on a dialectic of perceiving consciousness and external reality. As a result, her book quotes passages from the *novelas contemporáneas* merely as illustrations for her theory. Therefore, it serves more as a catalog of narrative devices used by Galdós than as a discussion of how these various devices function in unison within the individual texts. Furthermore, in the course of her investigation she makes two important statements with which I cannot agree. First, she says that the distinction between free indirect speech and free indirect thought "does not appear to be a particularly useful one for describing the function of free indirect style in Galdós's novels" (75). On the contrary, I will show that the interior views afforded by free indirect thought are used by Galdós for substantially different effects than are produced

---

[31] Kay Engler, *The Structure of Realism: The Novelas Contemporáneas of Benito Pérez Galdós,* North Carolina Studies in the Romance Languages and Literatures 184 (Chapel Hill: North Carolina UP, 1977).

by free indirect speech's exterior views. Second, Engler shows a
serious misunderstanding of Booth's concept of the unreliable narrator. She states that "unreliability is inherent in the 'first-person'
narrator, an inevitable consequence of the choice of that form of
narration" (140-41). Consequently she declares all omniscient narrators to be reliable and all protagonist-narrators to be unreliable.
Engler clearly is confusing the limited narrator with an unreliable
one. Neither ignorance of certain facts nor the inability to enter the
minds of the characters constitutes unreliability. Rather, unreliability is the product of a narrator's rejection of the norms and values
held by the implied author. Although Engler does speak of values
and norms in the text, she confuses those norms and values existing
within the plane of the story (i.e. those values held by the characters within the fictional milieu of nineteenth century Madrid) with
the norms and values proposed by the implied author through the
configuration of all the components within the story and the discourse. As I will show, the omniscient narrators of *La de Bringas*
and *Fortunata y Jacinta* are not reliable, but the protagonist-narrator of *El amigo Manso* most decidedly is. Jennifer Lowe also discusses the discursive devices in Galdós's contemporary novels,
though in a much briefer and less linguistically oriented manner
than Engler.[32] In focusing on the various forms that a character's
spoken and unspoken thoughts can assume, Lowe specifically refers
to Galdós's use of these devices for character portrayal. Other
scholars limit their discussion of Galdós's narrative techniques to
those discursive devices found in specific novels. For example,
Geoffrey Ribbans deals with *Fortunata y Jacinta*; Harriet Turner examines that novel along with *El amigo Manso*; and Robert Fedorchek looks at *Tormento* and *La de Bringas*.[33] These studies will
be included in my discussion of the individual novels.

---

[32] Jennifer Lowe, "Spoken and unspoken: Soliloquy, Monologue, and Aside in
some of Galdós' 'Novelas contemporáneas'," *Revista Canadiense de Estudios Hispánicos* 8 (1983): 110-20.
[33] Geoffrey Ribbans, *Pérez Galdós: Fortunata y Jacinta*, Critical Guides to Spanish Texts 21 (London: Grant & Cutler, 1977) 37-55 and "Dos paseos de Fortunata
por Madrid y su integración dentro de la estructura de la novela," *Hispania* 70
(1987): 740-45; Harriet S. Turner, "Strategies in Narrative Point of View: On
Meaning and Morality in the Galdós Novel," *Homenaje a Antonio Sánchez Barbudo:
Ensayos de literatura española moderna*, ed. Benito Brancaforte, Edward R. Mulvihill, Roberto G. Sánchez (Madison, Wisconsin UP, 1981) 65-76; Robert Fedorchek,
"Rosalía and the Rhetoric of Dialogue in Galdós' *Tormento* and *La de Bringas*," *Revista de Estudios Hispánicos* 12 (1978): 199-216.

I have chosen to examine the discursive features of Galdós's *segunda manera* by focusing on its earliest examples, beginning with the first contemporary novel and continuing through his masterpiece, *Fortunata y Jacinta*. In my discussion of these novels I will explain how individual discursive devices influence the reader's response toward the various characters, and how that response in turn affects the reader's appreciation of the social, political, religious, and ethical issues played out through the interaction of the characters and through the attitudes of the narrators, both reliable and unreliable. When appropriate, I also will refer to the galleys of these novels in order to show how Galdós's final revisions altered the affective quality of certain scenes. Throughout my discussion I will keep in mind James Phelan's observation that "the relation between ideology and a particular element of narrative technique is always mediated by the relation of that element to the rest of the narrative. The individual elements of narrative need to be considered in themselves in order for us to understand their complex potential for participating in the rhetorical transaction of narrative, including the inculcation of ideology. To make those analyses pay their full dividends, however, we must bring them together so that we may assess the particular contribution and mutual interaction of different narrative elements in the transaction as a whole."[34] Indeed, it is important to keep in mind that the reading process entails a complex interaction of all the elements involved, and that the dynamics of that interaction adjust to the individual works concerned. Consequently, I will examine each of the novels separately in order to contextualize the discursive devices within their particular realm of operation. But since I also am concerned with discovering what constitutes the discursive dimension of Galdós's *segunda manera*, I will draw similarities between the ways that certain narrative techniques function from one novel to the next.

In my first chapter I compare the discursive devices of *La desheredada* with those found in the *primera época* novels in order to show that this first novel of the *segunda manera* initiated a mode of writing for Galdós that not only is narratologically more complex than previously, but also conveys character consciousness with greater subtlety and naturalness. Galdós's preference for indirect

---

[34] James Phelan, "Narrative Discourse, Literary Character, and Ideology," *Reading Narrative*, ed. James Phelan (Columbus: Ohio State UP, 1989) 145.

thought in his *primera época* novels is replaced by a larger array of interiorization devices in *La desheredada*. Direct thought, both tagged and free, grants the reader unmediated access to the characters' minds, while free indirect thought is extensively used for both its ironic and sympathy producing effects. Innovative techniques such as theatrical formatting, present tense narration, and filtered descriptions also enhance the character-oriented nature of the *segunda manera*. In *La desheredada* Galdós develops his protagonist through a combination of reliable narration (criticizing her impracticality and classist outlook) and inside views (underscoring her attitudes while creating an intimate connection with the reader). This results in the reader's ability to reject Isidora's elitism without condemning her completely. In *Fortunata y Jacinta* Galdós uses a different narrative strategy. Although he continues to develop his characters through the various discursive devices seen in *La desheredada*, he now combines these devices with narration that is not entirely reliable. Furthermore, the reader's affective response to the characters is influenced by the interior views given to Fortunata, Jacinta, and Maxi, as compared to the overwhelmingly exterior treatment of Juanito. Galdós's use of free indirect speech further contributes toward the reader's negative assessment of both Juanito and the narrator. Consequently, it is Juanito, rather than Fortunata, who receives the reader's censure for their adulterous activity. Much of the intricacy of the characterizations in *Fortunata y Jacinta* is the consequence of a complex combination of semi-reliable narration, interiorization devices, and distancing techniques.

In my second chapter I deal with the interrelated set of narratives comprising the Centeno-Tormento-Bringas trilogy. In these three novels the discursive presentation of recurring characters is used to portray them as evolving entities. The interplay of story elements and discursive devices influences the reader's reception of Centeno, Amparo, and Rosalía de Bringas as they move from one text to the next. Indeed, the critical controversies concerning these three characters can be explained in terms of the amount of weight given to either the story or the discourse by the individual critics. Thus, for example, the differing opinions concerning the identity of the protagonist of *El Doctor Centeno* can be resolved by looking beyond the story level of the text. By adding the discursive dimension we see that the uneven distribution of interior views for Felipe and Miquis in parts one and two results in a dual-focused narrative

with two complementary protagonists. Similarly, the strong dis-
agreements concerning the assessments of Amparo and Rosalía may
be linked to the degree to which the individual reader allows the
negative actions of these women to be softened by their interiorizations. As Centeno, Amparo, and Rosalía develop over the course of
these novels, their words, thoughts, and actions are juxtaposed with
those of the other characters in ways that reveal the implied author's attitudes on social, political, religious, and ethical issues.
These attitudes, in turn, contribute toward the cohesiveness of the
trilogy as a whole. Despite Galdós's use of reliable narration in
the first two novels and unreliable narration in the last, the trilogy
is unified in its condemnation of hypocrisy, impracticality, social
climbing, and political opportunism.

In my third chapter I turn to the first-person narratives *El
amigo Manso* and *Lo prohibido* in order to show how Galdós's
segunda manera creatively subverts the constraints associated with
autobiographical fiction. Unlike the first-person *episodios* which
preceded them, these novels do not remain within the conventionally recognized rules of fictional autobiography. Due to the self-referential frame-story format of *El amigo Manso*, Galdós is able to
grant Manso in the frame all of the privileges of editorial omniscience while making Manso in the embedded story suffer all of the
limitations of protagonist narrators. Despite these limitations, however, throughout the story Manso is fully in accord with the implied
author's condemnation of the self-interested hypocrisy prevalent
among the middle and upper levels of Restoration society. Consequently, Manso is a reliable narrator. As such, he profoundly differs
from the narrator of *Lo prohibido*. Although both Máximo Manso
and José María Bueno de Guzmán are protagonist-narrators, and
although both *El amigo Manso* and *Lo prohibido* criticize Restoration era values, Galdós is able to engage the reader in substantially
different ways by making one narrator reliable and the other unreliable. Whereas the first novel achieves our acceptance of the implied
author's stance through our acceptance of the narrator, the second
novel accomplishes the same results through our rejection of the
narrator. This process is structurally facilitated by the segmented
diary pretext of *Lo prohibido*, which allows the degree of narrator
reliability to vary from one segment to the next depending on the
narrator's situation. This narrative segmentation also serves to expand the role conventionally assigned to first-person narrators.

Overall, in my analysis of Galdós's *segunda manera* I will show how the polyphonic nature of the relationship between the characters and the narrator of each novel actively involves the reader in the process of inferring what Bakhtin calls the text's "unified truth" by engaging the reader's affective response to the multiple consciousnesses contained within it. I will do this by showing how elements of the discourse, such as interior or exterior views and varying degrees of narrator reliability, function in tandem with the story elements of each text. My pluralistic approach to Galdós's *segunda manera* will help to clarify the interrelated nature of the narrative transaction, where author, text, and reader each play a fundamental role. Indeed, Galdós's own awareness of this collaborative process is evident in the following comment: "Las obras de uno y otro género, así las muy pesadas y con cariño escritas como las compuestas a vuela pluma, no son más que la mitad de una proposición lógica, y carecen de sentido hasta que no se ajustan con la otra mitad, o sea el público." [35]

---

[35] Benito Pérez Galdós, prólogo, *Los condenados, Obras completas: Novelas, Teatro, Miscelánea,* ed. Federico Carlos Sainz de Robles (Madrid: Aguilar, 1961) 6: 695-96.

CHAPTER 1

NEW TRENDS: *LA DESHEREDADA*
AND *FORTUNATA Y JACINTA*

In his essay on the first volume of *La desheredada* Leopoldo
Alas makes two major observations concerning Galdós's new mode
of writing in that novel.[1] First, he notes Galdós's shift toward naturalism and praises his ability to employ much of Zola's theory while
avoiding its extremes. Second, he mentions Galdós's skillful handling of a narrative technique that conveys the inner workings of his
characters' minds. The first of these observations has received a
great deal of critical attention. The second, unfortunately, has not.
By focusing on the naturalistic content of *La desheredada* scholars
have largely ignored the subtle changes in narrative style which differentiate this novel from the ones that precede it. The narrative
style of Galdós's *segunda manera* is characterized by a more sophisticated use of interiorization devices coupled with the introduction
of experimental techniques not seen in the *primera época* novels.
This chapter will examine the various facets of narrative voice displayed in *La desheredada*, comparing them to the narrative style of
the *primera época* novels, and then showing how the techniques
used in *La desheredada* are further developed in Galdós's masterpiece, *Fortunata y Jacinta*. In addition, these narrative devices will
be discussed in terms of the affective response they elicit and
rhetorical functions they serve in both *La desheredada* and *Fortunata y Jacinta*.

---

[1] Leopoldo Alas (Clarín), *Galdós, Obras completas* (Madrid: Renacimiento,
1912) 1: 95-104.

Alas's comment concerning Galdós's presentation of his characters' thoughts is a fitting point of departure for my discussion of the interiorization devices in *La desheredada*:

> Otro procedimiento que usa Galdós, y ahora con más acierto y empeño que nunca, es el que han empleado Flaubert y Zola con éxito muy bueno, á saber: sustituir las reflexiones que el autor suele hacer por su cuenta respecto de la situación de un personaje, con las reflexiones del personaje mismo, empleando su propio estilo, pero no á guisa de monólogo, sino como si el autor estuviera dentro del personaje mismo y la novela se fuera haciendo dentro del cerebro de éste. En el capítulo del insomnio de Teodora [sic] hay un modelo de esta manera de desarrollar el carácter y la acción de una novela. Sólo puede compararse á este subterráneo hablar de una conciencia, lo que en el mismo género ha escrito Zola en L'Assomoir, para hacernos conocer el espíritu de Gervaisia. (103)

Since it is commonly acknowledged that Galdós, like other nineteenth-century writers, cultivated the use of free indirect style to convey character consciousness in his novels, Galdosian scholars tend to ignore his other forms of representation. However, when we look at the example provided by Alas – "Insomnio número cincuenta y tantos" (vol. 1, ch. 11) – we find that he is not referring to free indirect style. Rather, the chapter Alas indicates as being innovative is entirely composed of a single and uninterrupted passage of free *direct* thought. That is, Isidora's exact thoughts are recorded in first person reference and present tense orientation but they are not indicated as being her thoughts by either a tag (Isidora pensaba) or quotation marks.[2] The unmarked status of this passage sets it apart from the interior views found in Galdós's earlier works. Although the *primera época* novels do contain lengthy passages of characters' thoughts, these are always tagged and punctuated. A typical example is seen in volume 1, chapter 26 of *Gloria* where the eponymous protagonist also is unable to sleep because "velaba el pensamiento." Both *Gloria* and *La desheredada* contain insomnia scenes, but the latter novel presents the character's thoughts in a more complex manner.

---

[2] Seymour Chatman, *Story and Discourse: Narrative Structure in Fiction and Film* (Ithaca: Cornell UP, 1978) 181-86.

The extent of that complexity can best be appreciated by first comparing the "Insomnio número cincuenta y tantos" chapter with yet another insomnia scene: the "Penelope" section of James Joyce's *Ulysses*. Both record the mental ramblings of sleepless women – Isidora and Molly respectively – in an extensive passage of free direct thought. Dorrit Cohn, in her discussion of the "Penelope" section, calls this type of narration "autonomous monologue" because the narrator's voice is totally obliterated by that of a character for an entire chapter.[3] The autonomous monologues of Isidora and Molly share a number of additional traits as well. The beginning of each coincides with the beginning of its respective chapter. There is no preparatory narrative in either text to explain to the reader that the untagged and unquoted passage contains the thoughts of a character rather than the comments of the narrator. Furthermore, the reader is thrust into the mind of that character while she is in the midst of her thoughts. The effect, as Cohn notes, is akin to starting a narrative *in medias res* (221). The reader must provide the connections that will link the autonomous monologue to the surrounding text. Although Galdós does give some guidance with his title, the reader still has a number of gaps to fill in. After determining that the passage is not attributable to the narrator's voice, the reader must ascertain the identity of the character, classify her as the insomniac, establish that she is alone, and decide that her words are silently addressed to herself. The non-communicatory nature of self-directed thought also poses additional challenges for the reader. Since Isidora is the listener of her own thoughts, she does not need to make her thoughts intelligible to anyone else. Therefore, she does not have to supply any of the referential information that would aid the understanding of an outside party. She can allude to anything within her experience without explaining its context. Furthermore, she can mentally skip from one topic to another and between past, present, and future without transitions. Consequently, the reader is required to provide the unwritten portion of the text.

As Cohn states, "[t]he constant oscillation between memories and projects, the real and the potential, the specific and the general, is one of the most distinctive marks of freely associative monologic

---

[3] Dorrit Cohn, *Transparent Minds: Narrative Modes of Presenting Consciousness in Fiction* (Princeton: Princeton UP, 1978) 218.

language"[4] (227). Although Isidora's autonomous monologue displays mental fluctuations of this type, they are far easier to follow than Molly's. Not only are Molly's thoughts more disjointed, but the situation is further complicated by a degree of grammatical confusion not seen in the Galdosian passage. The paucity of connecting verbs and the absence of all punctuation make the reader grapple with the surface level of Molly's monologue before even reaching its content. But despite the more accessible nature of Isidora's insomnia scene, her thoughts are sufficiently discontinuous to require the reader's participation in assigning meaning to her words. The beginning of the monologue alludes to events already witnessed or known by the reader. Therefore, the reader can supply the missing contextual material as Isidora's thoughts flit from the Aransis palace (past), to Mariano's imprisonment (present), to her heart palpitations (immediate present), and then back to the palace (imagined future). The passing hours are marked off one by one in her mind by the clock chimes which repeatedly interrupt her thoughts and send them in new directions. Finally, Isidora's thoughts turn to Joaquín Pez, and the reader must now piece together details of their relationship that had not been presented previously in the text. We learn that Joaquín has sworn to marry Isidora and has offered to lend her money. More importantly, we also find out about a specific past event that displays a heretofore unrevealed aspect of Joaquín's character:

> Hace dos semanas que no veo a Joaquín, y me parece que hace mil años. ¡Estuve tan fuerte aquel día!... ¡Me fingí tan incomodada! Verdad es que él fue atrevido, atrevidísimo... Es tan apasionado, que no sabe lo que se hace... Estaba fuera de sí. ¡Qué ojos, qué fuerza la de sus manos! ¡Pero que seria estuve yo!... Con cuánta frialdad le despedí..., y ahora me muero porque vuelva.

Here Galdós is using the narrative technique of presupposition, which Chatman explains is a way of conveying information "that is offered as a *datum*, something that 'goes without saying,' already understood."[5] Joaquín's physical assault on Isidora, though not dra-

---

[4] Cohn is not using the term monologic in the Bakhtinian sense. Rather, she simply is referring to the monologue format of the passage.

[5] Chatman offers the example "I'm glad to see that Jack has stopped drinking heavily" as a presuppositional statement that conveys the undisputed information that Jack drank heavily in the past. See *Story and Discourse* 210.

matized in the novel, must be accepted by the reader as fact. Indeed, two chapters later Joaquín specifically refers to this event during his calculated attempt to break down Isidora's resistance with money before trying to seduce her once again with "palabras ardientes" in the familiar tú form of address. Neither Joaquín nor Isidora need to explain their references to the rather violent confrontation between them because they both had participated in it. The reader, however, is required to reconstruct the scene from the details provided first by Isidora's thoughts and then by Joaquín's spoken words. Given Joaquín's ungentlemanly conduct in the past, it is not surprising that Isidora reacts with alarm when Joaquín locks her in his study after she refuses his advances a second time. Consequently, the melodramatic excess of Isidora's behavior is mitigated somewhat by our knowledge of Joaquín's brutishness during his earlier, presupposed encounter with Isidora.

In addition to the thoughts themselves, autonomous monologues normally contain evidence of the character's emotional state and physical situation as well. Typically, the character is mentally agitated, and this condition is conveyed through exclamatory statements (223-24). Virtually half of Isidora's statements are encased in exclamation marks, and they express not only her hopes and fears about the future, but also her mounting frustration over her inability to sleep. Her tossing and turning in bed is indicated through her thoughts, as are the sounds she hears – Melchor fiddling with his pipe in the next room, the clock chimes, street noises, Doña Laura's voice – and the things she sees in her room at daybreak. Since Galdós does not use the truncated syntax seen in Molly's monologue, the reader can clearly discern Isidora's movements and understand the sources of the sounds she hears. But like Joyce's passage, Isidora's monologue contains no descriptions or instructions from the narrator. The reader is directly engaged with the unmediated consciousness of a single character.

Both Ricardo Gullón and William Shoemaker view Galdós's rendering of Isidora's insomniatic thoughts as anticipating Joyce's interior monologues in *Ulysses*.[6] But whereas Shoemaker speaks of Galdós's "genuine stream of consciousness techniques," Gullón

[6] William H. Shoemaker, *The Novelistic Art of Galdós*, 3 vols. (Valencia: Albatros, 1980) 2: 164; and Ricardo Gullón, *Galdós, novelista moderno* (Madrid: Gredos, 1966) 264-66.

praises Galdós's ability to give order to his characters' thoughts rather than use Joyce's discontinuous narrative presentation. Though these statements seem contradictory, they simply result from each scholar focusing on a separate facet of Galdós's technique. Isidora's thoughts are freely associated but are not fragmented, therefore Galdós's passage appears more structured than Joyce's despite the similarity in their characteristics. Although Isidora's thoughts are not as chaotic as Molly's, the autonomous monologue in which they are found displays the same overall awareness of the conceptual process involved in self-directed thoughts. In *La desheredada*, published the year before Joyce's birth, Galdós approximated the inner workings of the mind through Isidora's darting thoughts and non-contextualized language. These characteristics are not seen in Galdós's handling of the insomnia chapter in the *primera época* novel *Gloria*.

Volume 1, chapter 26 of *Gloria* contains two insomnia scenes which are strung together. The chapter opens with a narrative description of Gloria's evening habits, during which the narrator specifically refers to Gloria's sleepless condition and the thoughts that fill her mind. The thoughts themselves are tagged and punctuated with quotation marks. Although she is not actually speaking aloud, the tags contain verbs like *hablaba, expresaba*, and *decía*. As Jennifer Lowe has explained in her discussion of Galdós's interiorizations, he often uses *pensar, decir, hablar, exclamar*, and similar verbs of expression interchangeably to indicate mental activity.[7] It is the situational context which alerts the reader to the silent nature of the utterance. Here, for example, the narrator says that "soltaba los diques al pensamiento para que, sin detenerse, corriese fuera." Her thoughts during the first night of insomnia deal with the events of that day. Rather than employ the non-contextualized language appropriate to self-directed thought, however, Galdós reproduces an entire dialogue between Gloria and Morton. Gloria's thoughts seesaw back and forth between her words and his, with awkward tags (me dijo, yo le respondí, etc.) impeding the flow of the passage. As she thinks of the encounter, she describes his actions and her mental reactions to them, providing logical and clear links between

---

[7] Jennifer Lowe, "Spoken and unspoken: Soliloquy, Monologue and Aside in some of Galdós' 'Novelas contemporáneas'," *Revista Canadiense de Estudios Hispánicos* 8 (1983): 110-11.

her feelings for Morton and the memory of her dead brothers. Although Galdós introduces presuppositional events in her thoughts – her meetings with Morton – he has Gloria recall them in a communicatory manner. That is, even though Gloria's thoughts are directed to herself, they contain referential indicators typically used in other-directed speech. She sets the scene for her own declaration of love by explaining the chronology of events and quoting the exact words of Morton's response. It is as if she were describing the events to someone else and had to provide sufficient background information in order for the listener to understand her behavior. Her explanatory tone finally culminates in a series of outwardly-directed questions restating her moral position: "yo pregunto al cielo y a la tierra, a los hombres y a Dios: «¿Por qué este hombre no ha de ser mi marido? ¿Por qué no ha de estar unido a mí, siendo los dos uno solo en la vida usual, como somos uno en la del espíritu, y lo seremos siempre, sin que nada ni nadie lo pueda impedir?... A ver, ¿por qué? Respóndame, ¿por qué?»" The narrator enters at this point to make the transition to the next insomnia scene, which we are told by the narrator has "un tono distinto." Once again Gloria recalls a recent event: that evening's conversation in which her father had spoken of religious matters. In her thoughts Gloria now refutes his opinions with her own well-structured argument. But rather than allow these thoughts to flow naturally into other issues, Galdós has the narrator interrupt this direct thought passage and formally introduce the mental shift that occurs when Gloria's rebellious thoughts begin to emerge. The narrator continues to resurface during the remainder of the chapter, which ends with a narrative description of the dawn's light entering Gloria's room. Throughout this chapter Gloria's thoughts are focused and clearly link past events to present circumstances. There is none of the past-present-future confusion typical of freely associated thoughts. Furthermore, contextual material is provided for the scenes which were not directly witnessed by the reader. The narrator frequently appears to further clarify the situation. Indeed, it is the narrator's voice, rather than that of Gloria herself, which begins and ends the chapter.

The differences in Galdós's handling of the insomnia chapters in *Gloria* and *La desheredada* are indicative of the change that occurs in Galdós's narrative voice techniques as he progresses from his *primera época* to his *segunda manera* novels. This change is characterized by a general movement toward a more subtle, natural, and spontaneous expression of the characters' minds. Galdós achieves this through the use of narrative voice techniques that are of a higher level of complexity and sophistication than those seen in the early novels. As discussed above, one such technique is free direct thought, which allows the reader access to a character's mind without an introductory tag or quotation marks to announce the beginning and end of the passage. Galdós also produces a variation on this form by omitting the tag but retaining the quotation marks. In either case, the absence of the tag requires the reader to bridge the gap that separates the narrator's words from the characters' thoughts.

This does not mean that Galdós abandons the use of tagged direct thought in his *segunda manera* novels. On the contrary, the *segunda manera* novels contain considerably more passages of tagged direct thought than do the *primera época* novels, which instead rely heavily on the technique of indirect thought coupled with narrative description. In statements of indirect thought the reader has no contact with the characters' minds. Rather, the narrator tells the reader what the characters are feeling or thinking. In chapter 37 of *La Fontana de Oro*, for example, throughout Clara's nocturnal adventure it is the narrator who relates her thoughts, impressions, and emotions as she wanders through the streets of Madrid. That is, instead of a transcript of the character's mental process during this ordeal, we just receive a narrative account of what she did, thought, and felt. The following selections from this lengthy scene will help to illustrate how indirect thought differs from its direct counterpart:

> Mucho horror inspiraba a la huérfana la casa de las de Porreño, aunque no tenía otra. Así es que su primer impulso al verse en la calle fue huir, correr sin saber adónde iba para no ver más tan odiosos sitios. Anduvo corto trecho, dobló la esquina y se paró. Entonces comprendió mejor que antes lo terrible de su situación. Al ver que no podía dirigirse a ninguna parte, porque a nadie conocía, le ocurrió esperar cerca de la casa a que entraran Elías o su sobrino. . . Parecíale que iba a salir por la reja cercana una gran mano negra, que la cogería llevándosela dentro: ¡qué horror!. . . La calle le parecía tan grande que no conocía distancia alguna a que referirla, pues para ella las casas hacían horizonte, y aquella gente que venía se le representaba como un mar agitado sordamente, y avanzando, avanzando como si quisiera tragarla. . .

Había visto alguna vez la Cibeles; *pero la oscuridad de la noche, la soledad y el estado de excitación y dolencia en que se encontraba su espíritu hacían que todos los objetos fueran para ella objetos de temor, todos con extrañas y fantásticas formas.* Los leones de mármol le parecía que iban corriendo con velocísima carrera, galopando sin moverse de allí. . . *La infeliz tenía muy extraviados los sentidos a causa del terrible trastorno de su espíritu* . . . Sentía gran postración en todos sus miembros, y, además, un frío intenso, que, creciendo por grados, llegó a producirle una convulsión dolorosa. Arropóse lo mejor que pudo, y pensó en el medio de volver a la casa para esperar a Lázaro en la puerta. Entonces le ocurrió súbitamente la idea de dirigirse a casa de Pascuala.

Indirect thought statements are not pure interior views of the characters because we receive the information totally from the narrator, an outside observer, rather than from the characters themselves. The relationship between the reader and the character is mediated by the presence of the narrator. Indeed, the narrator may even provide interpretive comments such as those I have italicized in the above scene. In contrast, direct thought – both tagged and free – permits the reader an unimpeded view of the character's actual thoughts. In direct thought we see inside the character's mind; in indirect thought we do not. The technique of indirect thought, favored by Galdós in the *primera época*, is largely replaced by the direct thought forms in his *segunda manera* novels, resulting in a mode of presentation that is less narrator-oriented and more character-oriented.

Furthermore, in the *segunda manera* novels Galdós expands his use of a technique that allows his characters' consciousnesses to merge with the narration: free indirect thought. Whereas in the *primera época* novels free indirect thought is used sparingly, in the *segunda manera* novels it becomes a significant component of Galdós's narrative presentation. In these passages the narrator's past tense orientation and third person reference are retained, but the perspective, tone, and at times even the vocabulary belong to the inner world of a character. As the subjective mind of a character fuses with the general narration, the reader slips into that mind with no discernible grammatical impediments. This technique requires the reader to recognize that a shift in point of view has occurred, and then distinguish between the sentences of the passage that are attributable to the narrator, and those that belong to the character. On the infrequent occasions that free indirect thought is used in the *primera época* novels, Galdós aids the reader in this task by providing qualifying statements, as seen in the following examples from *La Fontana de Oro*. The first pertains to Clara's thoughts while making a flower arrangement for her uncle. The second and third examples concern Lázaro's mental confusion over Bozmediano's relationship with Clara. For clarity, I have italicized the narrator's statements.

> ¡Oh! Sin duda, él, al entrar, se había de poner alegre viendo las flores. Las flores le gustarían mucho. ¡Qué sorpresa tendría!... *Esto pensaba ella.* (ch. 8)

> *Sintióse conmovido ante la generosidad desinteresada de aquella persona; pero pronto empezaron las dudas y la confusión.* ¿Quién era aquel joven? ¿Le había favorecido por generosidad o por miras ocultas? No le conocía. ¿Por dónde sabía su nombre y que estaba preso? *Lázaro no pensó mucho en esto.* (ch. 21)

> *Lázaro iba a pronunciar el nombre de Clara, pero se contuvo, porque multitud de pensamientos que se le agolpearon a la imaginación le hicieron detener un buen rato fija la vista en el militar. Aquel tropel de pensamientos fue una serie de rapidísimas nociones que le borraban unas y otras, sucediéndose con precipitado vértigo.* Ella le conocía, le había visto; Bozmediano era una agradable persona: éste le había puesto en libertad; ella se lo rogó tal vez; ella le tenía lástima; él quiso complacerla. ¿A qué precio? ¿Con qué fin? ¿Desde cuándo? (ch. 21)

In these passages the narrator explicitly states that the reader is entering the thoughts of the characters. He clearly marks the beginning and/or ending of the characters' thoughts. As Galdós enters his *segunda manera*, however, he relies less on these blatant narrational cues and instead uses more subtle indicators, as seen in the following example of Isidora's first visit to Joaquín's home in volume 1, chapter 13. Once again, I have italicized the narrator's statements:

> *Entró en casa de Joaquín, y el criado la encerró en un gabinete mientras pasaba recado al señorito.* ¡Qué hermosos y finos muebles, qué cómodos divanes, qué lucientes espejos, qué blanda alfombra, qué graciosas figuras de bronce, qué solemnidad la de

aquel reloj, sostenido en brazos de una ninfa de semblante severo, y sobre todo, qué magníficas estampas de mujeres bellas. *La escasa erudición de Isidora no le permitía saber si aquellas señoras eran de la Mitología o de dónde eran; pero la circunstancia de hallarse algunas de ellas bastante ligeras de vestido le indujo a creer que eran diosas o cosas así.* ¡Y qué bonito aquel armario de tallado roble, todo lleno de libros iguales, doraditos, que mostraban en la pureza de sus pieles rojas y negras no haber sido jamás leídos! «Pero ¿qué harán en los rincones aquellos dos señores flacos? ¡Ah, esa pareja se ve mucho por ahí. Son Mefistófeles y Don Quijote, según me ha dicho Miquis. Yo no haré nunca la tontería de tener en mi casa nada que se vea mucho por ahí. Vamos, que aún puedo yo dar lecciones a esa gente.» *Mirando y remirando, los ojos de Isidora toparon con el Cristo de Velázquez, y estaba ella muy pensativa, tratando de averiguar qué haría nuestro Redentor entre tanta diosa, cuando entró Joaquín.*

The narrator here simply introduces the scene by mentioning Isidora's entrance into the room. Then, without any formal indication of a switch in perspectives, Isidora's impression of what she sees takes over the narrative in the form of free indirect thought. This is briefly interrupted by the narrator bringing up the issue of Isidora's lack of formal education. This narrative statement subtly reminds the reader that the description of the room is being filtered through Isidora's perspective. After this intrusion by the narrator, Isidora's free indirect thoughts begin again, and they merge into a passage of free direct thought. This blending of two forms of interiorization in the same segment is common to the *segunda manera* novels. It provides a way for Galdós to capture both generalized feelings and concrete thoughts. *La desheredada*, however, is a transitional novel in respect to the mixing of interiorizations with narrative passages. In the *segunda manera* novels following this one, Galdós often dispenses entirely with narrative statements in the interior views. He simply dips into his characters' minds and presents them on the page without warning. Free indirect thought, used with or without direct thought passages, stands independent from the surrounding narrative. This technique is particularly prevalent in the Centeno-Tormento-Bringas trilogy, which I will examine in my next chapter.

The reasons behind Galdós's bolder use of free indirect thought in *segunda manera* novels is a matter of conjecture. Since this was a relatively new literary technique, perhaps Galdós felt that the audience of his early *primera época* novels was unprepared for the sudden appearance of free indirect thought in the text. Indeed, a mere ten years before Galdós began his novelistic career, Flaubert had been brought up on charges of immorality stemming from the public's inability to distinguish subjective free indirect style passages from objective authorial statements in *Madame Bovary*.[8] Or maybe Galdós himself needed a period of time to become familiar and comfortable with the possibilities of free indirect thought. If so, he may have been influenced by his reading of several novels from Zola's Rougon-Macquart series just prior to writing *La desheredada*. Zola's liberal and complex use of free indirect thought may have inspired Galdós's creativity in that area. But as Stephen Gilman points out, Galdós does not imitate Zola's constant use of free indirect thought. Rather, Galdós "saves it strategically for maximum narrative effect."[9]

One such effect is irony. Free indirect thought, as the title to Roy Pascal's study of the subject indicates, has a dual voice: that of the character and that of the narrator as well. The point of view and tone belongs to the character, but the grammatical structure of the passage links it to third person narration. The closer that the narrator captures the actual idiom of the character, the more the narrator's presence becomes effaced. But it never disappears completely. This residual presence can give an ironic resonance to the free indirect thought passage whenever the opinions of the narrator do not agree with those of the character whose consciousness is being conveyed. This continually happens in *La desheredada*. Indeed, as Mikhail Bakhtin points out, "hybrid constructions" such as free indirect thought inherently place the narrator's attitudes and values into dialogue with the socio-ideological belief systems of the characters.[10] Thus, free indirect thought requires active participation by the reader because the ironic nuances of this device will be lost on a reader who fails to realize the ideological differences between the character's opinions and the narrator's attitudes. Since the narrator of *La desheredada* occasionally expresses overt criticism of Isidora's

---

[8] Roy Pascal, *The Dual Voice* (Manchester: Manchester UP, 1977) 98.

[9] Stephen Gilman, *Galdós and the Art of the European Novel: 1867-1887* (Princeton: Princeton UP, 1981) 101.

[10] See the discussion of Turgenev's novels in M. M. Bakhtin, "Discourse in the Novel," *The Dialogic Imagination*, trans. Michael Holquist, ed. Caryl Emerson and Michael Holquist (Austin: U of Texas P, 1981) 315-19.

elitist views and fiscally irresponsible behavior, the reader is made aware that Isidora's system of values is in serious conflict with that of the narrator. Therefore, when free indirect thought is used to express Isidora's perspective of something she sees, the inherent irony of that technique emerges because the reader juxtaposes Isidora's views with those of the narrator. For the most part, it is Isidora who is ironized in the process. But others can be the targets of that irony as well. For example, in the passage just quoted above concerning Joaquín's home, Isidora is impressed by the richly bound books that show no evidence of use because to her they represent a level of wealth that permits the purchase of costly books for mere decoration. Thus, although the third person narrative form of this free indirect thought passage primarily conveys the narrator's implicit criticism of Isidora's fascination with conspicuous consumption, it also points out the Pez family's lack of intellectual rigor.

Galdosian scholars have long considered the narrator of *La desheredada* to be an advocate for solid middle-class values such as hard work, personal responsibility, and practicality. Recently, however, Stephanie Sieburth has challenged this view with a radical rereading of the narrator's position. In the first two chapters of her book, *Inventing High and Low*, she presents the narrator of *La desheredada* as a social climbing and elitist proponent of high art who metaphorically links Isidora's pursuit of an aristocratic title with his own desire to transcend his bourgeois roots and achieve literary legitimacy. [11] She further characterizes the narrator as being critical and fearful of modernity because it is hostile to high art and because it dissolves class distinctions which should be retained. I cannot agree with these interpretations for two reasons, both of which pertain to the manner in which Sieburth addresses Galdós's novelistic material. First, Sieburth disregards the long-standing distinction in literary criticism between the narrator and the author. Her general definition of a narrator "as the creator of the text's characters and of the world he narrates" posits the narratologically untenable position of making all narrators – first or third person, heterodiegetic or homodiegetic, omniscient or limited – the authors of the novels they narrate and responsible for all of the elements contained in them. It is only by blurring the boundaries between

---

[11] Stephanie Sieburth, *Inventing High and Low: Literature, Mass Culture, and Uneven Modernity in Spain* (Durham: Duke UP, 1994) 27-99.

real authors, implied authors, and narrators that Sieburth is able to speak of the narrator of *La desheredada* as a writer responding to the demands of a consumer economy and negotiating a place for his novel within the high-low cultural division of Spanish society.[12] Second, Sieburth admits that she presents a one-sided view of *La desheredada*'s narrator which "will not do justice to the side of the narrator that believes in progress and mocks, condemns, or parodies the Old World" (42). Thus, Sieburth's assertions concerning the narrator's negative views of modernity and of bourgeois ascendancy are achieved by discounting textual evidence that would support an alternative interpretation. To my mind, the procedural difficulties involved in Sieburth's approach undermine her assessment of the narrator's values and beliefs.

My own view of the narrator's position on social class stands in sharp contrast. Whereas Sieburth sees the narrator as championing Isidora's claims to nobility and sharing in her rejection of her bourgeois origins, I see the narrator as critical of Isidora precisely because she has turned her back on the middle class in favor of the aristocracy. Passages of narrative commentary are not abundant in *La desheredada*, but when they do appear, they often target the hypocrisy and vanity of middle-class social climbers engaged in an endless process of mimicking those on a higher rung of the social ladder. A typical example occurs in volume 1, chapter 8, section 3 where the narrator states that "hay un verdadero delirio en los pequeños por imitar el modo de presentarse de los grandes." This dissatisfaction with their actual social status leads all members of the middle class – from the petty bourgeois shop girl to the haut bourgeois industrialist – to spend beyond their means in an attempt to look as much like the titled nobility as possible.

By defining her world in terms of an aristocratic lifestyle which she aspires to but cannot afford, Isidora exhibits much the same behavior as the *cursis* who bear the brunt of the narrator's explicit criticism. But the narrator only infrequently makes direct comments

---

[12] In support of her definition of the narrator-as-creator Sieburth merely cites isolated statements, without any explanation of their contexts, from Käte Hamburger, *The Logic of Literature*, trans. Marilynn J. Rose (Bloomington: Indiana UP, 1973) 189 and Susana Reisz de Rivarola, "Ficcionalidad, referencia, tipos de ficción literaria," *Lexis* 3 (1979): 119. Since Sieburth's rereading of *La desheredada* is based on her unorthodox conception of the narrator, a more thorough justification of that position is needed.

targeting Isidora specifically. Rather, double-voiced free indirect style frequently is used instead to implicitly register the narrator's displeasure toward Isidora's actions and attitudes. An early example appears in volume 1, chapter 7, where Isidora is on a shopping spree. Narrative description records what she does, but her mental reactions to what she sees are rendered in free indirect thought:

> Entró en una tienda de paraguas a comprar una sombrilla. ¡Le pareció tan barata...! Todo era barato. Después compró guantes. ¿Cómo iba a salir sin guantes, cuando todo el mundo los llevaba? Sólo los pordioseros privaban a sus manos del honor de la cabritilla.

The passage continues in this vein as Isidora spends nearly all of the money from her uncle on a variety of luxury items such perfume, embossed writing paper, earrings, hairpins, and a fan. Purchasing these unnecessary objects – "¡de que tenía tanta falta!" according to Isidora – soon leaves her without sufficient funds to pay for her room and board. Although the narrator never remarks directly about Isidora's buying habits, his tacit disapproval of her thoughts while shopping imbues the entire passage with an ironic tone. The ironic impact of Isidora's free indirect thoughts is redoubled when they appear within a scene that also features the narrator's friend and confidant, Augusto Miquis, who echoes the sentiments of the narrator concerning Isidora's impracticality, high-society values, and unbridled imagination. Nowhere is this disparity between Isidora's opinions and those of the narrator more clearly shown than in the Castellana carriage procession scene of volume 1, chapter 4, section 4, which begins with Miquis's view of the situation:[13]

> Miquis veía lo que todo el mundo ve: muchos trenes, algunos muy buenos, otros publicando claramente el *quiero y no puedo* en la flaqueza de los caballos, vejez de los arneses y en esta tris-

---

[13] For the historical and political background to this scene see Brian J. Dendle, "Isidora, the *mantillas blancas*, and the Attempted Assassination of Alfonso XII," *Anales Galdosianos* 17 (1982): 51-52 and Peter A. Bly, *Galdós's Novel of Historical Imagination: A Study of the Contemporary Novels* (Liverpool: Francis Cairns, 1983) 4-7. Also, for a discussion of how Galdós uses this scene to rewrite the motifs common to the 19th century novel see Ignacio-Javier López, *Realismo y Ficción: La desheredada de Galdós y la novela de su tiempo* (Barcelona, PPU, 1989) 83-87.

teza especial que se advierte en el semblante de los cocheros de
gente tronada; veía las elegantes damas, los perezosos señores,
acomodados en las blanduras de la berlina, alegres mancebos
guiando faetones, y mucha sonrisa, mucha confusión de colores y
líneas. Pero Isidora, para quien aquel espectáculo, además de ser
enteramente nuevo, tenía particulares seducciones, vio más de
los que vemos todos.

This last sentence, with its first person plural form of the verb *ver*,
instructs the reader to adopt the viewpoint which Miquis and the
narrator share, in opposition to Isidora's impression of the spectacle. Isidora's free indirect thoughts which follow the narrator's comments further exemplify the contrast between her aristocratic pre-
tensions and the disdain felt by the narrator and Miquis for both
ostentatious displays of wealth and the social climbers who attempt
such displays:

> ¡Qué gente aquella tan feliz! ¡Qué envidiable cosa aquel ir y
> venir en carruaje, viéndose, saludándose y comentándose! Era
> una gran recepción dentro de una sala de árboles, o un rigodón
> sobre ruedas. ¡Qué bonito mareo el que producían las dos filas
> encontradas, y el cruzamiento de perfiles marchando en direc-
> ción distinta! Los jinetes y las amazonas alegraban con su rápida
> aparición el hermoso tumulto; pero de cuando en cuando la
> presencia de un antipático simón lo descomponía.

This description of the event is a projection of Isidora's viewpoint,
and as such it not only provides us with a picture of the things she
sees, but also her feelings toward them. [14] Simultaneously, we receive information about the physical object and about the character
viewing it. Isidora's perceptual perspective (the procession before
her eyes) is filtered through her conceptual perspective (her elitism
and snobbery). But since her conceptual perspective differs from
that of either the narrator or Miquis, Isidora becomes ironized in
the process. In this way, Galdós undercuts the second major effect
inherent in free indirect thought: sympathy.

---

[14] Peter A. Bly, *Vision and the Visual Arts in Galdós: A Study of the Novels and Newspaper Articles* (Liverpool, Francis Cairns: 1986) 104 and Michael A. Schnepf, "Galdós's *La desheredada* Manuscript: Isidora in the Prado Museum," *Romance Quarterly* 37 (1990): 323, link Isidora's impression of the procession to the paint-ings she viewed in the Prado in the scene immediately preceding this one.

The sympathy producing potential of free indirect thought stems from its status as an interiorization device. As Seymour Chatman has observed, all devices which grant the reader access to a character's consciousness – free indirect thought, free direct thought, tagged direct thought – create an intimate connection between that character and the reader.[15] When that connection is sustained in interior views throughout the text, the reader's emotional distance from the character is greatly reduced and identification with the character's point of view is possible. But as Wayne Booth has pointed out, there is a danger in this identification process. A reduction in emotional distance can result in a reduction of moral and intellectual distance as well.[16] In *La desheredada* Galdós avoids this problem by counterbalancing Isidora's interiorizations with the implicit and explicit criticism of her by both the narrator and Miquis. These strong voices in favor of practicality and moderation warn the reader not to identify with Isidora. Although our access to Isidora's thoughts allow us to empathize with her throughout the text, we are kept from fully sympathizing with her because of the ironic juxtaposition of her opinions against those of Miquis and the narrator.

Yet, her numerous interior views do allow us to see her as she sees herself, and therefore we can understand her actions in ways that the characters who chastise her cannot. In this novel's polyphonic interaction of voices, we frequently hear Isidora's own voice emerge above those of the narrator and the other characters. And in that voice we find what Bakhtin considers to be a hallmark of the polyphonic hero, namely the unwillingness to be defined by others.[17] *La desheredada* is the story of a woman who has been led to believe that she has a secret identity very different from her public persona. This situation sets up a contrast between her internal reality – who she sees herself to be – and the external reality of those around her. Galdós highlights this basic conflict by conveying a major portion of the text through interior views of Isidora. Since Isidora primarily lives within the fantasy world of her mind, the text

---

[15] Chatman, *Story and Discourse* 157.

[16] Wayne C. Booth, *The Rhetoric of Fiction*, 2nd ed. (1961: Chicago: U of Chicago P, 1983) 249-50.

[17] Mikhail Bakhtin, *Problems of Dostoevsky's Poetics*, trans. and ed. Caryl Emerson, Theory and History of Literature 8 (Minneapolis: U of Minnesota P, 1984) 47-77.

allows us to enter that realm through passages of tagged and free direct thought as well as free indirect thought. Through these interiorizations we watch as Isidora translates external reality to conform to her own personal reality. Thus, we sense her wonderment at seeing the trappings of wealth which she considers her legitimate due. Likewise, we feel her disdain for everything she considers to be common and beneath her true station. We literally see the world through her eyes, and this access to her inner world permits us to understand the reasons behind her seemingly self-destructive actions. Miquis's attempts to modify Isidora's behavior by sending her to Emilia's home to learn lessons of thrift and industry fail because, as Lou Charnon-Deutsch has noted, Miquis wants to bring Isidora closer to the ideal of bourgeois womanhood. [18] But Isidora does not regard herself as bourgeois. Rather, she patterns herself on the aristocratic model of womanhood, which is characterized by good taste and refinement, a contempt for all that is vulgar, and a generosity that manifests itself in patronage of the arts and charity toward the poor. Isidora is simply waiting for recognition of her rank so that she can assume her proper place in the world – a place where her elitist values would be deemed appropriate by her peers. [19] This world view – instilled in her by her uncle and reinforced by her reading of serial novels – is based on her faith in the authenticity of the documents proving her noble heritage. Isidora's every thought and action is governed by her belief that she is a member of the aristocracy.

When that belief is shattered at the end of the novel, Isidora's genuine anguish, confusion, and self-doubt are conveyed through free indirect thought passages in which the irony is now underplayed in order for the sympathetic aspect of the device to surface instead. In particular, her free indirect thoughts filling the central portion of volume 2, chapter 15, section 2 show her realistically assessing her situation for the first time in her life. By reserving all

---

[18] Lou Charnon-Deutsch, *Gender and Representation: Women in Spanish Realist Fiction*, Purdue U Monographs in Romance Languages 32 (Amsterdam: John Benjamins, 1990) 152-53.

[19] In *Galdós y la literatura popular* (Madrid: Sociedad General Española de Librería, 1982), Alicia Andreu notes that "la actitud clasista de Isidora" is also found in Faustina Saez de Melgar's *La Cruz del Olivar*, which Andreu cites as the model for *La desheredada*. In that popular novel, the author "proyecta todo un mundo ficticio basado en la superioridad de las clases privilegiadas" 118.

sympathetic interiorizations until after Isidora learns that she is the victim of her father's deception and her uncle's credulity, Galdós keeps us emotionally detached from Isidora throughout most of the novel. But at its close, we are made to feel the consequences of a life based on dreams instead of reality. Since these interior views allow us to directly experience the devastating disappointment and emotional upheaval she undergoes upon finding that her high-born status was a hoax, we finally sympathize with her and know that she is left with no foundation on which to now base her behavior. Her thoughts throughout the novel show the extremes in which she sees the world – noble/common; beautiful/ugly; priceless/worthless; decent/ordinary – and once she abandons her claim to the uppermost reaches of that world, she has no alternative but to descend to its depths. A mid-ground simply does not exist for her. Isidora is the unwitting casualty of her father's dissatisfaction with his position within the petty bourgeoisie. As a result, she is unable to return to those middle-class roots. Since she is not a lady of nobility, she can only see herself as a woman of the streets. Consequently, we can understand her actions at the close of the novel to be the outcome of her forcibly altered conceptual perspective. But it is important to note that Isidora is not plunged into prostitution by the author as a punishment for rejecting middle-class values. Rather, she herself chooses a life of prostitution over other options which are open to her and which would restore her to a petty bourgeois lifestyle. Through her final act of self-determination, Isidora continues to stand in defiance of the narrator's values. By allowing Isidora this freedom, Galdós reaffirms the polyphonic structure of the novel. Isidora's voice is never submerged into that of the narrator. In Bakhtin's terminology, Isidora has the "final word" on who she is, and it is through interiorization devices revealing her consciousness that the reader sees how she comes to voice that word (DP 48).

By far the majority of the interior views in *La desheredada* belong to Isidora, but the reader also is allowed to dip into the minds of the other characters on occasion. Of particular note are two interior views of Mariano which reveal the motivations behind the boy's attempted assassination of the king. Volume 2, chapter 14, section 2, contains a direct thought passage recording Mariano's impressions as he watches one of the habitual processions of coaches on the Castellana. Since an earlier version of this spectacle was featured in volume 1, chapter 4, section 4, the reader immediately makes the connection between the scenes and compares Mariano's reaction against that of his sister. The differing conceptual perspectives of the two siblings produce substantially different views of the event. Whereas Isidora stared in awestruck admiration as she watched the rich display of coaches and their well dressed passengers greeting each other, Mariano mentally berates these "bloodsuckers" of the people for their lavish lifestyle supported by the misery of the working poor. The following condensed version of Mariano's thoughts gives the general flavor of the entire passage:

> Ya empieza a pasar la pillería. Allá va un coche..., y otro y otro. Toma, aquel es de ministro. *Chupagente...* Ahí va otro. ¡Cuánto habrá robado ese hombre para llevar cocheros con tanto galón!... Anda, anda, y allí va un cochero montado en el caballo de la derecha, con su gorrete azul y charreteras... ¡Eh!, y en el coche van dos señoras... ¡Vaya unas tías, y como se revuelcan en los cojines! *Oigan ustés,* ¿de dónde han sacado tanto encaje? Y qué abrigaditas con sus pieles... Pues yo tuve anoche mucho frío, y ando con los zapatos rotos. Paren, paren el coche, que voy a subir un poquito. Estoy cansado. ¡Valientes tías!... ¡Puño, cuanto coche! Alla va don Melchor acompañando a dos niñas. Sí, para ti estaban, bruto. Son las niñas de Pez. Y el señor Pez va también con la gran tripa llena de billetes de Banco, que ha tragado... Más coches, más coches, más. Bien dice el maestro que lo bueno sería que toda esta gente no tuviera más que un solo pescuezo para ahorcarla toda de una vez... ¡Vivan los pobres!, digo yo, y caiga el que caiga. ¡Abajo los ladrones!

His language is peppered with the coarse phrases which characterize his idiom, and he uses some of the pat political terms taught him by Juan Bou. Overall, Mariano's thoughts reflect a proletariat-oriented philosophy which sharply contrasts with Isidora's aristocratic-based perspective. Neither, however, reflects the moderate – and middle class – voice represented by Miquis and the narrator. As J. M. Labanyi has noted, "In *La desheredada*, Galdós is defending the liberal notion of a free-enterprise society against both the stratified social order of the *ancien régime* (represented by the Aransis family) and new communistic visions of a classless society (represented by Juan Bou and Mariano)."[20] The implied author uses

---

[20] J. M. Labanyi, "The Political Significance of *La desheredada*," *Anales Galdosianos* 14 (1979): 54.

Miquis as an exemplary model to advocate a meritocracy based on hard work, responsibility, and practicality. Unlike either Isidora or Mariano, Miquis sees the sham behind the glitter of the procession and recognizes the entire spectacle to be an exercise in vanity. Although Miquis later enters the upper levels of society through his professional achievements, he is neither impressed by it (like Isidora) nor hates it (like Mariano and Bou). Rather, he retains a critical distance and uses humor to deflate the pomposity of the aristocracy and the *nouveaux riches*. But Isidora envies the lifestyle of the rich and famous, and so does Mariano, although he hides his feelings behind the guise of revolutionary zeal. He is constantly in search of money and resents the wealthy for their unwillingness to allow him into their inner circle. This envy and personal resentment is revealed in Mariano's second long interiorization in volume 2, chapter 16, where Mariano's free indirect thoughts culminate in his decision to take revenge on society by attacking its personified form: the king.[21] By using free indirect thought instead of direct thought in this passage, Galdós is able to communicate to the reader the complexity of Mariano's emotions in a way that Mariano could not do himself given his lack of verbal skills. This same strategy is used again in *El doctor Centeno* for many of the interior views of Felipe who, like Mariano, isn't sufficiently articulate to verbalize his thoughts in a direct form.

The brief interiorizations of two other characters, Augusto Miquis and Joaquín Pez, also are of interest because they are used in conjunction with two techniques that form part of Galdós's narrative repertoire: present tense narration and theatrical formatting. The first of these techniques is also found in the *primera época* novels, but the second appears for the first time in *La desheredada*. I will examine each case separately.

Miquis's interior views in volume 2, chapter 10, sections 1 and 3 provide a rare look at his innermost feelings as he battles with his conscience against the sexual temptation which Isidora represents. Miquis's thoughts are presented both directly and in a free indirect form. His vacillation adds a dimension to his personality not yet

---

[21] In "The Medical Background to Galdós' *La desheredada*," *Anales Galdosianos* 7 (1972): 70-73, M. Gordon suggests that this plot element may have been inspired by Francisco Otero González, a youth of a similar background and temperament to Mariano's, who made a real-life attempt on Alfonso XII's life in 1879.

seen in the text and contributes toward making his portrayal more complex. The division inherent in Miquis's nature – practical and responsible on one hand but passionate and playful on the other – is graphically represented in the text by Galdós's sudden use of the present tense to narrate a portion of this chapter's opening section. Miquis's free indirect thoughts immediately preceding the present tense segment show him at his weakest moment. But he literally is saved by the bell when his fiancee's father makes an unexpected visit. Whereas Miquis's entire office meeting with Isidora prior to this interruption is related in past tense narration, Muñoz's arrival signals a change to the present tense.

> Y él volvió a pasearse y a mirarla... ¡Qué hermosa estaba! ¿Quién le metía a él a moralista ni a redentor de samaritanas? Soltó una carcajada en lo recóndito de su ser, allí donde su alma contemplaba atónita la imagen de la ocasión. «Pero me caso el lunes, el lunes...» Miró el retrato de su novia.
>
> De pronto suena la campanilla, entra un señor y pasa a la sala... Es el papá de la novia de Miquis, que viene a consultarle un punto de Higiene. Augusto deja a Isidora en su despacho y tiene que resistir una hora la embestida de su suegro, el cual le habla de Sanidad y de la fundación de la Penitenciaría para jóvenes delincuentes.
>
> Cuando su suegro se marcha, Miquis vuelve al despacho. Está aturdido; la visita le ha dejado insensible. Hay en su cuerpo algo de efecto de una paliza; pero está fortificado interiormente. Isidora aguarda ansiosa. Está pálida y ha llorado un poco, porque no puede apartar del pensamiento que su hijo y su padrino no tienen qué comer aquella tarde.
>
> – ¡Cuánto has tardado! Es pesadito ese señor. En fin, amigo, yo siento molestarte. Acuérdate de lo que te dije al entrar.
>
> Miquis hace una rápida exploración en su alma, encuentra en ella algún desorden y dispone que todo vuelva a su sitio. «Soy un hombre sublime – dice para sí –, un hombre de honor y de caridad; soy también un hombre que se casa el lunes.»
>
> Isidora le había dirigido al entrar una súplica angustiosa, elocuente expresión salida de los más sagrados senos del alma humana. Juntando el quejido de la necesidad a la súplica del pudor, Isidora le había dicho: «Dame de comer y no me toques.»
>
> Miquis abre su bolsa a la desvalida hermosa y con magnánimo corazón le dice:
>
> – Mañana estarás en casa de Emilia.

The sound of the bell that jolts Miquis out of his sexual fantasizing coincides with a similarly jarring shift in verb tenses for the reader. In this way Galdós creates an almost cinematic effect of freezing the scene between Miquis and Isidora, and leaving it suspended in time while the actions between Miquis and his visitor are projected into the foreground. Miquis leaves his desire for Isidora behind while he assumes his role as a respected doctor and future husband. The tense shift dramatically represents Miquis's suppression of his passionate side and the re-establishment of his responsible side. [22] As will be seen in my discussion concerning the more extensive use of this technique in *El doctor Centeno*, *Tormento*, and *Fortunata y Jacinta*, Galdós typically reserves the present tense for his characters' emotionally intense moments. In this way, he is able to take advantage of the vividness and immediacy associated with present tense narration in order to allow the reader to experience the personal drama along with the character. [23]

Joaquín Pez's only major interior views appear in the two chapters of *La desheredada* that are written as if they were scenes from a play. As Roberto Sánchez notes, these chapters represent the first tentative steps toward what Galdós calls his "sistema dialogal." [24] This practice will eventually result in such dialogue novels as *Realidad* and *El abuelo*. Indeed, it is in the prologue to this latter novel

---

[22] I cannot agree with Stephanie Sieburth's assessment of Miquis's behavior here as displaying "sexual aggressivity" and showing his "dark side." Neither can I agree that in his next encounter with Isidora a few days after his wedding he is "prepared . . . both to wrong a brand-new wife and to abuse a long-time friend in need." Although Miquis is tempted by Isidora's beauty, he consciously stops himself from acting on that impulse on both occasions. In fact, he actually flees from Isidora on the second encounter in order to keep himself from giving in to her offer to sell herself to him. Miquis chooses to remain faithful to his wife despite his sexual attraction to Isidora. Thus, Miquis again serves as a model of behavior, this time to male readers who may find themselves in a similar situation. See "The Dialectic of Modernity in *La desheredada*," *A Sesquicentennial Tribute to Galdós 1843-1993*, ed. Linda M. Willem (Newark DE: Juan de la Cuesta, 1993) 38-39.

[23] For a discussion of the effects traditionally associated with the historical present see Carol Joy Van Ess-Dykema, "The Historical Present in Oral Spanish Narratives," diss., Georgetown U, 1984, 31-32; or Nessa Wolfson, "The Conversational Historical Present Altercation," *Language* 55 (1979): 169.

[24] Roberto G. Sánchez, "«El sistema dialogal» en algunas novelas de Galdós," *Cuadernos Hispanoamericanos* 235 (1969): 155-67. It is also interesting to note that *La desheredada* originally was published with a "lista de personajes" preceding both volume 1 and volume 2, as was the practice in Galdós's dialogue novels. Enrique Miralles's edition of *La desheredada* (Barcelona: Planeta, 1992) reproduces this roster of names on pages 6 and 254.

that the rationale for his use of theatrical formatting is stated. Through his "sistema dialogal," explains Galdós, the characters "manifiestan su contextura moral con su propia palabra, y con ella, como en la vida, nos dan el relieve más o menos hondo y firme de sus acciones. La palabra del autor narrando y describiendo no tiene, en términos generales, tanta eficacia, ni da tan directamente la impresión de la verdad espiritual."[25] This technique allows the characters to reveal themselves to the reader without narrative intrusions, thereby contributing to the character-oriented presentation of the *segunda manera* novels. Furthermore, the "sistema dialogal" permits Galdós to expand his repertoire of interiorizations beyond those devices normally allowed in a novelistic context. Soliloquies and asides, common in dramatized performances, are inserted in the novel via the "sistema dialogal," thereby creating two new avenues by which the reader can have access to the characters' thoughts. In volume 2, chapter 12 Isidora, Pez, and don José display "la verdad espiritual" of their relationship through these theatrical interiorization devices. Joaquín Pez, seen largely through exterior views in all other chapters of the novel, here is given a long and intimate interiorization at a moment of personal crisis. His thoughts reinforce the reader's assessment of him as self-centered and egotistical. But we also see that he, like Isidora, is a victim of an upbringing that ill prepared him for the realities of life. Galdós uses Pez's anguished thoughts to critique social climbing parents who instill unrealistic expectations and unattainable desires in their children. Once again the reader is allowed to see the consequences of a life based on mere fabrication. But any sympathy that the reader may feel for Pez is immediately undercut by his extreme selfishness in allowing Isidora to once again sell herself to save him. His thoughts during his conversation with don José in section 3 clearly show him rationalizing his financial exploitation of Isidora's love for him. Don José's asides allow Galdós to explicitly censure Joaquín's actions without using the narrator to do so.

Galdós's attempts to efface the narrator through his *sistema dialogal* is merely one facet of a general trend toward less intrusive narrative presentation in the *segunda manera* novels. My discussion of *La desheredada*'s interiorization devices has mentioned many more. By

---

[25] Benito Pérez Galdós, *El abuelo, Obras completas: Novelas*, ed. Federico Carlos Sainz de Robles, 3 vols. (Madrid: Aguilar, 1970) 3: 800-01.

decreasing indirect thought passages while increasing direct thought passages, for example, Galdós provides the *segunda manera* reader a larger degree of unimpeded access to the minds of the characters. This increase in interiorizations is supplemented by the addition of free direct thought, free indirect thought, theatrical soliloquy, and aside. Taken together, these devices point to a clear narratological departure from the writings of Galdós's *primera época*.

To concentrate exclusively on interiorization devices, however, would do a disservice both to the complexity of Galdós's discoursive style and to the subtlety of his rhetorical strategies. As Bakhtin has observed, "Self-consciousness can be made the dominant in the representation of any person. But not all persons are equally favorable material for such a representation" (DP 50). Indeed, the withholding of interior views can be a particularly effective way of avoiding the reader's empathetic identification with certain characters. In *La desheredada*, for example, all of Isidora's lovers are portrayed either primarily or entirely through exterior views. When they do have interiorizations, they are brief and unflattering. In general, we observe these characters from a distance, learning about them from the narrator's comments and through their own spoken words and actions. As they are revealed to us through these exterior views, we become aware of their negative traits, and we come to disapprove of their behavior and the values they hold. In volume 1, chapter 12, section 3, for example, the narrator tells us about Joaquín's womanizing and his immoderate spending habits. Afterwards we hear his dialogues with his father where he clearly shows that he doesn't believe in the legitimacy of Isidora's claims to the Aransis name despite his repeated assurances to her to the contrary. We see Joaquín lie to Isidora in order to obtain both her sexual favors and her money. Thus, we know that Joaquín is a libertine and a cad well before Isidora realizes as much. Similarly, our initial exposure to Melchor in volume 1, chapter 8, section 3 is through the narrator's description of how his family spoils him and uses their meager income to indulge his whims. This is immediately followed by two brief free indirect thought passages – his only interior views – where Melchor first shows his own high opinion of himself by mocking his hard-working but unschooled uncle's way of pronouncing words, and then shows his ingratitude toward his parents and his dissatisfaction with his middle-class lifestyle by complaining that he lacks the money to buy what his upper-class friends own.

But Melchor's character is largely developed through his actions. In particular, we see him engaged in get-rich-quick schemes of dubious legality. It is interesting to note that both Melchor and Joaquín also share traits with Isidora. Like her, they are vain, self-centered, snobbish, and profligate with money. Thus, by implicitly drawing parallels between Isidora and these two men, Galdós is able to subtly condemn not only the individual behavior and attitudes of each, but also the values that all three characters hold in common.

The remaining lovers, however, exhibit a level of dishonesty that places them at a moral distance far removed from Isidora. Galdós uses these characters to level criticism at the more serious problems of society: political corruption, crime, adultery, and violence. Thus, Galdós portrays both Botín and Gaitica through "character-narration," an exteriorization device which allows for a stronger expression of reproach than would have been possible through simple narrative commentary. In character-narration the direct speech of one character is used to tell a story about another. Consequently, the speaker's opinions can color that narration. This occurs in volume 2, chapters 5 and 6, where first don José and then Joaquín give examples of Botín's hypocrisy (feigning religiosity while carrying on an extra-marital affair) and dirty-dealing (involving his government connection). Due to their hostility toward Botín, both don José and Joaquín use strong language and a harsh tone, resulting in a derogatory portrait of Isidora's third lover that the narrator can implicitly approve of without having to comment on directly. Similarly, the criminal activities and violent behavior of Gaitica are character-narrated, this time by Emilia. In volume 2, chapter 17, section 3 she calls Gaitica "ese salvaje, ese canalla, ese asqueroso reptil, ese inmundo," and then after asking Miquis to excuse her language because "faltan palabras apropiadas" to express Gaitica's baseness, she goes on to say that "ese basurero animado" savagely beat Isidora and scared her face with a knife. By conveying this information through the outrage of such a positive character as Emilia, Galdós generates greater reader sympathy for Isidora and against Gaitica than would have resulted from the narrator's description of the events. These character-narrations of Gaitica and Botín produce damning portraits which are reinforced by the scenically-presented actions of these two men. Gaitica's whipping of Mariano's face in volume 2, chapter 14, section 2 foreshadows the disfiguring wound he inflicts on Isidora, and Botín's humiliation of Isidora in volume

2, chapter 7 displays the same ruthlessness he exhibits in his business dealings.

Through the exterior portrayals of Joaquín, Melchor, Botín, and Gaitica, Galdós was able to raise the reader's awareness of a wider variety of social ills than are represented by Isidora alone. Indeed, Isidora's complex portrayal – which uses interior views for both ironic and sympathetic purposes – makes her a less effective vehicle for social criticism than her unambiguously negative lovers. Without any empathetic or sympathetic attachment to these men, the reader can feel the full weight of the implied author's scorn for their behavior. Furthermore, by seeing all four of them functioning within the upper levels of respectable society – Joaquín and Botín have titles, and even Melchor and Gaitica take part in the Castellana procession – the reader is implicitly encouraged to examine his or her own extra-textual behavior and social connections. In short, Galdós's use of exterior views plays a vital role in the overall rhetorical strategy of the text because the reader's affective response to the characters is as much influenced by being denied access to their minds as being granted it. Indeed, the key element of that strategy lies in the effects created through the *interplay* of interior and exterior views.

* * *

The *segunda manera*, begun with *La desheredada*, finds its full development a mere five years later in *Fortunata y Jacinta*, a novel which in many ways resembles *La desheredada*. Fortunata's intense devotion toward the unworthy Juanito is prefigured in Isidora's constancy to Juanito's friend and fellow señorito, Joaquín. Both women, abandoned by their paramours, must live by offering their sexual favors to men whom they do not love. The sexually charged but unconsummated relationship between Isidora and Miquis anticipates the affair between Fortunata and Feijoo. The advice offered by these two men, though socially practical, does not take into consideration the emotional well-being of the women they are trying to save. The marriage partners they propose – Bou for Isidora and Maxi for Fortunata – simply are unsuited for the task. These two "fallen women" become social outcasts, yet they both have their champions. In Ballester's eloquent defense of Fortunata we hear echoes of José Relimpio's inarticulate but similarly heartfelt declarations of Isidora's unsullied honor. As Germán Gullón has observed, Galdós even makes use of a small detail to link these two women: the charm Miquis finds in Isidora's eating of an orange is later repeated in the allure that Juanito feels when he sees Fortunata sucking on an egg. [26] As we shall see, the similarities between Isidora and Fortunata extend to their narrative voice presentation as well, with extensive interior views used to generate an empathetic response in the reader toward these two women. But unlike Isidora's interiorizations, where irony frequently undercuts the reader's sympathy, Fortunata's interior views invite the reader's full emotional engagement. Before discussing these interiorization devices, however, it is necessary to focus on the narrator of *Fortunata y Jacinta*.

One of the most important tasks that faces the reader of any novel is to determine the degree to which the narrator exhibits what Wayne Booth has described as reliability. In order to do so, the reader must constantly evaluate the narrator's opinions against the implied author's social, political, religious, and ethical attitudes and assumptions as they emerge over the course of the text. It is important to keep in mind that the values of the society depicted in a novel may be at odds with the values that the implied author condones. Chatman's distinction between story and discourse becomes a useful tool in sorting out this matter. The values held by the characters merely pertain to the realm in which the characters reside – the story. They do not constitute the values of the text as a whole. It is only through the configuration of all the elements in both the story and the discourse that the implied author projects the range of social, political, religious, and ethical values advocated by the text. The reader is asked to construct the implied author's views from evidence in the text. Given the polyphonic nature of Galdós's novels, that task is not easily achieved. The reader's active participation in the text is needed to bring together all of the views expressed in the text, and after so doing, the reader must use these diverse perspectives and opinions to discern what Bakhtin calls the "unified truth" of the text (DP 81). The narrator's perspective is an important issue in this process, not only because it is one of the many voices in the text, but also because of the slant that that perspective can give to the entire story. Thus, the narrator's reliability

---

[26] Germán Gullón, "Originalidad y sentido de *La desheredada*," *Anales Galdosianos* 17 (1982): 39.

or unreliability must be taken into consideration. Yet, literary scholars often fail to make the distinction between the narrator's degree
of omniscience and his degree of reliability. Indeed, reliability is
often equated with omniscience, while unreliability is confused with
a limited point of view. This problem is easily cleared up if we remember that reliability is based on the values held by the narrator
rather than his degree of omniscience. If his attitudes are in accord
with the implied author's, he is reliable; and if he differs entirely
from the implied author, he is unreliable. If, however, only some of
the narrator's attitudes conflict with those of the implied author, he
is unreliable just in those areas and reliable in all others. This semi-
reliable narrator is the most difficult to detect because he is the
source of both trustworthy and misleading information. It is just
this type of semi-reliable narrator which is found in *Fortunata
y Jacinta*. Geoffrey Ribbans divides the statements of *Fortunata y
Jacinta*'s narrator into two categories: those dealing with facts are
reliable, but those expressing a judgment are not to be trusted completely. [27] Indeed, it is within this area of value judgments that the
reader must be careful to examine each individual narrative opinion
in order to ascertain how far the narrator is from the implied author. Over the course of the novel it becomes clear that the narrator's unreliability is confined to one area alone: his social class. His
entire narrative is slanted in favor of the lifestyle of the upper middle class. The narrator accepts without question all aspects of that
lifestyle, and herein lies his point of contention with the implied author. Unlike the narrator's uncritical view of the middle class, the
implied author projects a more nuanced opinion which values the
middle class for its dynamic role in the development of Spanish society, but is critical of certain behaviors and attitudes associated
with the haute bourgeoisie. Over the course of the novel, both the
story and the discourse will contribute toward the reader's identification of these behaviors and attitudes as being detrimental to
Spanish society.

The narrator's upper middle-class bias is established early in the
novel, within the first of its four volumes. According to its premise,
Fortunata y Jacinta is a retrospective account of events which oc-

---

[27] Geoffrey Ribbans, "Notes on the Narrator in *Fortunata y Jacinta*," *A Sesquicentennial Tribute to Galdós 1843-1993*, ed. Linda M. Willem (Newark DE: Juan de
la Cuesta, 1993) 95.

curred some fifteen years earlier as told by the chronicler-narrator, who specifically states that his information is gleaned from personal experience and through conversations with named informants. His interest in qualifying small details of which he is uncertain (which university class was the scene of the egg frying incident; how many days were spent in Sevilla during the honeymoon; etc.) further emphasizes his attempt to appear objective and accurate. However, his objectivity is undercut by his choice of informants: Villalonga (a mutual friend of Juanito and the narrator, and also Juanito's partner in his slum adventures); the Santa Cruz family (Juanito, Jacinta, don Baldomero, and doña Barbarita); Zalamero and Arnáis (linked to the Santa Cruz family through business, friendship, and family ties); Estupiñá (the Santa Cruz family retainer); and Rafaela (Jacinta's personal maid). All these informants, including the narrator himself, are part of the Santa Cruz circle of influence and therefore reflect the values held by the *nouveau riche*, upwardly mobile, commercially oriented Santa Cruz dynasty. The prejudicial effect of their influence on the narrator's outlook is reflected in his statement that the class system in Spain is "una dichosa confusión de todas las clases" where money and upbringing rather than birth are the main factors in determining one's position in society (vol. 1, ch. 6, sec. 5). A dinner given by the Santa Cruz family is presented as a symbolic representation of this harmonious blending of the classes: "siendo de notar que el conjunto de los convidados ofrecía perfecto muestrario de todas las clases sociales" (vol. 1, ch. 10, sec. 5). However, of the twenty-five member guest list, twenty-four are of the upper and middle classes. The only member of the lower class, Estupiñá, had long since severed allegiance to his own class in order to establish himself under the patronage of his benefactor. Therefore, the narrator's concept of an intermingled social system refers only to the class barriers which were being broken down between the newly moneyed middle class and the impoverished aristocracy, not between the middle and lower classes. Indeed, it is precisely the recently acquired wealth of the middle classes which formed the basis for their upward social mobility. The *pueblo* is excluded from this mixing of classes because it has neither the funds nor the "educación académica" – which the narrator erroneously states is given to all Spaniards – to move up the social ladder.[28] At various points

---

[28] For a discussion of Spain's failure to provide adequate public education in the nineteenth-century see Ángel Bahamonde and Jesús A. Martínez, *Historia de*

elsewhere in the text the narrator reflects a romantic attitude toward the *pueblo*, similar to that of Juanito and Villalonga, when he describes the colorful dress, speech, and customs of its people. Also, when he says that "el pueblo, en nuestras sociedades, conserva las ideas y los sentimientos elementales en su tosca plenitud, como la cantera contiene el mármol, materia de la forma. El pueblo posee las verdades en bloque, y a él acude la civilización conforme se le van gastando las menudas, de que vive" (vol. 3, ch. 7, sec. 3), he echoes not only the sentiments but the very words used earlier by Juanito: "¡Pueblo!... lo esencial de la humanidad, la materia prima, porque cuando la civilización deja perder los grandes sentimientos, las ideas matrices, hay que ir a buscarlos al bloque, a la cantera del pueblo" (vol. 2, ch. 7, sec. 6). As John Sinnigen has observed, this attitude equates civilization with the middle and upper classes, and sees the *pueblo* as a primitive resource to be exploited for the benefit of civilized society.[29] At best this attitude views the *pueblo* as a type of noble savage to be admired from a distance. Occasional contact, such as the kind Juanito and his cohorts have with the denizens of the *cava baja*, is not intended to alter the "legitimate" social relations among the middle and upper classes. The *pueblo*, romanticized but socially shunned, largely remains outside the realm of the class fusion taking place between the other segments of society. The narrator is oblivious to the marginalized status of the *pueblo* because he defines social mobility entirely in terms of his own class. Comfortably ensconced in the bourgeoisie, he exhibits the same classist attitude as his friends. Also like his friends, he belongs to the generation of idle and indulged *señoritos* who, through no effort of their own, reaped the benefits of the hard work and industrious habits exhibited by their fathers and grandfathers.

The narrator fully ascribes to the norms of social acceptability operating in his peer group, where a man is primarily judged by his wealth, appearance, quick wit, and conversational ability. Juanito is praised as being in abundant possession of all these qualities, and

España: Siglo XIX (Madrid: Cátedra, 1994) 484-87 and Germán Rueda, *Historia de España: El reinado de Isabel II* (Madrid: Temas de Hoy, 1996) 44-48.

[29] John H. Sinnigen, "Individual, Class, and Society in *Fortunata y Jacinta*," ed. Robert J. Weber (London: Tamesis, 1974) 55.

although the narrator acknowledges that Juanito is vain, this character flaw is presented as a natural consequence of having so many socially desirable traits. Indeed, throughout volume 1 the narrator downplays or excuses Juanito's failings. For example, his unemployed status and large monetary expenditures are glossed over while his generosity and ability to prudently handle his monthly allowance are stressed. Also, his neglect of his studies is justified by his preference to live life rather than read about it.[30] Above all, the narrator dismisses Juanito's womanizing activities as minor infractions by modern standards. They are, he says, mere "barrabasadas" that "parecerían hoy timideces y aun actos de ejemplaridad relativa" (vol. 1, ch. 1, sec. 2). According to the narrator, Juanito's disgraceful treatment of the women in his life is excusable since it falls under the category of the socially sanctioned sexual double standard. Overall, the narrator presents Juanito's behavior and attitudes as being appropriate to his station in life, and he generally views Juanito in a good light.

However, throughout volume 1 Juanito's actions and words call into question the narrator's evaluation of this character. Juanito's selfishness and cruelty, evident in his eventual abandonment of Fortunata, is also shown in his treatment of other characters earlier in the story. Indeed, at the early stages of the novel Juanito's self-centered and mean-spirited behavior is better gauged when it is not directed toward Fortunata – still a shadowy figure in volume 1 – but rather toward two characters who have fully engaged the reader in the text's opening chapters: Ido del Sagrario and Estupiñá. Although Ido's first appearance in *Fortunata y Jacinta* is in the very scene where he is ridiculed by Juanito, he is by no means a stranger to the Galdosian reader. This totally inoffensive and pitifully eccentric character had been featured in two previous novels. Through both *El doctor Centeno* and *Tormento* the reader has come to know that Ido is a kindhearted, idealistic, and honorable man who constantly endeavors to raise his family out of poverty. We bring that knowledge to the scene in volume 1, chapter 8, section 4 in which

---

[30] For a discussion of the issue of vicarious vs. lived experience see Peter B. Goldman, "Juanito's *chuletas*: Realism and Worldly Philosophy in Galdós's *Fortunata y Jacinta*," *The Journal of the Midwest Modern Language Association* 18.1 (1985): 82-101.

Juanito takes advantage of Ido del Sagrario's mental imbalance by feigning serious concern for his troubles in order to mock him in front of Jacinta and the servants. As a result, it is Juanito rather than Ido who is lowered in our estimation. The same process occurs with Estupiñá. This somewhat quirky character is presented as honest, loyal, and basically simple. He places a great deal of importance on personal honor, and his dedication to the Santa Cruz household is evidenced in his adoration of Barbarita and Juanito. His only "shameful" incident occurred when he inadvertently became drunk one night and publicly knelt and prayed before a *sereno* believing him to be a priest administering a sacrament. This incident caused him great embarrassment and "nada afligía tanto su honrado corazón como la idea de que Barbarita se enterara de aquel chasco del Viático" (vol. 1, ch. 3, sec. 2). The reader brings this generally positive view of Estupiñá to the scene at the end of chapter 8 in the first volume where Juanito is recovering from a cold and causes all those around him, family and friends alike, to attend to his whims. After Estupiñá relates various amusing bits of gossip during his visit, the bored Juanito purposely ridicules Estupiñá in Barbarita's presence by questioning him about the drunken incident. Once again Juanito shows his willingness to obtain pleasure at another person's expense.

Throughout volume 1, then, the reader's confidence in the narrator's reliability has been undermined by his non-objective choice of informants and by the discrepancy between the narrator's estimation of Juanito and the reader's evaluation of him. The gap that exists between the narrator's statements and the reader's acceptance of them is filled by the reader's understanding that the narrator's class prejudices cause his viewpoint to be slanted toward an uncritical endorsement of the social values held by the upper middle class. However, since the narrator's unreliability is confined to that specific bias, he is fully capable of making valid judgments on matters outside its realm (as seen later in his assessment of Lupe and Nicolás, for example). Therefore, he is a semi-reliable narrator. That is, his opinions are sound except when speaking of Juanito and those of his social circle.

In short, the choice of this particular type of narrator serves several purposes in *Fortunata y Jacinta*:

1. Since the narrator's untrustworthy tendencies are revealed in volume 1, the reader is alerted that the narrator's areas of unreli-

ability need to be defined in order to fully appreciate the remainder of the text. The reader must first determine if the narrator is totally unreliable or only partially so. Once the reader establishes that the narrator is semi-reliable, the reader must continue to actively partic- ipate in the text on a long term basis. Unlike reliable narrators who are openly accepted, and unreliable narrators who are quickly iden- tified and rejected, the semi-reliable narrator demands constant vig- ilance by the reader because at any moment he can lapse into a new area of unreliability. Therefore, semi-reliable narration, in addition to being difficult to discern, requires ongoing reader engagement with the world of the text.

2. Since this is a retrospective narration, the narrator is privy to information which is unknown to the reader until the entire story has been told. Before he begins his narration, the narrator is aware of Juanito's actions and their consequences, but he condones Juani- to's behavior nonetheless. Perceiving this unreliable aspect of the narrator early in the text, the reader is able to quickly reject the su- perficial social values that the narrator holds and which are person- ified by the idle, rich, selfish *Delfín*. Thus, Galdós implicitly crit- icizes this lifestyle through the unreliable aspects of the narrator.

3. The bourgeois-centered view of class relations exhibited by the narrator and the members of his social circle presents a patron- izing vision of the *pueblo* as an exoticized "other" excluded from the dynamic interaction of classes occurring in nineteenth-century society. The short-sightedness of this attitude is revealed through the text's use of Fortunata to bring about a true "confusión de clases" through the mixing of the *pueblo* and the bourgeoisie in the birth of her son. Thus, Galdós implicitly challenges the extra-textu- al values of flesh-and-blood readers who come to the text with a view of the *pueblo* similar to that of the narrator. Rather than use a narrator who openly preaches the mingling of the lower and middle classes, Galdós uses the characters and plot to show how the narra- tor's bourgeois condescension toward the *pueblo* is unjustified.

4. The narrator's status as a character grants him familiarity with certain practicalities of Spanish life. As a member of the ed- ucated middle class, he affords the reader a multifaceted view of Madrid. His is the world of commerce (he knows the banking, trades, and fashions of the capital); his is the world of politics (he knows the political gossip as well as the grand motives behind the movements affecting Spain); his is the world of the café (he de-

scribes the eclectic conversations and the social hierarchies governing *tertulias*). Like many of his class, however, he has only superficial knowledge of the slums, so he presents a picture which is limited to the observable facts – the activity, color, poverty, sounds, filth,
etc. He relates a subjective view of life in Madrid during a period
when the middle class was gaining power.

5. The narrator's selective reliability forces the reader to de-
pend heavily on other narrative voice techniques to either confirm
or refute the narrator's evaluations of the various characters. As we
shall see, Galdós's complex handling of discursive techniques in
Fortunata y Jacinta complements the semi-reliable narration of the
text, resulting in a highly sophisticated integration of the various
facets of the narrative voice operating in the text.

Given the semi-reliable nature of this narrator, we cannot accept his judgments at face value. We need more information, and to
this end Galdós provides the reader with a large number of characters holding a variety of social, economic and ethical positions. To
use Stephen Gilman's phrasing, each character is a mirror of private
awareness whose point of view conveys a more or less distorted
view of reality.[31] By paying attention to what each character does,
says, and thinks, the reader can shift between a variety of perspectives – adopting what Iser calls a wandering viewpoint – constantly
evaluating the validity of each.[32] In this way the reader of *Fortunata
y Jacinta* engages in an on-going process of forming inferences
which correct the false expectations which have been aroused by
the semi-reliable narrator. "Rectification" is the term Geoffrey Ribbans uses to refer to such reversals of previously presented evidence, a technique which Galdós often links to the development of
the characters and themes of his various novels.[33] Of particular importance in this inferential process are the numerous interior views
present in this novel. These are excellent indicators of personality
because novelistic convention requires them to be truthful manifes-

---

[31] Stephen Gilman, "Narrative Presentation in «Fortunata y Jacinta»," *Revista
Hispánica Moderna* 34 (1968): 298.

[32] Wolfgang Iser, *The Act of Reading: A Theory of Aesthetic Response* (Baltimore: Johns Hopkins UP, 1978) 108-14.

[33] Geoffrey Ribbans, "Social Document or Narrative Discourse? Some Comments on Recent Aspects of Galdós Criticism," *Galdós's House of Fiction*, ed. A. H.
Clarke and Eamonn Rodgers (Llangrannog: Dolphin, 1991) 72.

tations of the thoughts and feelings of the characters.[34] The reader
can rely on these interiorizations to infer personal traits which may
not be evident from the characters' speech alone. As we interact
with the text by pulling together evidence about the characters
from their words, actions, and thoughts, we begin to construct the
social, political, religious, and ethical attitudes of the implied author. No one character is the spokesman for the novel. No one
character possesses completely positive characteristics. Therefore,
we must determine the configurative meaning of the text – its unified truth – based on the combination of perspectives expressed in
it. Narrative voice techniques provide the reader the necessary access to those perspectives. Through the interplay of inside views
(especially direct and free indirect thought) and exterior views (especially direct and free indirect speech) Galdós develops his characters and directs the reader's appreciation of the norms and values
represented in the text.

   Of the four key characters in the novel, only Juanito is presented to the reader predominantly through exterior views. This is in
stark contrast to the interior presentations of Fortunata, Jacinta,
and Maxi. We come to know these three characters intimately
through their thoughts, but we know Juanito basically through
what he says and does. And it is the disparity between Juanito's
words and his actions which reveals his essentially deceitful nature.
Furthermore, by largely denying Juanito interior views Galdós
maintains an emotional distance between Juanito and the reader.
This distance aids the reader in objectively assessing Juanito despite
the narrator's slanted portrayal of him, especially in volume 1 where
Juanito is described in positive terms not only by the narrator but
by Barbarita as well. Indeed, the first four chapters of the novel are
filled with Barbarita's presence. In this way, the narrator attempts to
influence the reader's initial impression of Juanito by presenting
him through the opinions of a character even more biased in his
favor than is the narrator himself. Barbarita's tone invades the text
through her words and thoughts which focus on her son's supposed
qualities. As soon as Juanito becomes a functioning character in the
novel, however, his own words and actions counter the positive

---

[34] Chatman *Story and Discourse* 157: "thoughts are truthful, except in cases of
willful self-deception."

view of him provided by his mother and the narrator. Above all, Juanito's credibility is effectively destroyed in his intimate conversations first with Jacinta and later with Fortunata.

In recording what Juanito says, Galdós primarily uses direct speech (either tagged or free), but on occasion he uses free indirect speech instead. The overall effect of this last technique is mimicry, and as such, it exaggerates the character's manner of speaking and emphasizes both what is said and how it is said. Therefore, chatty gossip appears more malicious, social conversations seem trivial, complaints sound whiny, flattery seems more obvious, and self-justification less successfully hides its true motivations. Indeed, throughout his novels – *primera época* and *segunda manera* alike – Galdós often highlights the negative traits of his unsympathetic characters through their free indirect speech passages. [35] This important characterization device has been overlooked by Galdosian critics because of their failure to separate free indirect style into its spoken and unspoken components. [36] Whereas free indirect thought provides an interior view of the character, free indirect speech gives an exterior one. Consequently, the sympathetic effect associated with interiorizations is present for free indirect thought, but absent in free indirect speech. However, free indirect speech does retain the "double-voiced" nature of all free indirect style. It conveys the perspective of one of the characters, but a shadow of the narrator's presence is perceived in the third person grammatical format. As we have seen in *La desheredada*, this double-voicing can be used for ironic effect. In *Fortunata y Jacinta* Galdós uses free indirect speech to ironize not only Juanito, but the narrator as well. This is possible due to the unreliability of the narrator concerning Juanito and those of his ilk. All of Juanito's free indirect speech passages occur in response to the questions Jacinta poses to him about his affair with Fortunata, as seen in the following example:

---

[35] In this practice Galdós resembles Jane Austen, who regularly satirizes her characters through free indirect speech. See Anne Waldron Neumann, "Characterization and Comment in *Pride and Prejudice*: Free Indirect Discourse and the 'Double-voiced' Verbs of Speaking, Thinking, and Feeling," *Style* 20 (1986): 364-94.

[36] Only Kay Engler has made this distinction, but she does not perceive any functional difference in Galdós's use of these two techniques. See *The Structure of Realism: The Novelas Contemporáneas of Benito Pérez Galdós*, North Carolina Studies in the Romance Languages and Literatures 184 (Chapel Hill: North Carolina UP, 1977) 75.

¡Si lo que la *nena* anhelaba saber era un desvaneo, una tontería...! cosas de muchachos. La educación del hombre de nues-
tros días no puede ser completa si éste no trata con toda clase de
gente, si no echa un vistazo a todas las situaciones posibles de la
vida, si no toma el tiento a las pasiones todas. Puro estudio y educación pura... No se trata de amor, porque lo que es amor, bien
podía decirlo, él no lo había sentido nunca hasta que le hizo tilín
la que ya era su mujer. (vol. 1, ch. 5, sec. 1)

Unlike direct speech which records exact words, free indirect
speech captures the overall tone and content of what is said. Juanito's classist and sexist attitudes, as well as his flip manner, mirror
the narrator's demeanor as he excused Juanito's behavior in the
opening chapters of the novel. Therefore, these free indirect speech
passages underscore the negative traits of both Juanito and the narrator.

The negative portrayal of Juanito is reinforced as the novel progresses and Juanito's lying manipulation of both his wife and mistress becomes evident. Examples are found in volume 3, chapter 2,
section 3, where he represents himself to Jacinta as nothing more
than Fortunata's benevolent protector, and in the opening section
of the next chapter where he breaks off relations with Fortunata
using the false excuse that his parents had found out about them.
Although he successfully conceals the truth from Jacinta and Fortunata, he cannot do the same with the reader. In addition to recording Juanito's spoken words, Galdós also provides brief interior
views of Juanito in both scenes in order to show his real motives: to
appear morally justified in his actions and to free himself from an
affair that had ceased to interest him. His direct, indirect, and free
indirect thoughts show him calculating his strategy in order to get
the upper hand in each argument. These interior views are typical
of those granted Juanito. They are few in number, non-sympathetic,
and unflattering. Juxtaposed against the words he speaks to Jacinta
and Fortunata, these thoughts highlight his vanity, selfishness, and
deceit. At only one point in the novel does Juanito display any remorse for his actions – his drunken honeymoon confession – but
his anguish fails to elicit much sympathy in the reader because we
are aware of the ordeal that he is putting Jacinta through. Even this
confession is selfish because in it he unburdens himself at Jacinta's
expense. Reader sympathy is with Jacinta instead as her free indi-

rect thought passages show her confusion as to whether or not she should believe her husband's ravings. Furthermore, any value that Juanito may have gained from his late-night repentance is negated the next morning when the now-sober Juanito recants all responsibility for his abandonment of Fortunata and recasts his behavior as being necessary in order to disengage himself from ties binding him to his social inferiors.

Although the two eponymous heroines of this novel are rivals for the affection of Juanito, Galdós does not make them rival each other for the affection of the reader. Rather, he distributes their interiorizations in such a way as to generate a sympathetic response in the reader toward both women. The vast majority of the interior views in volume 1 belong to Jacinta, and it is through them that we feel her emotional pain due to Juanito's infidelity and her childless state. By granting us frequent access to Jacinta's thoughts, Galdós insures our involvement in Jacinta's plight from the very first days of her marriage. But Jacinta's dominant position at the opening of the novel is offset at its conclusion where, in volume 4, Fortunata's interiorizations become the most numerous. In particular, her thoughts express the emotional bond which she is forming with Jacinta and which eventually will be solidified through the gift of her child. Reader compassion for Fortunata reaches its height at the end of the novel where her interior views show us the maternal love and nobility of spirit that characterize the last days of her life. In the central portion of the novel – volumes 2 and 3 – both women share in the distribution of interior views as their thoughts display their attempts to deal with each other and the demands of society. In short, Galdós allows us to experience the novelistic world through the carefully balanced perspectives of the two female protagonists, and in the process we come to understand the motivations which govern their behavior.

As Ricardo Gullón has demonstrated, Fortunata is the pivotal character upon which all the major relationships of the text turn.[37] It is interesting to note, then, that this fundamental character is introduced relatively late in the novel, well into volume 1, and receives an initially negative portrayal which, furthermore, is achieved entirely through exterior views. After seeing her eating a raw egg amid the squalor of her slum surroundings, we hear about her affair

---

[37] Ricardo Gullón, *Técnicas de Galdós* (Madrid: Taurus, 1980) 138-57.

with Juanito during his honeymoon confession to Jacinta. Immediately, our loyalties to the familiar Jacinta incline us to dislike this potential threat to the marital harmony of the Santa Cruz household. Also, because of his class biases and friendship with Juanito, the semi-reliable narrator does not provide us with background information on Fortunata which might favorably dispose us toward the underprivileged young woman. Clearly, our original negative impression of Fortunata must be reversed, and since the narrator is unwilling to provide testimony of Fortunata's worth, she must do so herself. To achieve this Galdós uses the discourse in two ways: first, by granting Fortunata a large number of sympathetic inside views; and second, as René Schimmel has observed, by portraying her in scenes rather than through description.[38] It is in volumes 2, 3, and 4 of this novel that Fortunata wins over the reader by presenting her own case through her thoughts and words. Her verbal interaction with others shows her basic honesty and goodness, and her interiorizations reinforce this impression. Nevertheless, she still must counterbalance the reader's disapproval of her socially unacceptable sexual behavior. In order for Fortunata to be perceived as a positive character, the reader must be brought to pardon her numerous liaisons with men and her ongoing affair with the married Juanito. This is done by redefining the morality of her actions – by transforming them into manifestations of a constant and dedicated love for one man, a love which is misplaced but not immoral.

The principal manner of gaining acceptance for this unorthodox position is through a sustained and sympathetic interior presentation of Fortunata which provides the reader with an intimate understanding of her attempts to deal with the realities of her situation. Fortunata, more than any other character, must contend with numerous outside forces trying to control or modify her behavior – forces which are not in agreement with one another. The conflicting moral advice given her by Guillermina and Nicolás on the one hand and Mauricia on the other is further complicated by the willingness of Feijoo and Lupe to help Fortunata to cuckold Maxi discretely and with social impunity. As she is emotionally buffeted about by the diverse influences in her life, her confusion is displayed in her interior views. Both her direct thoughts and her free indirect

---

[38] René Schimmel, "Algunos aspectos de la técnica de Galdós en la creación de Fortunata," *Archivum* 7 (1958): 82-83.

thoughts are characterized by questions addressed to herself and by exclamations denoting her reactions to problems. Through these interiorizations we share her frustrations over whether or not she should marry Maxi; what she should feel toward Jacinta; how she can deal with the various stages of Maxi's madness; whom she can trust; what she can do to counter Aurora's lies; etc. The bulk of Fortunata's interior views are rendered in direct thought, thereby allowing the reader to hear the actual words that pass through her mind. This unmediated entry into Fortunata's consciousness helps to establish the bond that gradually forms between her and the reader. We witness her thought process as she tries to formulate satisfactory answers to her problems.

An interesting and highly effective variation of the direct thought technique occurs during Fortunata's stay at Las Micaelas. While in church one day she projects her thoughts onto the holy sacrament, thereby imagining the host itself – *la idea blanca* – to be speaking to her, but from her own point of view and "con familiar lenguaje, semejante al suyo" (vol. 2, ch. 6, sec. 7). This allows her to be the audience to her own interior monologue which, significantly, concerns the need for her to accept her lot in life, to recognize Jacinta's claim on Juanito, to forget him, and to marry Maxi. Her susceptibility to the persuasive powers of outside pressures takes an extreme form in this passage, where not only the content but the very form in which she conceives it indicates the source of the influence – the religious training she is receiving. Ultimately however, no matter how strong an influence may appear, its power over Fortunata is only transitory, and our access to her inner thoughts allows us to view the various influences as they take root and then eventually give way to others. Due to her lack of personal conviction in a set of core values, she is subject to conflicting arguments which cause her thoughts to sway from one direction to another in hopes of finding solutions to her problems. She does, however, tenaciously adhere to the one belief which she sustains throughout the course of the text – that any action associated with genuine love can't be sinful. This constitutes a justification of her behavior and a legitimizing of her position as Juanito's wife through natural rather than civil law. A large percentage of her interior views are explicitly centered on this belief, and it also is revealed in conversations with various characters who either accept or reject this concept of sinless love.

Fortunata's belief in her natural right to Juanito forms the underpinnings for her first two meetings with Jacinta in sections 3 and 5 of volume 3, chapter 6. Both scenes center on Fortunata's thoughts as she grapples with her ambivalent feelings toward Jacinta, whom she both respects and resents. The reader's censure of her violent behavior toward Jacinta in section 5 is mitigated somewhat by the ability to see the situation from Fortunata's perspective. We are allowed to feel sorry for both Fortunata and Jacinta without having to choose between them. Although Jacinta is the victim of Fortunata's attack, it is on Fortunata that the text focuses, both during and after the event. As Fortunata physically departs the building, the reader also leaves Jacinta behind. At this point Fortunata's mental state is depicted in a combination of discoursive techniques: free indirect thought is interspersed with direct thought, indirect thought, and narrative summary. Through this discoursive mixture Galdós is able to capture the mental turmoil that Fortunata experiences. The constant shifting between different narrative techniques mirrors Fortunata's thoughts as they jump between anger, fear, and remorse. Galdós typically employs this combination approach for the discoursive presentation of disturbing moments in Fortunata's life. [39] A similarly complex presentation of Fortunata's thoughts and feelings is seen in volume 3, chapter 7, section 4 after her second confrontation with Jacinta leaves her in a state of agitation and confusion:

(1) Bajó Fortunata los peldaños riendo... Era una risa estúpida salpicada de interjecciones.
(2) – ¡A mí, decirme...! Si no me echan, la cojo... le levanto... pero no sé, no recuerdo bien si le arañé la cara! ¡A mí decirme! Si le pego un bocado no la suelto... Ja, ja, ja...
(3) Le temblaron tanto las piernas, que al llegar a la calle apenas podía andar. La luz y el aire parecía que le despejaban algo la cabeza, y empezó a darse cuenta de la situación. (4) ¿Pero era verdad lo que había dicho y hecho? (5) No estaba segura de haberle pegado; pero sí de que le dijo algo. (6) ¿Y para qué la otra la había llamado a ella *ladrona?*... (7) Subió por la calle de la

---

[39] Geoffrey Ribbans, "Dos paseos de Fortunata por Madrid y su integración dentro de la estructura de la novela," *Hispania* 70 (1987): 742-44 discusses a similar combination of discoursive techniques which are used to convey Fortunata's thoughts after Juanito breaks off their second affair.

Paz, pasando a cada instante de una acera a otra sin saber lo que hacía. (8) «¿Pero yo qué he hecho?... ¡Oh! Bien hecho está... ¡Llamarme a mí *ladrona*, ella que me ha robado lo mío!»... (9) Se volvió para atrás, y como quien echa una maldición, dijo entre dientes: (10) «Tú me llamarás lo que quieras... Llámame tal o cual y tendrás razón... Tú serás un ángel... pero tú no has tenido hijos. Los ángeles no los tienen. Y yo sí... Es mi idea, una idea mía. Rabia, rabia, rabia... Y no los tendrás, no los tendrás nunca, y yo sí... Rabia, rabia, rabia...»

This presentation begins with a narrative description of Fortunata's actions (1), then moves to a brief direct speech by Fortunata (2), before returning to more narrative description (3). Fortunata's two passages of free indirect thought (4 and 6) are interrupted by an indirect thought statement by the narrator (5). More narrative description precedes (7) and interrupts (9) Fortunata's direct thoughts (8 and 10). Following this material are two additional direct thought passages (too long to reproduce here) introduced by narrative description. Thus, this hodge-podge of interiorization devices reflects the chaotic nature of Fortunata's feelings as she struggles against what Bakhtin calls the "finalizing secondhand definitions" of her by others (59). She responds to Jacinta's labeling her a "ladrona" by redefining the entire concept of marriage though her "pícara idea." By viewing herself as Juanito's legitimate wife, she rejects society's judgment of her and sets into motion her plan to bear the Santa Cruz heir. Rather than being the "cantera" which the middle-class can mine for its own purposes, Fortunata asserts her will over the class barriers tacitly upheld by the narrator. It is she who decides to conceive a child, and through that child she gains a position for both herself and the *pueblo* within middle-class society. Furthermore, as Catherine Jagoe has shown, Fortunata's process of self-definition achieves the goal of subverting the patriarchal conception of "el ángel del hogar" by appropriating that term and using it to legitimize her love for Juanito and her bearing of his son.[40]

When Fortunata retires to her bed after both her confrontations with Jacinta, her thoughts become clouded by what is described as

---

[40] Catherine Jagoe, *Ambiguous Angels: Gender in the Novels of Galdós* (Berkeley: U of California P, 1994) 102-19.

a "somnolencia" and an "embriaguez." Interestingly, Galdós uses this state of semi-consciousness to introduce the only dream that Fortunata has which is presented scenically rather than in narrative summary. In this dream she wanders about the streets of Madrid looking at shops and street vendors. Suddenly, she sees a shabbily dressed Juanito who has been ruined financially and is reduced to working as a clerk. Fortunata tells him that she will support him and that they can live happily together in an upper flat. This dream is important since it shows the extent of Fortunata's desire to transform her situation.[41] As with the holy sacrament scene in Las Micaelas, Galdós conveys Fortunata's feelings stylistically as well as through content. This dream sequence occurs in the *present* tense even though the narrative as a whole exists in the realm of the past. Elsewhere in the text the present tense is confined to records of direct speech. This sudden switch from past to present tense projects the dream into the present of the reader and allows us to experience it exactly as Fortunata does. This dream is an act of wish fulfillment which Fortunata realizes through a negation of her own reality. As the scene dissolves, the reality of the dream becomes intertwined with Fortunata's waking life, resulting in the use of present tense verbs to describe Fortunata's awareness of Maxi's clothes in her room and doña Lupe's voice as she scolds Papitos. This scene closes the fourth section of chapter 7 in volume 3. The next section immediately resumes the use of past tense verbs. The choice to convey this dream sequence in the present tense was a conscious decision made by Galdós during his correction of the galley proofs. Based on the Beta manuscript, this portion of the galleys was printed in past tense verbs. However, Galdós crossed out each of these and replaced them with the present tense before the galleys went to print.[42] What effects were achieved through this modification? In addition to lending an immediacy to the scene from the standpoint of the reader, it makes the dream exceptionally vivid for Fortunata herself. Indeed, for a moment after awaking she thinks that the actions actually had happened ("Le había visto, le había hablado"),

---

[41] For both a Freudian and a Jungian interpretation of this and other dreams in the novel see Mercedes López-Baralt, "Sueños de mujeres: La voz de *anima* en *Fortunata y Jacinta*," *Hispanic Review* 55 (1987): 491-512.
[42] The *Fortunata y Jacinta* galleys are stored at the Casa-Museo Pérez Galdós, calle Cano 6, Las Palmas de Gran Canaria. Volumes 1 and 2 are in *caja* 21, and volumes 3 and 4 are in *caja* 22. This scene is on pages [2]76-79 of volume 3.

and later when she is with Juanito in the next section, the impression of the dream remains strong enough for her to initially speak about it as if it were reality ("Te vi en la calle Imperial... No, digo, soñé que te vi"). As in *La desheredada,* Galdós uses present tense narration to set off an emotionally charged scene from the surrounding narrative, thereby drawing the reader's attention to the importance of the event to one of the characters.

Indeed, Galdós frequently uses characters as focal points through which he is able to communicate not only the events of the text but their emotional impact as well. For example, in volume 4, chapter 3, section 1 the final break-up between Juanito and Fortunata is presented to the reader entirely through Fortunata's thoughts as she recalls their conversation. In this way Galdós is able to simulate a scenic representation of the occurrence, but deliver it from Fortunata's point of view. Furthermore, by relaying this event through a retrospective memory, Galdós can allow Fortunata to mentally comment on the entire experience. Consequently, we receive Fortunata's feelings about Juanito's words not when they were said, but rather, after she has had time to reflect upon them and put them within the larger context of her on-again-off-again relationship with Juanito. This segment is too long to reproduce in its entirety, but the following example is representative of the whole:

> Otra vez sentía retumbar en su oído las tremendas palabras de *aquél*: «Si vueles a pronunciar delante de mí, *etc...*» Y el comentario parecía producirse en el cerebro paralelamente a la repetición de la filípica: «¡Ah!, tuno, no hablabas antes de ese modo. En junio, sí, bien me acuerdo, todo era *te quiero y te adoro,* y bastante que nos reíamos de la *mona del Cielo,* aunque siempre la teníamos por virtuosa. ¿Que es sagrada, dices?... ¿Entonces, para qué la engañas? ¡Sagrada! Ahora sales con eso. *Cojo mi sombrero y no me vueles a ver...* Eso es que tú lo quieres hace tiempo. Estás buscando un motivo, y te agarras a lo que dije. *Te comparo con ella, y si pierdes en la comparación, échate a ti misma la culpa.* Eso es decirme que soy un trasto, que yo no puedo ser honrada aunque quiera... ¡Cómo me requemaba oyendo esto y cómo me requemo ahora mismo! Se me aprieta la garganta, y los ojos se me llenan de lágrimas. ¡Decirme a mí esto, a mí, que me estoy condenando por él...! Pero, Señor, ¡qué culpa tendré yo de que esa niña bonita sea ángel! Hasta la virtud sirve para darme a mí en la cabeza. ¡Ingrato!»

Reproducción de algo que ella le había contestado: «Mira; no lo tomes tan a pechos. Podrá ser mentira ¿Yo qué sé? No creerás que lo he inventado yo. Para que veas que no me gustan farsas contigo; eso que te incomoda tanto, es cosa de Aurora...»

Y él: «Como yo la coja, la arranco la lengua. Es una víbora esa mujer, una envidiosa, una intrigante. Andate con cuidado con ella.»

Comentario: «De veras que estuve muy imprudente. No se debe hablar mal de nadie sin tener seguridad de lo que se dice.» Desde aquel momento no me volvió a mirar como me mira siempre. Le chafé su amor propio. Es como cuando se sienta una, sin pensarlo, sobre un sombrero de copa, que no hay manera, por más que se le planche después, de volverlo a poner como estaba. Esta sí que no me la perdona. Perdona él todo; pero que le toquen a su soberbia no lo perdona. «¿Estás enfadado?» – «¡Si te parece que no debo estarlo...!» – «Hazte el cargo de que no he dicho nada.» – «No puedo; me has ofendido; te has rebajado a mis ojos. Como tú no tienes sentido moral, no comprendes esto. No calculas el valor que se quitan a sí mismas las personas cuando hablan más de la cuenta.» – «No me digas esas cosas.» – «Se me salen de la boca. Desde que calumniaste a mi pobre mujer, la veneración y el cariño que le tengo se aumentan, y veo otra cosa; veo lo miserable que soy al lado suyo; tú eres el espejo en que miro mi conciencia y te aseguro que me veo horrible.»

In keeping with the self-directed nature of her thoughts, Fortunata does not provide mental tags to differentiate her part of the conversation from his. Neither does she contextualize the presuppositional reference to the month of June, which the reader must construct from the evidence in the text as being the beginning of the couple's final affair. As with Isidora's *insomnio número cincuenta y tantos*, this scene provides data which the reader must sort out. Both Isidora and Fortunata are speaking to themselves, and therefore do not have to systematically link together information for an audience. Unlike Isidora's *insomnio* scene, however, some guidance is provided by the narrator. Nevertheless, the reader's responsibility for filling in the gaps of this segment remains substantially greater than what is required to read Gloria's remembrances of her conversations with Morton in chapter 26 of *Gloria*, from Galdós's *primera época*.

Another way that Galdós relays the emotional effect of an event is to allow a character's perspective to fuse with the narrative itself, resulting in what can be called "filtered descriptions." [43] In these passages the presentation of external reality is filtered through the impressions of the character who experiences the event. These descriptions do not convey the thoughts or speech of the character, as would a free indirect style passage, but they do capture the character's point of view. As Chatman has observed, point of view is subject to three types of engagement: perceptual (through the character's physical senses); conceptual (through the character's attitudes, feelings, and worldview); and interested (through the personal stake the character has in the situation). [44] All three forms come into play in the filtered description of Jacinta's "visita al cuarto estado" in volume 1, chapter 9, section 1. This entire scene is written so as to reflect Jacinta's sensations as she moves through the bustling market *en route* to Ido del Sagrario's house, and the descriptions are subjectively tinged by her perspective. The orientation of the scene from Jacinta's viewpoint is explicitly announced by the narrator prior to the description of the marketplace: "Recibía tan sólo la imagen borrosa de los objetos diversos que iban pasando, y lo digo así, porque era como si ella estuviese parada y la pintoresca vía se corriese delante de ella como un telón." She perceives her surroundings as a jumbled mixture of sights and sounds where details rather than whole objects dominate. Since she is only aware of bits and pieces of the activity around her, the pace seems frantic, the figures appear to be grotesquely distorted, and the colors are intensely vivid. This walk along the calle de Toledo is her first exposure to the poverty in which the lower class lives. In this neighborhood, so close to her own in distance but so far from her own in appearance, nothing seems familiar. For Jacinta, raised in a protected middle-class environment, the *cava baja* is another world which disorients her and fills her with apprehension. Consequently, she registers what she sees and hears in negative terms. That is, the impressions she receives from her physical senses (her perceptual perspective) are influenced by her middle-class attitudes (her conceptual perspective). Thus, the voices of the women hawking their goods seem so harsh that they hurt her ears, while her eyes are assaulted by the

---

[43] This term is derived from Seymour Chatman's discussion of character-based point of view in *Coming to Terms: The Rhetoric of Narrative in Fiction and Film* (Ithaca: Cornell UP, 1990) 143-44.

[44] Chatman, *Story and Discourse* 151-58.

vivid colors of the clothing on display. Seen through Jacinta's "mareada vista," each color projects some undesirable trait, from "el naranjado que chilla como los ejes sin grasa" and "el bermellón nativo, que parece rasguñar los ojos" to "el cobalto, que infunde ideas de envenenamiento" and "ese amarillo tila, que tiene cierto aire de poesía mezclado con la tisis, como en *La Traviatta* [sic]." As the scene progresses, one color comes to dominate and everything takes on a blood-red hue, above all the tavern doors that she sees at every turn. Suddenly Jacinta is aware of the potential danger of the area and becomes afraid. That is, her conceptual perspective has caused her to move from simply disliking her surroundings to being fearful of them. As soon as Jacinta notices the large number of infants and mothers in the area, however, she fixes her attention on nothing else. Her interest perspective becomes so powerfully engaged by the presence of these children that it totally overrides her fears and the sense of danger which her conceptual perspective had generated just moments before. This scene, then, becomes more than a description of Jacinta's surroundings. Rather, it primarily serves as a characterization device which simultaneously shows Jacinta's upper middle-class sensibilities and her frustrated maternal desire.

A more elaborate form of filtered description is found in Maxi's moneybox scene in the first chapter, fifth section of volume 2. Except for the insertion of a brief direct thought displaying Maxi's rational assessment of the situation – "¡Qué tonto soy! Si esto es mío, ¿por qué no he de disponer de ello cuando me dé la gana?" – the entire lengthy paragraph beginning the scene is composed of a narrative description of Maxi's actions from his point of view. Here, however, Maxi's conceptual perspective actually transforms the objects being described. To achieve this Galdós includes in his description what Ann Banfield calls "embeddable subjective elements" – words and phrases which convey Maxi's impressions of the act.[45] Therefore, the moneybox is seen as "la infeliz víctima, aquel antiguo y leal amigo, modelo de honradez y fidelidad." As the box is broken it groans and spills its "tripas de oro, plata y cobre" on the bed, soiling it with "manchas de sangre." The broken pieces "semejaban pedazos de un cráneo." Maxi is referred to as an "ase-

---

[45] Ann Banfield, *Unspeakable sentences: Narration and representation in the language of fiction* (Boston: Routledge and Kegan Paul, 1982) 202-03.

sino" and a "criminal" while the moneybox is "la muerta." These
subjective elements permit the reader to experience the simple action of breaking a moneybox as an act of violence and aggression.
In this passage Maxi's rational thoughts and his feelings are juxtaposed to show that they are at odds with each other, thereby conveying the intensity of Maxi's internal conflict, and consequently
arousing reader sympathy for this weak and frightened character in
his first moment of defiance. As soon as the moneybox is broken,
the discourse switches to free indirect thought embedded with direct thought to further insure reader involvement in the scene. We
now directly experience Maxi's mental panic and fear that he will
not be able to hide what he has done from Lupe.

Sympathetic interiorizations of Maxi are common in *Fortunata
y Jacinta*. Since Maxi is a highly articulate character, his interior
views are dominated by discursive forms which faithfully reproduce his words. Therefore, direct thought – both spoken and unspoken – appears more frequently than does free indirect thought,
and these interiorizations record the progress of Maxi's madness
through its various stages. So detailed are these representations of
Maxi's thoughts that they have provided data for a number of critical studies on Maxi's madness. [46] Maxi continually directs statements to himself and others, but often no one pays any attention to
what he is saying. Therefore, many potential dialogues become
monologues when Maxi is in the presence of others. Ignored by
those around him, and unable to assimilate into society, he retreats
into his own world. Throughout the text Maxi's interiorizations
serve the dual function of reducing the reader's emotional distance
while documenting the evolution of Maxi's gradual withdrawal
from society as he becomes more and more involved in the private
world of the mind. It is fitting that the closing paragraph of the entire novel features Maxi speaking his thoughts aloud to a "ser invisi-

---

[46] See Joan Connelly Ullman and George H. Allison, "Galdós as Psychiatrist in
Fortunata y Jacinta," *Anales Galdosianos* 9 (1974): 7-36; E. Dale A. Randolph, "A
Source for Maxi Rubín in *Fortunata y Jacinta,*" *Hispania* 51 (1968): 49-56; Ángel
Garma, "Jacqueca, seudo-oligofrenia y delirio en un personaje de Galdós," *Ficción*
(1958): 84-102; rpt. from *Acta Neuropsiquiátrica Argentina* 3 (1957): 143-54; Geoffrey Ribbans, *Pérez Galdós: Fortunata y Jacinta,* Critical Guides to Spanish Texts 21
(London: Grant & Cutler, 1977) 102-06; and Thomas R. Franz, "Galdós the Pharmacist: Drugs and the Samaniego Pharmacy in *Fortunata y Jacinta,*" *Anales Galdosianos* 22 (1987): 33-46.

ble" rather than to his companions in the carriage. At peace with himself, he no longer needs to interact with others on their level.

Whereas the four main characters of this novel are given a narrative presentation that is either predominantly interior (Fortunata, Jacinta, Maxi) or exterior (Juanito), the secondary characters are developed through a more balanced mixture of interior and exterior devices. An examination of the narrative techniques used for Lupe, Nicolás, Mauricia, and Moreno-Isla will exemplify how Galdós's skillful handling of interior and exterior views helps to cultivate the reader's response toward these characters in particular and secondary characters in general.

The narrator's comments and descriptions of Lupe and Nicolás make them appear ridiculous. Although Nicolás is a man of the cloth, his dominant characteristics are physical rather than spiritual. His appellation, "el peludo" conveys his unattractive appearance, his table manners are said to be nauseating, and his unpleasant smell is explicitly mentioned several times. Above all, his gluttony, which becomes a running joke throughout the text, seems all the more humorous since he repeatedly refers to his delicate constitution and special dietary requirements. Whereas the narrator uses exaggeration to make Nicolás appear grotesque, his description of Lupe takes the form of a parody that presents her ugliness as if it were beauty by speaking of the "vello finísimo" of her mustache and the "verruguita muy mona, de la cual salían dos otros pelos bermejos que a la luz brillaban retorcidos como hilillos de cobre" (vol. 2, ch. 3, sec. 3). The narrator also likens her missing breast to the unfeeling part of her heart which is dominated by greed. In addition to this unflattering presentation by the narrator, both Lupe and Nicolás reveal themselves through direct thought passages which contradict the public persona they wish to project. For example, in the initial conversation that Nicolás has with Fortunata in volume 2, chapter 4, section 4, his seemingly sincere words are contrasted against his inner thoughts showing his conceit and hopes for self-glorification. Likewise, we learn through Lupe's direct thoughts and her conversations with Fortunata that she has selfish motives for her charitable actions toward Mauricia. Also, in the final section of volume 2 when Lupe and Nicolás find out about Fortunata's affair with Juanito, their spoken words provide negative self-portraits showing that they are less concerned about Maxi than their own loss of face. In this scene the gravity of Fortunata's adultery is undercut by this negative portrayal of Lupe and Nicolás, which highlights Lupe's haughtiness and Nicolás's slovenly appearance. Finally, both Lupe and Nicolás are placed in situations where they are laughed at by other characters. Nicolás is the victim of two tricks played on him by Lupe and Papitos, one with the hidden strawberries and the other with the spoiled fish. These not only show him to be easily duped, but also underscore his gluttony. Similarly, Lupe is subjected to ridicule by Papitos who publicly airs her false-breasted garment on the clothesline, and she is the butt of Feijoo's humorous story to Fortunata concerning Lupe's mistaken impression that Feijoo had once been interested in her romantically. Nevertheless, there is a major difference between Lupe and Nicolás which is reflected in the discursive techniques used to portray them. Whereas Nicolás is a totally negative character, Lupe is not. As the narrator tells us, she is generally good except where money is concerned: "Su corazón no era depravado sino en lo tocante a préstamos; era como los que tienen un vicio que fuera de él, y cuando no están atacados de la fiebre, son razonables, prudentes, y discretos" (vol. 2, ch. 3, sec. 4). Since this assessment of Lupe does not fall within the realm of the narrator's unreliability, we can accept it as valid. How, then, is Lupe's characterization softened to allow us to respond to her better qualities? This is done by permitting her several interior views showing her genuine love for Maxi and her concern for his welfare. These sympathetic interiorizations help to offset somewhat the effect of the more numerous interior views displaying her negative traits. Lupe is not a positive or sympathetic character, but she does have some worthwhile qualities. Nicolás, on the other hand, is totally without merit, and therefore all his interiorizations – like those of Juanito – are unflattering.

As for Mauricia, the narrator is openly critical of her in his commentary, and in order to reinforce this negative impression, he occasionally permits other characters to take his place in the narration of Mauricia's actions. Without exception, these characters hold equally unfavorable opinions of Mauricia. Therefore, these character-narrations reinforce the censuring point of view already presented to us by the formal narrator. Mauricia is introduced through Severiana's disparaging account of her neglect and final abandonment of her daughter (vol. 1, ch. 9, sec. 8); Mauricia's violent behavior at the Protestant home is told by Maxi and commented upon disapprovingly by Lupe and Nicolás (vol. 3, ch. 5, sec. 3); and finally, Mauricia's death is related by Lupe who cynically dismisses her possible religious conversion as nothing more than a drunkard's plea for more alcohol (vol. 3, ch. 6, sec. 9).[47] This completely negative appraisal of Mauricia is not acceptable to the reader, however, because of her close personal relationship with Fortunata. Since Fortunata is a highly sympathetic character, the bond she feels for Mauricia suggests the possibility of some inner qualities which may have been overlooked in Mauricia by others. Although the narrator, along with the various characters, constantly contrast Mauricia's "evilness" with Guillermina's "saintliness," Fortunata is instinctively able to discern the basic goodness in Mauricia. Indeed, this positive aspect of Mauricia is felt so strongly by Fortunata that she begins to confuse Mauricia and Guillermina in her mind. In Bakhtinian terms, Fortunata's consciousness becomes "the field of battle for others' voices" (DP 88), and like one of Dostoevsky's heroes, Fortunata plays out her dialogic interaction of good and evil through paired characters (DP 28). The result is a hybrid vision of the two women – doña Mauricia and Guillermina la Dura – which challenges the polarized viewpoints held by those around her and calls into question the socially-sanctioned definitions of evil by which she herself is also judged.[48] In addition, through the doubling of Mauricia and Guillermina, Fortunata counters the narrator's single-dimensional portrayal of each. Not only is Mauricia less demonic than the narrator acknowledges, but Guillermina is also less saintly. Indeed, the egotism and arrogance Guillermina displays while carrying out her charitable activities call into question the unselfishness and compassion of her behavior. Ricardo Gullón, John Sinni-

---

[47] For a discussion of these and other character-narrated stories see John W. Kronik, "Narraciones interiores en *Fortunata y Jacinta*," *Homenaje a Juan López Morillas: De Cadalso a Aleixandre: Estudios sobre literatura e historia intelectual españolas*, ed. José Amor y Vázquez, David Kossof (Madrid: Castalia, 1982) 275-91.
[48] Several scholars have dealt with the Mauricia/Guillermina duality. Ricardo Gullón, *Técnicas* 159-69 and Gustavo Correa, *El simbolismo religioso en las novelas de Pérez Galdós* (Madrid: Gredos, 1962) 110-15 have analyzed the angelic-demonic polarity of the two women, while Lucille V. Braun, "The Novelistic Function of Mauricia la Dura in Galdós' *Fortunata y Jacinta*," *Symposium* 31 (1977): 280-84 and Francisco Romero Pérez, "The Grandeur of Galdós' Mauricia la Dura," *Hispanic Journal* 3.1 (1981): 113 have demonstrated how each woman contains elements of both good and evil. Peter B. Goldman and Andrés Villagrá, "Personajes y transformaciones en *Fortunata y Jacinta*," *Romance Quarterly* 39 (1992): 66-69 view Mauricia's transformation into Guillermina as an example of the dialectical union that is often seen in Galdós's novels.

gen, and J. L. Brooks all point out that Guillermina's charity is filtered though her bourgeois ethics, creating a patronizing attitude
toward the poor which sometimes manifests itself in cruelty and
consistently regards the *pueblo* as morally as well as socially inferior.[49] Thus, the narrator's positive view of Guillermina and his
negative assessment of Mauricia may simply reflect his own class biases.

Clearly, Mauricia's behavior is erratic. She exhibits a rebellious
and sometimes violent disregard for social conventions. Yet she is
capable of genuine concern for others and can feel remorse for her
past actions. Furthermore, her religious beliefs, though somewhat
unorthodox, are firmly ingrained. Although the dramatic nature of
her negative personality traits makes them appear paramount, her
positive tendencies manifest themselves on occasion. Of particular
importance is her late night chapel escapade while at Las Micaelas
(vol. 2, ch. 6, sec. 9). Significantly, the reader sees the scene from
Mauricia's point of view through a lengthy interiorization recount-
ing her compassionate, albeit drunken, attempt to reunite the infant
Jesus with his mother. This scene begins with Mauricia speaking
her direct thoughts aloud "como quien sostiene un diálogo." In her
mind she is conversing with the Virgin, whom she promises to help.
Her subsequent dream is scenically presented in a mixture of narration, direct speech, and both direct and free indirect thought. Had
the dream been entirely narrated instead of incorporating Mauricia's perspective, any positive impact would have been lost. It simply would have been the account of an alcohol-induced delusion.
By experiencing it from Mauricia's point of view, however, we know
her motives and recognize them as inappropriate but oddly admirable. Not only do her efforts to reunite the Holy Mother and
Son show her compassion for others, but as Lucille Braun and
James Whiston have observed, her actions also display her own
sense of loss over Adoración.[50] Although she had been characterized as an unloving mother by Severiana's neighbors, the entire

---

[49] See Ricardo Gullón, *Técnicas de Galdós* (Madrid: Taurus, 1980) 162-64; John
H. Sinnigen, "Individual, Class, and Society in *Fortunata y Jacinta*," ed. Robert J.
Weber (London: Tamesis, 1974) 55; and J. L. Brooks, "The Character of Doña
Guillermina Pacheco in Galdós' Novel, *Fortunata y Jacinta*," *Bulletin of Hispanic
Studies* 38 (1961): 86-94.

[50] Braun 285 and James Whiston, "The Materialism of Life: Religion in *Fortunata y Jacinta*," *Anales Galdosianos* 14 (1979): 73.

focus of this dream suggests otherwise. Overall, Mauricia's interior views, coupled with Fortunata's affection for her, cause us to reevaluate the negative opinions of her held by the narrator and some characters. We see her as a colorful character, street-wise and tough, but capable of caring for others. The complexity of her character precludes the possibility of assigning the simplistic and restrictive label of "evil" to her.

Before concluding this discussion of *Fortunata y Jacinta*, attention should be paid to the discursive presentation of Moreno-Isla, a character whose peripheral status belies his importance to the novel. Mentioned only in passing and appearing but briefly in the first three volumes of the novel, Moreno-Isla suddenly becomes the focus of an entire chapter, "Insomnio," in volume 4.[51] Throughout the bulk of the novel he simply is a type – the expatriated Spaniard who finds other European countries to be far superior to his own – whose antipathy for things Spanish makes him a caricature as well. However, Galdós raises him to the status of a fully realized character just before he dies. Galdós does this by opening Moreno-Isla's mind to us at the most introspective period of his life. We experience the last two days of his life through his thoughts as he interacts with those around him and as he grapples with his own despair during his evenings alone. The chapter opens with Moreno-Isla's lengthy direct thought passage in which his untagged free speech indicates his physical movements as he walks through the streets of Madrid. The scene is entirely oriented though Moreno-Isla's perceptual perspective. His running mental commentary on what he sees and hears is juxtaposed against his spoken words, revealing his anti-Spanish bias and displaying what Barbarita calls his "esplín." This interiorization merely reinforces his caricature, but the one that he has late that night brings a new depth to his characterization.

Section 3 is filled with a series of his direct thought passages strung together by indirect thought and brief narrative descriptions. Taken together, his thoughts display the non-contextualized and freely-associative characteristics of self-directed thought. Similar to

---

[51] For a broader discussion of how this chapter functions within the overall development of Moreno-Isla's character, see my article "Moreno-Isla's Unpublished Scene from the *Fortunata y Jacinta* Galleys," *Anales Galdosianos* 27-28 (1992-93): 179-83.

Isidora's *insomnio* scene, Moreno-Isla's sleepless thoughts jump from one topic and time period to another. In remembering the events of the day he experiences pity for the beggar he had shunned on the street. These and other memories are mixed with future plans and present impressions. Referents are not explained. For example, at one point, without warning, his thoughts turn to the lines and flowers on the wallpaper. Most notably, however, is the total absence of Jacinta's name in this section despite her overwhelming presence in his thoughts. The reader must ascertain that Jacinta is the "maldita mujer" who is tormenting Moreno-Isla. Although general critical opinion holds that Moreno-Isla's respect for Jacinta kept him from actively trying to seduce her during his last sojourn in Spain, evidence from his thoughts suggests otherwise. Through presuppositional sentences the reader becomes aware of events that had passed between these two characters but were not included in the plotline. We learn that Moreno-Isla had indeed broached the subject of a relationship with Jacinta on at least one occasion:

> Yo desgraciado; ella desgraciada, porque su marido es un ciego y desconoce la joya que posee. De estas dos desgracias podríamos hacer una felicidad, si el mundo no fuera lo que es, esclavitud de esclavitudes y todo esclavitud... Me parece que la estoy viendo cuando le dije aquello... ¡Qué risita, qué serenidad, y qué contestación tan admirable! Me dejó pegado a la pared. Tan pegado estoy, que no me he vuelto por otra, y cuando preparo algo para decírselo, ¡anda valiente!... le digo todo lo contrario. (vol. 4, ch. 2, sec. 3)

But Moreno-Isla's pursuit of Jacinta, begun merely as a sexual "campaña," has turned into a profound emotional attachment. His thoughts in this section testify that his feelings for Jacinta are unlike any he had ever experienced before, and when Moreno-Isla confesses to himself that "de esa mujer digo yo lo que hasta ahora no he dicho de ninguna, y es que si fuera soltera, me casaría con ella," we witness a genuine declaration of his love. In his anguish over not being able to have Jacinta he wonders if she ever thinks of him, concluding that he would be content just knowing that at some point she might say to herself "¡Qué bueno es este Moreno! Si yo fuera su mujer, no me daría disgustos, y habríamos tenido un chiquillo, dos o más." Of course, Jacinta finally does respond to

Moreno-Isla's love at the end of the novel when her thoughts re-
fashion Fortunata's child into an image of them both. But this is
only after Moreno-Isla has died.

The narrative presentation of that death has been examined in
detail by two scholars. Gonzalo Sobejano concentrates on Moreno-
Isla's thoughts just preceding the attack. Once again Moreno-Isla
thinks of a beggar with tenderness and suddenly becomes filled
with regret over his treatment of her. His inner world is filled with
sadness and loneliness as well, yet he mentally clings to the hope of
winning Jacinta's affection some day – a hope that is cut short by
death.[52] Harriet Turner focuses on the fatal moment itself, showing
how it is cinematically presented, beginning with a close-up in
which Moreno-Isla's thoughts signal the beginning of the attack,
then gradually pulling back the focus to show the physical position
of the dying man, and closing with a distanced long-shot of the
dead body and a narrative comment linking Moreno-Isla to humanity at large.[53] Both Sobejano and Turner stress the sympathy producing quality of Moreno-Isla's thoughts in this chapter. We feel his
pain as he looks back on a life ill-spent. We realize the sincerity of
his feelings for Jacinta. We see the compassion behind his harsh exterior. Over the course of a single chapter Moreno-Isla has under-
gone a transformation. His caricaturized type has been replaced by
an individualized character.

* * *

As illustrated by the above discussion of *La desheredada* and
Fortunata y Jacinta, Galdós's *segunda manera* employs a wide assort-
ment of interiorization devices that create a more character-cen-
tered narrative style than is exhibited in Galdós's *primera época*
novels. Beginning with *La desheredada*, direct and free indirect
forms of thought frequently replace narrator commentary and grant

---

[52] Gonzalo Sobejano, "Muerte del solitario: (Benito Pérez Galdós: *Fortunata y
Jacinta*, 4.ª, II, 6)," *El comentario de textos, 3: La novela realista* (Madrid: Castalia,
1982) 201-54; rpt. in *Fortunata y Jacinta de Benito Pérez Galdós*, ed. Germán Gullón (Madrid: Taurus, 1986) 313-53.

[53] Harriet S. Turner, "Strategies in Narrative Point of View: On Meaning and
Morality in the Galdós Novel," *Homenaje a Antonio Sánchez Barbudo: Ensayos de
literatura española moderna*, ed. Benito Brancaforte, Edward R. Mulvihill, Roberto
G. Sánchez (Madison: Wisconsin UP, 1981) 70-76.

the reader access to character consciousness. Furthermore, innovative discoursive techniques such as filtered description and theatrical formatting offer new ways of communicating the characters' points of view to the reader. Exteriorization devices such as character-narration and free indirect speech continue this trend toward a greater focus on the character. Nevertheless, the narrator remains an important component of Galdós's narrative strategies. Thanks to the double-voicing of free indirect style – both thought and speech – the narrator's opinions can be placed in contrast or agreement with those of the characters. In addition, narrator reliability or unreliability can be used in conjunction with interior and exterior views of the characters to influence the reader's reception of the social, political, religious, or ethical attitudes and assumptions present in the texts.

In *La desheredada* Galdós uses a reliable narrator to condemn Isidora's elitism and impracticality, and he reinforces this critique of Isidora's values through her irony-saturated free indirect thoughts. But Isidora's numerous interior views also establish an empathetic connection between her and the reader, which allows the reader to understand and feel compassion for Isidora despite the narrator's constant reproaches of her. Also, after Isidora learns the truth about her birth, her emotional devastation is conveyed in sympathetic interiorizations which grant her victim status and soften the critique leveled against her by Miquis and the narrator. Thus, we accept their censure of Isidora's classist attitudes and prodigal behavior, but we do not place all the blame on her. In contrast to *La desheredada*, we are not presented with a reliable narrator in *Fortunata y Jacinta*. Rather, the narrator's social biases hold us at a distance, obliging us to look beyond his opinions. Consequently, the extensive and penetrating interior views of Fortunata more easily sway the reader in her favor. By the end of the novel we not only excuse her socially censurable behavior, but we share in her posthumous *abrazo* with Jacinta. The generosity of her final act, affirmed by her unselfish thoughts, overrides all negative comments about her. Despite the narrator's efforts to portray Juanito favorably and Fortunata unfavorably, their interiorizations provide the reader with the necessary information to judge which of the characters has the greater merit.

Many of the narrative strategies seen in *La deheredada* and *Fortunata y Jacinta* also appear in the Centeno-Tormento-Bringas trilogy. In the next chapter, I will discuss how the sequential format of these novels allows Galdós to influence the reader's affective response to the recurring characters by changing how they are discoursively presented from one text to the next. Once again the narrator's degree of reliability also plays a part in the reader's reception of the behavior and attitudes of the various characters.

CHAPTER 2

RECURRING CHARACTERS:
THE CENTENO-TORMENTO-BRINGAS TRILOGY

Although Galdós does not designate them as such, *El doctor Centeno*, *Tormento* and *La de Bringas* commonly are referred to as a trilogy because of the recurring characters which link the plot of each of these novels to the one preceding it. Throughout this trilogy, a character who originally has a secondary or minor role is suddenly given prominence in a single text, only to recede into the background in the subsequent novels. When we examine the narrative voice techniques used to develop these major recurring characters, we find that the shift in character importance is accompanied by a shift in discoursive presentation as well. While functioning in their original capacity, these characters are portrayed through external views. But during their tenure as protagonists, they receive extensive interior views. Thus, Felipe Centeno, a secondary character with no interiorizations in the *primera época* novel *Marianela*, comes to the forefront in *El doctor Centeno*, where his portrayal is primarily internal. Similarly, Amparo receives a largely external presentation as a minor character in *El doctor Centeno* but is viewed internally in *Tormento*. And finally, Rosalía de Bringas moves from an external to an internal portrayal as she leaves her secondary status in *Tormento* to become the principal character in *La de Bringas*.

As I have shown in my discussion of *La desheredada* and *Fortunata y Jacinta*, an intimacy is established between the reader and those characters who are given prolonged interior treatments. Similarly, a sense of distance is felt by the reader toward characters whose thoughts are rarely or never revealed. Thus, through the skillful interplay of interior and exterior views Galdós is able to manipulate the reader's emotional response in favor or against each of his various characters. This practice is particularly evident in the case of recurring characters whose discoursive portrayal differs from one text to the next. In this chapter I will examine the narrative voice techniques which Galdós uses to depict Felipe, Amparo, and Rosalía as they appear over the course of the trilogy. In so doing, attention also will be paid to the manner in which the discoursive portrayal of these three characters compares to the presentation given the other characters with whom they come in contact. Furthermore, I will discuss how narrator reliability affects the reader's reception of the major recurring characters. Finally, I will show how the interaction between the two narrative levels of each text – the story and the discourse – contributes toward the complexity of all three characterizations, and consequently, helps to account for the wide range of critical responses which these sequential protagonists have received over the years.

FELIPE CENTENO

Critical studies concerning *El doctor Centeno* display a startling lack of agreement, due primarily to the novel's episodic structure and its title character who is often peripheral to the action of the story. Citing the work's loose organization, José Montesinos regards the work as a fusion of two separate novels, the first volume being merely an introduction to the second one which features Alejandro Miquis as its protagonist. Because of his focus on Miquis rather than Centeno, Montesinos places this work into the category of "novelas de la locura crematística" instead of his "novelas pedagógicas" classification. [1] But Centeno's central status is defended by scholars who regard this novel as a *Bildungsroman* which documents Felipe's growth process through his life experience with two masters. [2] However, Hazel Gold has suggested that the linear structure of Felipe's personal development is thwarted by the circular

---

[1] José F. Montesinos, *Galdós*, 3 vols. (Madrid: Castalia, 1968-73) 2: 62-78.
[2] Germán Gullón, "Unidad de «El doctor Centeno»," *Cuadernos Hispanoamericanos* 250-52 (1970-71): 582-85; and Francisco Caudet, "*El doctor Centeno*: La «educación sentimental» de Galdós," *Studies in Honor of Bruce W. Wardropper*, ed. Dian Fox, et al. (Newark DE: Juan de la Cuesta, 1989) 41-66.

structure also operating in the text.[3] Other critics cite an organizing theme, such as education or traditional values, to compensate for the lack of a clear-cut protagonist.[4] How can we reconcile these divergent critical positions? When we examine the narrative voice in this double volume novel, we find that Galdós varied his distribution of certain devices from one volume to the next. This change in narrative voice technique has an impact on the depiction of both Centeno and Miquis, and consequently affects the reader's perception of each character's importance in the text.

In volume 1 Felipe Centeno's portrayal is primarily internal. That is, the reader frequently has direct access to Centeno's consciousness through direct and free indirect thought. These extensive interiorizations play a large part in quickly establishing a personal relationship between him and the reader. In contrast, Alejandro Miquis's characterization in volume 1 is entirely external, achieved through dialogue and narrative description. Direct representation of Miquis's thoughts and emotions is totally absent. At the close of this volume the narrator states that he will continue to recount the adventures of Centeno and Miquis in the following volume, but that "en vez de un héroe, ya tenemos dos." Significantly, in volume 2 there is a sudden and dramatic shift toward interiorization for Miquis as well as Centeno. Thus, volume 2 features extensive inside views – conveyed through direct and free indirect thought – of both characters.

In the first volume Miquis actively engages in daily activities while Centeno largely observes. Centeno's passive role is offset, however, by the powerful effect of the lengthy interior views which focus reader attention on him. In the second volume the situation is reversed. Because of his illness and financial ruin, Miquis becomes the passive character while Centeno deals with the everyday demands of life. Miquis's prominence in the text, however, is insured by allowing him interior views which were denied him earlier. Since Centeno's interiorization is no longer exclusive, the strength of his

---

[3] Hazel Gold, *The Reframing of Realism: Galdós and the Discourses of the Nineteenth-Century Spanish Novel* (Durham: Duke UP, 1993) 151-70.

[4] See, respectively, Gloria Moreno Castillo, "La unidad de tema en «El doctor Centeno»," *Actas del Primer Congreso Internacional de Estudios Galdosianos* (Madrid: Cabildo Insular de Gran Canaria, 1977) 382-88; and Geraldine M. Scanlon, "*El doctor Centeno*: a study in obsolescent values," *Bulletin of Hispanic Studies* 55 (1978): 245-53.

hold on the reader is somewhat diluted while that of Miquis is substantially augmented.

In short, if we look at the text as a whole composed of two interrelated volumes, we can say that Centeno and Miquis are co-protagonists who complement each other by alternating in emphasis
between the story and discourse (the discourse being the means of
expression used to transmit the content of the story to the reader)
from one volume to the next. In the first volume Miquis controls the
story through his numerous plot actions, while the focal point of
the discourse is on Centeno's interior views. In the second volume
it is Centeno's activities which move the story along, while Miquis's
mental musings are highlighted in the discourse. Thus, we can understand the critical contention that the novel does not have a clearly established protagonist. Yet, it is also easy to see how either
Miquis or Centeno can be chosen as the main character. Miquis's
initial activity within the plotline lends a high degree of importance
to his character, which later acquires additional depth through interior views. Conversely, the intimacy established between the reader
and Centeno early in the novel as a result of interiorization is continued into the second half where his actions also become gradually
more significant to the plot progression. An examination of narrative voice techniques, then, uncovers some possible reasons behind
the differing critical reception of the two major characters of the
text. Yet, it gives rise to an even more fundamental question. Why
is Centeno depicted internally throughout the entire text while
Miquis is granted interior views only in the second half? The following discussion will attempt to answer this question by pointing
out the effects which perhaps governed Galdós's choice of narrative
voice techniques to portray these two characters.

Unlike Alejandro Miquis, Felipe Centeno is a recurring character who already had been introduced in a previous novel. Despite
the minor role that he plays in *Marianela*, his character is well-de-
fined and reasonably developed. In this early work his portrayal is
entirely external, through his dialogues with Marianela and in narrative commentary. His conversations with Marianela reveal his desire to make something of himself, and the narrator openly praises
him for being the only member of his "familia de piedra" to rebel
against their dehumanized existence. Nevertheless, Centeno's higher aspirations are not entirely altruistic. His interest in educating
himself is primarily motivated by the financial rewards and prestige

that becoming a doctor would bring him, and it is to that end that he strikes out on his own for Madrid. At the close of *Marianela* the narrator promises the reader a future book about Centeno's adventures. *El doctor Centeno*, of course, is that book. Because of our previous acquaintance with Centeno, his character must display a certain continuity from one novel to the next. Yet, if he is to win our affection, his cocky personality, his greed, and his status-seeking must give way to his better qualities. Thanks to his numerous interiorizations in *El doctor Centeno*, we learn that these character flaws simply are attributable to his youth and naiveté, and therefore, they diminish as he matures. In contrast, his more positive traits – those we see in his tender moments with Marianela – are shown to be permanent and become more prominent as time goes on. His closeness with Marianela and his genuine concern for her welfare attest to his ability to respond compassionately to others. This potential for human growth finds its fullest expression in his relationship with Alejandro Miquis.

In *El doctor Centeno* it is important to keep in mind Chatman's distinction between perspective that resides in the narrator (i.e. the narrative slant) and perspective that belongs to a character (i.e. a narrative filter).[5] Although *El doctor Centeno* is told by an unnamed third person narrator, it is Felipe Centeno's perspective as an observer of events which dominates many of the scenes.[6] As Germán Gullón has aptly stated, Felipe "es el prisma humano a través del cual se filtran los hechos que ocurren en la novela."[7] This role as narrative filter is established in the very first chapter of the novel where the banquet given by don Florencio Morales y Temprado is described from Centeno's point of view. The narrator clearly announces the perceptual orientation of the scene by stating that Centeno "observaba todo, callado y circunspecto. Nada perdía su activa penetración; a su instintivo examen de las cosas, nada se escapaba" (vol. 1, ch. 1, sec. 3). Thus, the description of the banquet is filtered through Centeno's point of view. But the boy's perceptual perspective – what he sees, hears, and smells – is strongly affected by his interest perspective. Because of his overwhelming hunger,

[5] Seymour Chatman, *Coming to Terms: The Rhetoric of Narrative in Fiction and Film* (Ithaca: Cornell UP, 1990) 139-49.
[6] To use Genette's terminology, the narrator is extra-heterodiegetic.
[7] Gullón 580.

Centeno largely focuses on the food and those eating or serving it. In his joy over receiving such an abundant serving, he regards everyone around him as a representative of all that is good and beautiful. It is left to the reader to make more objective judgments concerning Centeno's dinner companions as the novel progresses.

Centeno functions as the empathetic vehicle for experiencing the events of the text since our knowledge of the novelistic world is largely derived from his impressions of it. Centeno's perspective frequently dominates as the narrator temporarily recedes, only to once again take charge of the narrative and make objective comments or value judgments. Thus, the naive viewpoint of the young boy works in conjunction with the worldly perspective of the narrator to provide the reader with a layered reading experience. Centeno is a boy living in an adult world, and his view of it is conveyed in filtered descriptions. We, along with the narrator, know that Centeno's understanding often is faulty or incomplete due to his youth and inexperience. Thus, we look beyond Centeno's assessments to find the whole picture, and the narrator helps us by providing the necessary clues to fill in the missing gaps. An example is seen in the characterization of Amparo. Centeno's idealistic vision of her conflicts with the narrator's indications of her romantic entanglement with the priest, Pedro Polo. Yet, because the reader sees her largely through the eyes of a highly sympathetic character, her portrayal tends to be positive despite the suggestion of sexual impropriety. Our emotional response to Amparo is influenced by Centeno's view of her, but unlike the boy we are able to temper that opinion with a degree of worldly understanding given us by the narrator. Thus, we reserve our judgment of Amparo until we receive more evidence which, of course, is forthcoming in the next installment of the trilogy. Overall, *El doctor Centeno* combines qualities of the limited perspective of first person narration (conveyed in descriptions filtered through Centeno) with the unlimited perspective of the omniscient third person narrator.[8] In this way we feel the immediacy of Centeno's experience, but Galdós is not hampered by the restrictions of Centeno's solitary perspective. The result is a far richer narrative than would have been possible had it been written in the first person. Despite the picaresque format of the novel, Galdós chose to dis-

---

[8] That is, through filtered descriptions the heterodiegetic narrative acquires some of the personalized feel of a homodiegetic narrative.

pense with the protagonist-as-narrator convention associated with that genre, thereby gaining greater flexibility in narrative voice technique.

A variation on the filtered description is found in section 4, chapter 2 of the second volume where Centeno eavesdrops on conversations between Miquis and a woman identified only as "la Tal." No dialogue is recorded. Instead, the scenes are relayed through *Centeno's* mental impressions of the words spoken by the woman. That is, the free indirect speech of "la Tal" is presented from Centeno's perceptual point of view. In this way we learn the content of the conversations along with some indication of the woman's manner of speaking. The following is an excerpt from the first of these conversations:

> ¿Qué lengua hablaba? Ya,... se comía la mitad de las palabras, y las otras las rematarba con un dejo... ¡ay! Era andaluza. . . La Tal charlaba, charlaba en su graciosa lengua andaluza... ¡Tanto tiempo sin verle! No hacía más que pensar en él... ¡pobrecito! Era menester que se pusiera pronto bueno... Ella estaba muy disgustada. ¡Le pasaban unas cosas..., pero unas cosas! No podía vivir. Aún creyó entender Felipe que lloriqueaba algo.

These scenes acquire a secretive feel since they are presented second hand through a hidden observer, and the unknown woman becomes all the more mysterious because we are denied direct contact with her. Indeed, she continues to be a shadowy figure throughout the text since the narrator does not intervene to give us even the most rudimentary information about her, such as her name. Her lack of clarity facilitates the reader's acceptance of the blurring which will occur later in the novel between "la Tal" and the heroine of Miquis's play, la Carniola. Indeed, due to these conversations it is Centeno who first suggests to Miquis the similarity between the real woman and her fictional counterpart.

Centeno's point of view also is conveyed through his thoughts, unequally divided between direct and free indirect passages. Direct thought – displaying Centeno's idiosyncratic syntax and vocabulary – appears infrequently in the text. More commonly we find passages recording his free indirect thoughts. On the whole these segments reflect some of Centeno's unpolished verbal style but do not fully imitate his speech. There is a practical reason for this emphasis on free indirect thought over direct thought. Rather than have the reader struggle to decipher numerous direct representations of Centeno's idiom, Galdós relies heavily on free indirect thought to capture the general flavor of the boy's manner of speaking without citing his actual words. Short passages of this type appear in virtually every chapter, however, one lengthy example is worthy of particular note. In volume 1, chapter 2, section 6 a very depressed Centeno is thinking about his failure in Polo's school. Centeno considers himself to be worthless because he cannot learn anything from Polo or Ido, whom he sees as "dos templos de sabiduría." He also chastises himself for thinking that instead of using books, he can learn by asking questions about everyday things that interest him. In this free indirect thought passage the double-voicing associated with this device is used to juxtapose Centeno's limited understanding of the situation against the narrator's larger appreciation of what is happening in the story. In the process, Polo's school is ironized because of its failure to respond to the natural curiosity of a student who is highly motivated to learn. Felipe's desire to learn about natural phenomena ("por qué las cosas, cuando se sueltan al aire, caen al suelo; . . . Qué virtud tiene una pajita para dejarse quemar, y por qué no la tiene un clavo; . . . por qué el aceite nada por el agua; . . . qué es esto de echar agua por los ojos cuando uno llora") finds no answers in what the narrator calls Polo's *inyectocerebral* method of teaching by rote memorization. As José Luis López Muñoz has observed, "Felipe Centeno habría sido el alumno ideal para Jesús Delgado." [9] Indeed, this former employee of the Dirección de Instrucción Pública was dismissed precisely because he advocated the kind of active, student-centered, hands-on learning Felipe craves. [10] Thus, through Felipe's naive view of himself as a "bobo," Galdós is able to comment not only on Polo's pedagogical techniques in particular, but also on Spain's educational system in general.

Present tense narration provides an additional method of communicating the events of the text from Centeno's perspective. Dur-

---

[9] José Luis López Muñoz, "Felipe Centeno, un héroe oscuro e inédito," *Papeles de Son Armadans* 73.219 (1979): 253.

[10] For a discussion of the philosophical basis for Delgado's progressive educational theories see Denah Lida, "Sobre el 'Krausismo' de Galdós," *Anales Galdosianos* 2 (1967): 11-15 and Scanlon 247-48.

ing periods of emotional intensity, it occasionally is used to provide a link to Felipe's consciousness. In effect, these are quasi-interior views which combine the properties of both direct and free indirect thought. That is, the present tense format of direct thought is coupled with the third person pronoun reference and untagged status of free indirect thought. Present tense narration has the appearance of a free indirect thought passage, but it features present and future tense verbs rather than the traditional imperfect and conditional tenses. By allowing the present tense to momentarily encroach on the domain of the past tenses and assume the function of telling the story, Galdós is able to give a feeling of intensity and immediacy to the events thus represented. This phenomenon can best be explained through an examination of the different temporal planes operating in the storytelling situation: the story NOW and the discourse NOW. The story NOW refers to the time period in which the characters engage in the events which take place, while the discourse NOW is the time period in which the narrator tells the story to the reader. In *El doctor Centeno* these time periods are 1863 and 1883, respectively. Since the narrator deals with events which already have occurred, the story NOW of the characters pre-dates the discourse NOW of the narrator and consequently is related in the past tense. But the discourse NOW also exists as a type of perpetual present which is shared with each new reader who enters into the storytelling situation.[11] The introduction of brief passages of present tense narration into a text which is otherwise narrated in the past suddenly reduces the distance between the reader and the fictional world by placing the reader and the characters on the same temporal plane – that of the story NOW. The reader lives the moment along with the characters, and therefore it appears more vivid. This effect accounts for the traditional use of the "historical present" by writers who wish to heighten the impact of dramatic scenes. Segments typically cast in the present tense by Galdós, however, differ from the norm because they involve emotionally intense situations that focus on the subjective reactions of the characters rather than the dramatic quality of the events. Consequently, they feature descriptive passages of events which in themselves are mundane, but which hold some special importance to the characters. In

---

[11] For a discussion of NOW see Seymour Chatman, *Story and Discourse: Narrative Structure in Fiction and Film* (Ithaca: Cornell UP, 1978) 62-63, 81-84.

such cases, it is the *personal* drama of the events which is conveyed. Galdós uses present tense narration as a vehicle for allowing the reader to experience the events of the story though the emotional filter of its participants. In *El doctor Centeno* that filter is Felipe; in *Tormento* it is Amparo.

The entire first section of *El doctor Centeno* is narrated in the present tense. It opens with the chronicler-narrator's remarks concerning Felipe, during which he formally announces himself as an "historiador" bringing information to his reading public. This introductory portion is told entirely in the voice of the narrator, but approximately midway through section 1 – when the boy lights up the cigar – Felipe's voice begins to seep into the narration. Throughout Felipe's cigar smoking experience and his subsequent fainting spell, the narrator's presence fades as Felipe's strengthens. Information concerning Centeno's external reality is sifted through the boy's consciousness and presented as a response to what he sees. Like free indirect thought, present tense narration can capture the essence of Centeno's verbal style while retaining the voice of the narrator. This combination is particularly effective in its final few paragraphs:

> Contempla la mole del Hospital. ¡Vaya que es grandote! La Estación se ve como un gran juguete de trenes de los que hay en los bazares para el uso de los niños ricos. Los polvorosos muelles parece que no tienen término. Las negras máquinas maniobran sin cesar, trayendo y llevando largos rosarios de coches verdes con números dorados. Sale un tren. ¿Adónde irá? Puede que a Rusia o al *mesmo* Santander... ¡Qué *tié* que ver esto con la estación de Villamojada! Allá va echando demonios por aquella *escañada*... Sin *ponderancia*, esto parece la gloria eterna. ¡Válgate Dios, Madrid! ¡Qué risa!... Al héroe le entra una risa franca y ruidosa, y vuelve a escupir.
>
> ¿Pues y la casona grande que está allí arriba, con aquella rueda de *colunas*?... ¡Ah, ya, ya lo sabe! Poquito el ciego se lo ha dicho. Ya se va *destruyendo*. ¡Sabe más cosas!... En aquella casa se ponen los que cuentan las estrellas y *desaminan* el sol para saber esto de los días que corren y si hay truenos y agua por arriba... Paquito le ha dicho también que tienen aquellos señores unas antiparras tan grandes como cañones, con las cuales... Otra salivita.
>
> Pero ¿qué pasa? ¿Los orbes se desquician y ruedan sin concierto? El Hospital empieza a tambalearse, y por fin da gra-

ciosas volteras, poniendo las tejas en el suelo y echando al aire
los cimientos descalzos. La Estación y sus máquinas se echan a
volar, y el río salpica sus charcos por el cielo. Éste se cae como
un telón al que se le rompen las cuerdas, y el Observatorio se le
pone por montera a nuestro sabio fumador, que siente malestar
indecible, dolor agudísimo en las sienes, náuseas, desvaneci-
mientos, repugnancia... El monstruo, vencedor y no quemado
por entero, cae de sus manos; quiere el otro dominarse, lucha
con su mal, se levanta, da vueltas, cae atontado, pierde el color,
el conocimento, y rueda al fin, como cuerpo muerto por rápida
pendiente como de tres varas, hasta dar en un hoyo.
    Silencio, nadie pasa... Transcurren segundos, minutos... (vol.
1, ch. 1, sec. 1)

By using present tense narration to introduce this character, Galdós
establishes an immediate bond between the boy and the reader,
who co-temporally experiences the lightheadedness of the novice
smoker. In addition, the present tense allows us to feel directly the
wonderment of this small-town boy as he comes in contact with the
big city for the first time.

    Present tense narration is similarly used near the end of the
novel (vol. 2, ch. 3, sec. 5) during the scene in which Centeno fulfills his ambition to be a doctor in the only way possible to him – by
performing an autopsy on a cat. Thanks to his many hours spent secretly perusing Cienfuegos's anatomy books, Felipe is able to examine the animal with a degree of naive sophistication. Hardly the
dunce he had been characterized as being by Polo, Centeno exhibits a self-taught command of rudimentary anatomy.[12] Centeno's
surgical preparations are recounted in the past tense, but the operation itself is told in present tense narration followed by Centeno's
verbalized thoughts. Every step of the procedure is relayed from
Centeno's point of view. Present tense narration permits us to see
the scene through Felipe's eyes, while his direct thoughts and
speech allow us to witness Felipe's ideas as they occur to him. Past
tense narration is reestablished only when Centeno's concentration

---

[12] In *Images of the Sign: Semiotic Consciousness in the Novels of Benito Pérez Galdós* (Columbia: U of Missouri P, 1990) 41-48, Akiko Tsuchiya has noted that Felipe's interest in certain subjects over others is a reflection of his search for a nat-ural correspondence between signs and referents. He enjoys anatomy and geogra-phy because these are based on motivated signs, but he dislikes the arbitrary signs of grammar and math.

suddenly is broken by the voice of his neighbor calling to him. The use of present tense in this segment not only underscores the importance of the event to Felipe, but it also allows the reader to participate in it vicariously and to feel the curiosity and enthusiasm that still resides in the boy despite all the hardships he has endured during his disillusioning stay at Polo's school. Galdós's choice to narrate the surgery in the present tense represents a change from his original plan. In the manuscript of *El doctor Centeno* he first described the operation with preterite and imperfect verbs, which he subsequently scratched out and replaced with their present tense counterparts. In so doing, Galdós created the effect of having Centeno's present and the reader's present come together in a commonly shared experience. [13]

Present tense narration is also used to convey Alejandro Miquis's point of view, but only in the second volume when he too is granted interior views. An interesting combination of present tense narration and free indirect thought is seen in chapter 3, section 7 when Miquis's illness has so unbalanced his mind that he confuses the people in his life with the characters in the play he is writing. In a long free indirect thought passage he sees himself as the Duque, while la Tal is transformed into his heroine la Carniola, and Centeno becomes Quevedo. In his delirious state Miquis imagines his room to be a stage set, with la Tal's visit signaling her entrance. As Miquis replaces the reality of his life with the fantasy of his play, the past tense verbs temporarily yield to those of the present. At first, the switch seems to represent nothing more than the common practice of using the present tense to summarize the plot of a play. But when the present tense continues into the description of what la Tal and Centeno are doing, it has the disorienting effect of placing the reader in the timelessness of Miquis's feverish mind where there is no distinction between his play and the world around him. Significantly, the past tense narration resumes as soon as Centeno and la Tal are out of Miquis's sight. By switching from the past to the present tense in this segment Galdós was stylistically able to fuse Miquis's perceptual perspective – what he sees in his

---

[13] The original manuscript of *El doctor Centeno* is located in the Biblioteca Nacional (Madrid), with a photocopy in the Casa-Museo Pérez Galdós (Las Palmas de Gran Canaria). The present tense segment pertaining to the cat surgery is on page 321.

real life – with the conceptual perspective of the fictional world he is creating in his mind. Furthermore, the present tense orientation of his delirium draws the reader into the NOW of the story to experience first-hand Miquis's slowly deteriorating grasp on reality. Indeed, all the later inside views of Miquis – through direct as well as free indirect thoughts – reveal the picture of a man who is gradually falling under the power of a double obsession: his play and its heroine. As Gustavo Correa and Rodolfo Cardona have shown, Galdós uses *El grande Osuna* to satirize 19th-century Romantic drama, which was rooted in the artificiality of the Calderonian tradition.[14] But Galdós satirizes the concept of the Romantic artist as well. Romanticism saw a connection between disease and art due to the consuming and devouring nature of both. Tuberculosis, in particular, was associated with a heightening of aesthetic appreciation and was seen as inspiring creative genius. The physically incapacitated writer would channel all natural urges into mental activity.[15] Thus, the consumptive Miquis is in the appropriate state of health to compose his play. His money gone and his strength declining, he is the personification of the suffering Romantic writer who, coincidentally, is composing a Romantic drama. Miquis dedicates all of his attention to perfecting *El grande Osuna*, and as a result, he becomes enamored with the woman who reminds him of its heroine. His sexual feelings for la Tal, unrealizable in his weakened state, take an artistic form instead. In his mind, Miquis substitutes his role as the Romantic artist for that of the Romantic hero, thereby becoming a robust adventurer instead of a diseased writer. Consequently, when la Tal needs rescuing from a jealous brute, Miquis attempts to save her, just as the duke saved la Carniola from Jacques Pierre. Thus, two versions of the same play are in operation for Miquis – one featuring the historical figures, and the other star-

---

[14] Gustavo Correa, "Pérez Galdós y la tradición calderoniana," *Cuadernos Hispanoamericanos* 250-52 (1970-71): 227-30; and Rodolfo Cardona, "Nuevos enfoques críticos con referencia a la obra de Galdós," *Cuadernos Hispanoamericanos* 250-52 (1970-71): 69-70.

[15] See Jeffrey Meyers, *Disease and the Novel, 1880-1960* (New York: St. Martin's Press, 1985) 7-8. In addition, Susan Sontag, *Illness as Metaphor* (New York: Farrar, Straus, and Giroux, 1977) 63, has noted that the "consumption" metaphor for tuberculosis in the nineteenth-century implied the squandering of resources, both corporal and economic. Thus, Galdós was able to use Miquis's illness not only to satirize Romanticism, but also to criticize Miquis's unrestrained spending habits and wild living which led to his physical decline.

ring Miquis and la Tal as their heroic counterparts. The first is com-municated to the reader through lengthy conversations between Miquis and Centeno which are reminiscent of the accounts made by Don Quijote to Sancho concerning chivalric novels. Some of these speeches are similar to dramatic monologues since only Miquis's words are recorded. But whereas this official, written play takes shape during these exterior views of Miquis, the other version develops within Miquis's mind and is revealed to the reader through interior views. This difference in discoursive presentation helps the reader to distinguish between the two versions later in the text when Miquis himself cannot.

Now we can return to our question of why Centeno's interior views span the entire novel while those of Miquis are contained within the second volume alone. By limiting interiorizations to Cen-teno in volume 1, Galdós insures the reader's interest in his charac-ter. This is necessary because Centeno serves as the naive counter-point to the worldly perspective of the narrator, and the combina-tion of both viewpoints constitutes the global vision of the text. Since this function continues throughout the novel, Centeno's inte-rior views likewise continue from one volume to the next. Miquis's role in the first volume is to serve as Centeno's means of entering the social world portrayed in the text. While Miquis interacts with other characters, Centeno silently observes and reflects on what he sees. Centeno's mental reactions record Miquis's physical actions. In the second volume, however, Miquis's thoughts also come to the fore. This occurs after Miquis is explicitly announced as co-protag-onist of the text. Miquis shares the spotlight with Centeno in vol-ume 2 by suddenly intruding on the boy's monopoly of interior views, thereby slightly diminishing Centeno's importance while in-creasing it for himself. As the boy continues his picaresque adven-tures and becomes adept at handling the demands of daily life, the master is freed to pursue literary fantasies which eventually bring him to the edge of madness. Thus, the second volume combines elements of *Lazarillo de Tormes* and *Don Quijote*. Within the pi-caresque tale Centeno is the major character and Miquis is the sec-ondary one, just as Lazarillo outshines the *escudero*. But within the Cervantine adaptation the roles are reversed and Miquis's position is of greater importance than that of Centeno, mirroring the rela-tionship between Don Quijote and Sancho. This added emphasis on Miquis's character is reflected in his abrupt switch toward interiorization, which implicitly signals his new status to the reader. Volume 2 becomes Miquis's story while, at the same time, it continues to be Centeno's story. Just as Centeno's prime importance in volume 1 is established through interior views, Miquis's additional value in volume 2 is marked by his interiorizations. Both characters are co-protagonists of the entire novel and primary protagonists of their own realms within that novel, and this situation is reflected in the narrative voice techniques used to portray them.

AMPARO

The second novel in the trilogy has as its protagonist a character who hardly appears in *El doctor Centeno* but has an important behind-the-scenes role in Pedro Polo's life. As she moves to center stage in *Tormento*, the reader is obliged to piece together the truth about her past and to complete the very sketchy personality profile begun in the earlier text. It is a critical commonplace to point out that, with the exception of her lost virginity, Amparo has all of the qualities of the ideal romantic heroine found in serialized fiction.[16] Like these heroines Amparo is a beautiful, poor, modest, domestic, hard-working, and obedient young woman whose very name suggests that she will be a supportive life companion. Unfortunately, she also has the typical heroine's passivity, a trait which may have led to her sexual liaison with Polo and which most certainly contributed toward the complications in her engagement to Agustín. Yet despite her past affair with a priest, scholars generally consider her to be neither immoral nor bad, and several studies discuss how Galdós uses Ido's *folletín* to highlight the inadequacies of a value system that would judge her as being so.[17] In particular, Alicia An-

---

[16] Recently Hazel Gold 101-22 has shown how that same type of character is one of the stock elements of the romantic theater as well.

[17] Galdós's parodic use of the conventions associated with serialized fiction has been discussed from a variety of perspectives in a number of studies. For the most thorough treatments see Alicia G. Andreu, *Modelos diológicos en Galdós*, Purdue Monographs in Romance Languages 27 (Amsterdam: John Benjamins, 1989) 21-29; Bridget A. Aldaraca, *El Ángel del Hogar: Galdós and the Ideology of Domesticity in Spain*, North Carolina Studies in the Romance Languages and Literatures 239 (Chapel Hill: U of North Carolina P, 1991) 139-59; Stephanie Sieburth, *Inventing High and Low: Literature, Mass Culture, and Uneven Modernity in Spain* (Durham: Duke UP, 1994) 100-36; Anthony Percival, "Melodramatic Metafiction in *Tormen-*

dreu and Bridget Aldaraca show how Galdós exposes some of the inconsistencies inherent in the bourgeois feminine ideal by using Amparo's plight to point out the practical difficulties involved in the concept of virtuous poverty which was idealized in serialized literature. Indeed, Amparo is often described as a victim, not only of Polo's sexual advances but also of a crushing economic situation from which she has few avenues of escape. Yet a strong minority opinion sees Amparo in a less favorable light. To Rodney Rodríguez she is a scheming opportunist who seduced and financially ruined Polo before abandoning him in search of a richer prey.[18] She is also criticized by Eamonn Rodgers, Peter Bly, and Lou Charnon-Deutsch for what they call her cruel and heartless rejection of Polo.[19] Rodríguez and Rodgers particularly stress the selfishness of Amparo's behavior because they characterize her affair with Polo as being based on honesty, trust, and affection.

Yet what exactly do we know about the past relationship between Polo and Amparo? Galdós is silent on this point. As Diane Urey has ably shown, the reader must use small clues in the text to fill in the missing gaps.[20] It is through this inferential process that the reader is able to ascertain that their relationship was of a sexual nature. But that fact is all we ever know for sure. Although the text requires us to guess that an affair had taken place between these two characters, it does not allow us to know what that affair was

to," Kentucky Romance Quarterly 31 (1984): 151-60; David Cuff, "The Structure and Meaning of Galdós' *Tormento," Reflexión* 2 3-4 (1974-75): 165-66; and Michael Nimetz, *Humor in Galdós: A Study of the Novelas Contemporáneas* (New Haven: Yale UP, 1968) 70-71.

[18] Various aspects of this argument have been put forth in three articles by Rodney T. Rodríguez, "The Reader's Role in *Tormento: A Reconstruction of the Pedro Polo Affair," Anales Galdosianos* 24 (1989): 69-78; "Las máscaras del engaño en *Tormento," Actas del VIII Congreso de la Asociación Internacional de Hispanistas* (Madrid: Ediciones Istmo, 1986) 2: 517-24; and "La unidad orgánica de la trilogía *Centeno-Tormento-Bringas," Actas del Tercer Congreso Internacional de Estudios Galdosianos* (Las Palmas: Cabildo Insular de Gran Canaria, 1989) 2: 179-85.

[19] Lou Charnon-Deutsch, "Inhabited Space in Galdós' *Tormento," Anales Galdosianos* 10 (1975): 40; Peter A. Bly, "From Disorder to Order: The Pattern of *Arreglar* References in Galdós' *Tormento* and *La de Bringas," Neophilologus* 62 (1978): 394; and two studies by Eamonn Rodgers, "The Appearance-Reality Contrast in Galdós' *Tormento," Forum for Modern Language Studies* 6 (1970): 382-98 and *From Enlightenment to Realism: The Novels of Galdós 1870-1887* (Dublin: Jack Hade, 1987) 95-112.

[20] Diane F. Urey, "Repetition, Discontinuity and Silence in Galdós's *Tormento," Anales Galdosianos* 20.1 (1985): 47-63.

like. What Wolfgang Iser calls the "areas of indeterminacy" concerning the affair cannot all be resolved because we are not given
enough information about the dynamics of their relationship. But
our urge to eliminate every single one of these indeterminacies can
become so strong that there is a danger of *overfilling* the gaps. Like
Marcelina, we want to know everything, and consequently we may
jump to conclusions or provide elaborate details that make the
broadly sketched picture of the lovers seem more complete. Geoffrey Ribbans's lengthy defense of Amparo speaks to this issue by
showing how the textual evidence cited by Rodríguez does not support his claim that Amparo seduced Polo. Ribbans also answers
those who sympathize with Polo over Amparo by demonstrating
how that position ignores Polo's betrayal of his triple responsibility
to Amparo as an older relative, as a trusted friend of the family, and
as a representative of the church. Finally, Ribbans counters the argument that the affair had been a period of mutual happiness for
the lovers by using textual evidence to construct an opposing sce-
nario in which Amparo, due to her youth and inexperience, was seduced by Polo and then pressured into resuming the affair after her
father's death.[21] This same interpretation of the events is held by
José Montesinos, who cites Polo's violence as a justification for such
a reading.[22]

All of this debate concerning the Polo-Amparo affair merely underscores the fundamental indeterminacy of the text on this matter.
The text leads us to the conclusion that Polo and Amparo were sexually involved, but the textual evidence does not indicate which of
the parties was the seducer, neither does it let us know what happened during the affair, nor does it give us the reason why the
lovers broke up. That is, certain indeterminacies are meant to be
clarified, and some are not.[23] We may speculate as to the nature of

---

[21] Geoffrey Ribbans, "'Amparando/Desamparando a Amparo:' Some reflections on *El doctor Centeno* and *Tormento*," *Revista Canadiense de Estudios Hispánicos* 17 (1993): 495-524.
[22] Montesinos 2: 105.
[23] Michael A. Schnepf, "The Manuscript of Galdós's *Tormento*," *Anales Galdosianos* 26 (1991): 45-47 points out that the original manuscript of this novel contains a few additional details concerning the affair, all of which cast Amparo in a
somewhat less sympathetic light while portraying Polo more sympathetically. However, it is important to remember that these deleted details were part of a larger
rewriting of the plotline and do not represent facts that were intended to be recon-
structed by the reader. While manuscripts and galleys provide fascinating insights

the affair, but all of our conclusions are ultimately unverifiable. Those readers, such as Rodríguez, who do attempt to resolve everything fall into the trap of overfilling the textual gaps. Furthermore, in their search for textual clues, these readers are so drawn to the story level of the narrative that they may resist the pull of the discourse, and consequently they may also fail to respond to the interiorization devices used to develop Amparo's character. Indeed, Amparo's portrayal in this trilogy is constructed though the carefully balanced interplay of her actions (within the story) and her thoughts (conveyed in the discourse). An emphasis on one narrative level over the other upsets that balance and results in a skewed reading of Amparo's character. To focus on the story is to condemn Amparo for her behavior with Polo and toward Agustín. To focus on the discourse is to empathize with her to such a degree that she is unconditionally forgiven. Only by taking into consideration both the story and the discourse are we able to avoid such black and white interpretations and come to the more subtly shaded readings that the texts afford. A detailed examination of Amparo's portrayal in both *El doctor Centeno* and *Tormento* will demonstrate how discourse and story combine to create a complex characterization for this heroine who, on the surface, seems nothing more than a one-dimensional romantic type.

In *El doctor Centeno* Amparo's presence is limited to the first two chapters, during which she appears only three times: at the banquet given by don Florencio Morales y Temprado; at a holiday celebration following one of Polo's masterful sermons; and at Felipe's dismissal from the Polo household after the incident with the bull's head. On the first two occasions Amparo is merely one of the many guests described at these gatherings. Although we are told about her actions and given bits and pieces of her conversations, we do not know her thoughts. It is not until her last appearance in this text (vol. 1, ch. 2, sec. 13) that her mind is momentarily opened to us. After unsuccessfully pleading with Polo to forgive Felipe, she comforts the boy, and thinking to herself "¡Qué mal hacen en no perdonarte!," she gives him her lottery winnings. Thus, the final impression we have of Amparo is a positive one, based on her act of

---

into the creative process, textual analysis must be based on the published novel alone. Indeed, Galdós's rewritten segments suggest a deliberate effort to shift sympathy away from Polo and toward Amparo.

kindness and charity toward a defenseless child, and reinforced by the intimacy of a brief interior view that shows the genuine expression of her "alma abrumada." Furthermore, this parting scene is described through Felipe's eyes. From his *perceptual* perspective he sees Amparo standing in the light of the setting sun, but his *interest* perspective converts her into "una hermosa y celestial figura. . . rodeada de rayos de oro, echando de su frente fulgores de estrellas" and speaking "con voz de serafines." Although Felipe's point of view is highly subjective, Amparo's treatment of the boy is fully in keeping with his angelic vision of her. Felipe idolizes Amparo, just as he idolizes Polo. But unlike Amparo, Polo betrays Felipe's faith and trust. Polo's condemnation of Felipe is hypocritical. It is based not on any transgression that the boy may have committed against a sacred image, but rather, it is based on Polo's fear that the boy will reveal the priest's late-night tryst outside of the pharmacy building. He seizes upon the accusation that Felipe is a liar, and he uses it to publicly discredit the boy. Amparo's protective and nurturing behavior towards Felipe stands in sharp contrast to Polo's cruelty and selfishness. No anguished interior views of Polo's mind are provided to soften our reaction to his actions. Instead, it is Amparo's kind thoughts that we hear. In this, the last time we see Amparo and Polo together before *Tormento*, both the events of the story and the interiorization in the discourse jointly work to incline the reader's sympathies toward Amparo and against Polo. [24] Lest we forget this scene as we follow Felipe in his adventures with Miquis, we are reminded of it in the second volume of *El doctor Centeno* when Felipe requests money from Polo to care for the ailing Miquis. Polo toys with the boy until he learns of Amparo's past generosity. Then, in a calculated attempt to surpass her spontaneous gesture, Polo gives Felipe exactly one peseta more than he had received from Amparo. Once again the contrast between Amparo and Polo is underscored by this hollow act of charity. Indeed, Polo's lack of concern for Felipe's welfare is evident when he refuses the boy's next petition for help. Throughout *El doctor Centeno* Polo's portrayal is

---

[24] In "Galdós's *El doctor Centeno* Manuscript: Pedro Polo and Other Curiosities," *Romance Quarterly* 41 (1994): 36-42, Michael A. Schnepf notes that Galdós also channeled the reader's sympathy away from Polo by deleting certain portions of the original manuscript, thereby making Polo's characterization more sinister in the published text.

exclusively external. We know what he does and says, but we don't
have access to his thoughts. Despite Polo's major role in the novel,
he has no sympathetic interior views to help offset his bizarre and
sometimes cruel behavior. But Amparo, though a minor character,
is allowed to reveal her thoughts to us at a point in the text where
her compassion for Felipe matches our own. As Felipe is dismissed
from Polo's school, we emotionally stand with Felipe and Amparo
rather than with Polo, Marcelina, and Claudia. Since these same
lines will be drawn in *Tormento*, our loyalties toward Amparo in
this scene can carry over to that next novel as well. This isolated use
of an interior view to portray Amparo sympathetically in *El doctor
Centeno* will be expanded to produce an extended interior treatment of her in *Tormento*, thereby increasing our intimate contact
with Amparo as she assumes a larger role in the narrative.

Douglass Rogers has commented that the discursive presentations of Amparo in *Tormento* and Isidora in *La desheredada* are similar because both heroines are given sustained interior views
through the use of free indirect style. [25] Indeed, it is true that the
minds of these women are presented to us largely through free indirect thought passages. Nevertheless, it also is important to distinguish between the kind of double-voicing present in each case. In
so doing we will see that Galdós uses the same discursive device to
create different effects in these two novels. Since free indirect style
(both speech and thought) combines a character's perspective with
the presence of the narrator, it is necessary to determine the narrator's feelings concerning each character in order to appreciate the
nature of the double-voicing. As I discussed in my previous chapter, the narrator of *La desheredada* is highly critical of Isidora's impracticality and elitist attitudes, and therefore whenever Isidora's
conceptual perspective is conveyed in free indirect thought, the
narrator's implied censure of that perspective also is communicated
through the third-person orientation of the passage. Therefore, in
La desheredada most of Isidora's free indirect thoughts contain a
strong element of irony based on the conflict between the her values and those held by the narrator. In *Tormento* a conflict of values
also is involved, but it exists between the integrity advocated by the

---

[25] Douglass M. Rogers, "Amparo, o la metamorfosis de la heroína galdosiana," *Selected Proceedings of the Mid-America Conference on Hispanic Literature*, ed. Luis T. González-del-Valle and Catherine Nickel (Lincoln: SSSAS, 1986) 142.

narrator on one hand, and the hypocrisy practiced by Spanish society on the other. The entire seventh chapter of the novel contains the narrator's overt criticism of how false appearances and personal connections are valued over honesty and hard work, not only during the time frame of the story in 1867-68, but also extending to the narrator's present some sixteen years later. In this last half of the nineteenth-century when societal norms demand that each individual present an image that is different from his or her true situation, concealment and deception become everyday occurrences, and the ethics of those actions is rarely questioned. But two characters – Agustín and Polo – do subject the values of their society to scrutiny and find them lacking in moral substance. Consequently, the narrator openly sides with Agustín when he rejects "la falsificación de su ser," as well as with Polo when he asserts his authentic self over the "yo falsificado" demanded of him by society. The third member of the novel's love triangle, Amparo, does not actively question the way her society operates, but she does grapple with the ethical dimension involved in its shams. Although she is guilty of engaging in a sexual relationship with a priest – a crime which transgresses both social and religious laws – she is not guilty of what the narrator considers to be the even greater crime of deliberately attempting to deceive Agustín. At issue here are Amparo's intentions, not her actions. All of her free indirect thoughts concerning Agustín show a total absence of guile, and therefore, the double-voiced nature of this device allows the narrator to implicitly approve of Amparo's efforts to think of a way to inform Agustín about her past without either hurting him or losing his love. Unlike Isidora, who is reproached by her narrator, Amparo is supported by hers. Consequently, the ironic element present in Isidora's free indirect thought passages is not included in those of Amparo.

With both heroines, however, Galdós does use free indirect thought to shorten the emotional distance between the reader and these characters. In the case of Isidora that intimacy is tempered by the narrator's irony, but with Amparo there is no such impediment to reader sympathy. On the contrary, many of Amparo's interior views – whether the style is direct, indirect, or free indirect – contain sympathy producing moments of introspection. Carol Hanbery MacKay, in her discussion of nineteenth-century British fiction, borrows the theatrical term "soliloquy" to refer to self-directed thoughts in which a character assesses his or her situation and engages in various forms of self-debate, self-confrontation, and self-appraisal. Typically, the language of these soliloquies is melodramatic, with self-apostrophes, rhetorical questions, and exclamations. [26] Such melodramatic devices are common to Amparo's thoughts, and their rhetorical excesses help to convey the desperation she feels. Although she mentally goads herself to speak, she is overwhelmed and silenced by her emotions. Through these soliloquies the reader directly experiences Amparo's fear, guilt, sincere repentance, anguished confusion, and isolation. We share her mental turmoil and feel her vulnerability. The frequency of these soliloquizing interior views increases during moments of personal tension, and they build toward the crisis point when Amparo chooses to take her own life. Overall, these interiorizations are aimed at cultivating a compassionate reaction in the reader toward Amparo's plight. They show her to be weak-willed but not bad-intentioned.

Amparo's first lengthy interior view occurs in chapter 12 where free indirect thought records her mental reaction to the money delivered to her by Felipe from Agustín. Based on the boy's detailed description of the many people and institutions that his master generously supports on an ongoing basis, Amparo first considers Agustín's monetary gift to be an act of charity. It is only on second thought that she wonders whether or not Agustín's romantic feelings for her lean toward marriage. Her confusion is understandable because Agustín had not declared himself verbally to her during their conversation at Rosalía's home, and he also had failed to include a letter of explanation in the envelope he sent her. Refugio's misinterpretation of the money as coming "de pie de altar" (i.e. from Polo) leads her to charge Amparo with hypocrisy. Since the reader knows the origin of the money, this false accusation serves as a contrasting element which underscores the truthfulness of Amparo's assertion that "es el dinero más honrado del mundo." Agustín's failure to make his usual visit to the Bringas household the next day keeps Amparo in the dark concerning his motives for sending her the money. It is not until two days later that Agustín finally asks Amparo to marry him. Her flustered response to this proposal includes two attempts to warn Agustín away from her. In chapter 20 she tells him "Yo no valgo lo que usted cree." When

---

[26] Carol Hanbery MacKay, *Soliloquy in Nineteenth-Century Fiction* (Macmillan, 1987) 12. For a larger discussion of soliloquies see 7-33.

Agustín ignores this first statement, she cautions him again by saying "Yo no valgo tanto como usted se figura."

Since these somewhat oblique references to her past prove inadequate, Amparo begins to think of ways to present her situation to Agustín more clearly. Chapter 23 opens with an indirect thought passage in which the narrator tells us that Amparo is upset about her engagement because she feels that she is deceiving Agustín with her silence but knows that she isn't strong enough to face him with a confession. The narrator goes on to say that Amparo truly does love Agustín and considers to be virtues what society calls his faults. Thus, Amparo's indirect thoughts confirm what she had told Agustín in chapter 20 concerning her opinion of him. She clearly is not attracted to him merely because of his wealth, and it is this affection that makes the idea of a confession so painful. As her free indirect thoughts turn to direct thoughts, we also see that she feels guilty for accepting Agustín's money if she can not marry him. After she concludes that Agustín will forgive her if she tells him the truth about her past, the discourse switches back to free indirect thought to record her mental rehearsal of what she will say. This segment is parallel to the direct thought passage in chapter 9 where Agustín similarly rehearses the words he intends to speak to Amparo. In both cases these imaginary conversations while each character is alone are followed by what actually transpires between the couple. These scenes of them together juxtapose what is said against what is thought. But although we see the spoken words of both Amparo and Agustín, we only learn the thoughts of one of them in each of these scenes. In chapter 9 it is Agustín's mind that we view as he struggles with the forgotten text of his proposal to Amparo, just as at the end of chapter 23 we see Amparo's thoughts as she laments her inability to voice the confession she had intended to make. After this unsuccessful attempt, Amparo decides to confess to a priest before confessing to Agustín. Although she does accomplish the former, Polo's letter informing her of his departure allows her to put off doing the latter. Her weak nature is shown in the contrast between her direct thoughts in chapter 24 and those in chapter 25. Before the letter arrives, her thoughts show her steeling herself for a frank talk with Agustín. But after receiving the letter she thinks: "Que se lo he de decir es indudable; pero me parece que ya no corre tanta prisa." She does not intend to deceive Agustín. She simply wants to delay the painful and unpleasant task she knows she must perform.

With her mind now relieved, in chapter 25 Amparo engages in a long discussion with Agustín about their future domestic life together. Their conversation is not stated in dialogue form, however. Rather, it is conveyed in a single extended free indirect speech passage where the sentences spoken by Agustín alternate with those spoken by Amparo. Although this segment is too long to reproduce here, the central portion represents the spirit of the entire conversation:

A él le gustaba que todo se hiciera con régimen, a la hora; así no habría barullo en la casa. Para eso ella se pintaba sola; todo lo dispondría con la anticipación conveniente para que en el instante preciso no faltase. ¡Y que ya andarían listos los criados, ya, ya!... Ella no les perdonaría ningún descuido... A él le gustaba mucho, para almorzar, los huevos con arroz y frijoles. El frijol de América era muy escaso aquí; pero Cipérez solía tenerlo... Ella se ejercitaría en la administración, llevando su libro de cuentas, donde apuntara el gasto de la casa. Cuando no se hace así, todo es enredo, y se anda siempre a oscuras... Irían a los teatros cuando hubiera funciones buenas; pero no se abonarían, porque eso de que el teatro fuese una obligación no agradaba ni a uno ni a otro. Tal obligación sólo existía en Madrid, pueblo callejero, vicioso, que tiene la industria de fabricar tiempo. En Londres, en Nueva York, no se ve un alma por las calles a las diez de la noche, como no sea los borrachos y gente perdida. Aquí la noche es día, y todos hacen vida de holgazanes o farsantes. Los abonos a los teatros, como necesidad de las familias, es una inmoralidad, la negación del hogar... Nada, nada; ellos se abonarían a estar en su casita. Otra cosa: a ella no le gustaba dar dinerales a las modistas, y aunque tuviera todos los millones de Rothschild, no emplearía en trapos sino una cantidad prudente... Además, sabría arreglarse sus vestidos... Otra cosa: tendrían coche, pues ya estaba encargado a la casa Binder un landó sin lujo para pasear cómodamente, no para hacer la rueda en la Castellana, como tanto bobo. Siempre que salieran en carruaje, convidarían a Rosalía, que se pirraba por zarandearse. Ambos concordaban en el generoso pensamiento de ayudar a la honesta familia de don Francisco, obsequiando sin cesar a marido y mujer, discurriendo una manera delicada de socorrer su indigencia sobredorada... Agustín pensaba señalarle un sobresueldo para vestir, calzar, educar a los pequeños y llevarlos a baños. Pero ¿cómo proponérselo? ¡Ah! Amparo se encargaría de comisión tan agradable. Por de pronto, los invitarían a comer dos veces por semana...

In this back and forth exchange of ideas, the reader must use the embedded pseudo-tags (él/ella; Agustín/Amparo) to determine who says what. By actively engaging in this deciphering process, we come to realize how similar Amparo and Agustín are in their tastes. They are of one mind, as the unbroken flow of their conversation in this passage graphically displays. A simple dialogue would not have brought this uniformity of opinion to our attention so forcefully. Thus, Galdós's use of free indirect speech in this scene serves to indicate how well suited Amparo and Agustín are for one another.

Elsewhere in the text Galdós uses another discursive technique – filtered description – to display the emotional attachment that also binds these two characters. As Amparo and Agustín are each described in the text from the other's point of view, we experience the pleasure felt by someone in love upon seeing the object of his or her affection. In chapter 27 Amparo is surrounded by the many luxuries present in Agustín's sumptuous apartment, yet her attention is focused instead on her fiancé's weather-beaten face, with its silver-speckled beard and a skin color that Amparo compares to the warm tone of the terra-cotta figures he collects. Likewise, in chapter 20 Agustín examines Amparo's appearance in loving detail as he contrasts her natural beauty with the shabbiness of the clothing she must wear. Neither Amparo nor Agustín speaks much in this novel. Indeed, silence is what Alicia Andreu considers to be the essential characteristic of their verbal communication. [27] But Galdós compensates for the paucity of dialogue between Amparo and Agustín by creatively using discursive devices such as filtered description and free indirect speech to subtly show that their relationship solidly rests on a base of genuine affection and like temperament.

But Amparo's decision to delay her confession to Agustín has serious repercussions for the future happiness of this couple. In chapter 27, convinced that it is now too late to confess to Agustín, she worries that he will "ver en ella perversión mayor de la que

[27] Alicia Andreu, "*Tormento*: Un Discurso de Amantes," *Hispania* 72 (1989): 226-32.

había" and that he will misinterpret her silence as disloyalty and deceit. Thus, her innocent intentions have now taken on the appearance of guilty motives – a serious situation in nineteenth-century Madrid where appearances carry more weight than the truth. Amparo becomes tormented by the thought that someone else will tell Agustín about her past, and when Polo's letter arrives promising "todas las babaridades posibles," her direct thoughts immediately turn to suicide. But she convinces herself that she might be able to persuade Polo to leave her alone by visiting him one last time. In this confrontation between the former lovers, only Amparo's thoughts are recorded. Polo's portrayal is entirely external. Through direct, indirect, and free indirect thought we learn of the various strategies Amparo conceives to try to control Polo's volatile temper and unpredictable behavior. These same interiorizations also show us the emotional pain she feels about having to lie about her feelings for both Agustín and Polo. Significantly, however, Amparo's thoughts are not shown when she briefly considers Polo's proposition to stay the night with him in return for his silence. We are only allowed to hear her rejection of this indecent offer. Throughout this scene Polo's treatment of Amparo is cruel and sadistic, and no interiorizations of Polo are provided to offset our negative reaction toward his physical and psychological bullying. Although he shows compassion in his care of Celedonia, this behavior merely serves as a contrast to further highlight his brutishness toward Amparo.

After this private meeting turns into a public scandal, Amparo resolves to kill herself in her apartment. But Francisco's unexpected appearance at her door causes her to move the location of her suicide to Agustín's home. The entire thirty-fourth chapter focuses on Amparo's few actions and many thoughts as she prepares herself for this final ordeal. While she imagines herself being found dead by Agustín, direct thought is used in the text. But when she actually takes what she believes is the poison, free indirect thought is used. This allows Galdós to convey the scene from Amparo's point of view while giving it the appearance of a third person account by the narrator. [28] Indeed, Amparo's suicide attempt is discoursively de-

---

[28] Indeed, as Diane Urey has noted, Germán Gullón mistakenly attributes to the narrator Amparo's feelings of death overcoming her. See Urey 63 n16 and Gullón, *El narrador en la novela del siglo XIX* (Madrid: Taurus, 1976) 113.

signed to convince the reader that Amparo really has poisoned herself. First, the narrator describes Amparo's preparation of the medicine: "La demente vertió el agua que estaba en el vaso, y, echando en él la mitad del contenido del frasco, se lo bebió." Next, Amparo's mental reactions appear in free indirect thought: "¡Gusto más raro! ¡Parecía... así como aguardiente! Dentro de cinco minutos estaría en el reino de las sombras eternas, con nueva vida, desligada del grillete de sus penas, con todo el deshonor a la espalda, arrojado en el mundo que abandonaba como se arroja un vestido al entrar en el lecho." Then suddenly there is a discoursive switch to present tense narration, which is interspersed not only with direct thought, but also with a present tense equivalent to free indirect thought:

Ocúrrele pasar a la habitación vecina. En su alcoba. ¡Soberbio, espléndido tálamo! Hay también un sofá cómodo. No bien da cuatro pasos en aquella pieza, advierte en sus entrañas como una pena, como una descomposición general. Cree que se desmaya, que pierde el conocimiento; pero no, no lo pierde. Ha pasado un minuto no más... Pero siente luego un miedo horrible, la defensa de la Naturaleza, el potente instinto de conservación. Para animarse, dice: «Si no tenía más remedio; si no debía vivir.» La flojedad y el desconcierto de su cuerpo crecen tanto, que se desploma en el sofá, boca abajo. Nota opresión grande, ganas de llorar... Con su pañuelo se aprieta la boca y cierra fuertemente los ojos... Se asombra de no sentir agudos dolores ni bascas. ¡Ah!, sí; ya siente como unas cosquillas en el estómago... ¿Padecerá mucho? Empieza el malestar; pero es un malestar ligero. ¡Qué veneno tan bueno aquel que mata tranquilamente! De pronto se le nubla la vista. Abre los ojos y lo ve todo negro. Tampoco oye: los pájaros cantan lejos, como si estuvieran en la Puerta del Sol... Y entonces el pánico la acomete tan fuertemente, que se incorpora y dice: «¿Llamaré? ¿Pediré socorro? Es horrible..., ¡morirme así!... ¡Qué pena! ¡Y también pecado!...» Escondiendo el rostro entre las manos, hace firme propósito de no llamar. Pues qué, ¿es su muerte acaso una comedia? Después se siente desvanecer..., se le van las ideas, se le va el pensamiento, se le va el latir de la sangre, la vida entera, el dolor y el conocimiento, la sensación y el miedo; se desmaya, se duerme, se muere... «¡Virgen del Carmen –piensa con el último pensamiento que se escapa–, acógeme...!»

Once again Galdós has used present tense narration to convey an emotionally charged situation for one of his characters. And once again we find that this technique was added at the galley stage. When we examine the *Tormento* galleys, we see that Galdós originally continued the past tense orientation of the narration until the very end of this chapter. But in the galleys he replaced all of the past tense verbs in the last paragraph with their present tense equivalents. [29] By so doing Galdós personalized the situation to a greater degree than would have been possible through standard past tense narration because present tense verbs are better able to convey the immediacy of an experience. Thanks to the free indirect thought introduction to this final paragraph, we are already in Amparo's mind. From that position, we now can respond to the present tense verbs in order to place ourselves on Amparo's temporal plane as well. Thus, Amparo's perspective is retained, but in an intensified form. As Amparo gradually loses consciousness, the present tense rendering of the experience puts us directly at the site at the moment it is occurring. Just as with Felipe Centeno's present tense segments, we live through the scene along with the character, thereby minimizing our emotional distance from the event. In this way Galdós's galley changes not only increase our empathy with Amparo, but also increase the impact of the surprise when we find out that the supposedly fatal preparation that Amparo drank was nothing more than a pain-relieving sedative. We have been duped, but not by the narrator. Rather, it is Galdós himself who tricked us by using discoursive devices that oblige us to experience this "death" through Amparo's point of view. Since she believes she is dying, we do too.

Amparo's central position in the novel ends with her suicide scene. Even though she does not die, she fades into the background. The new focus of the story is on Agustín, and the interiorizations in the discourse shift to him as well. Galdós avoids the vagaries of free indirect thought with Agustín in favor of a more clearly defined discoursive device – direct thought – in order to communicate the solitary purposefulness of Agustín's mental processes as he endeavors to work out his problem without the input of others. Through a series of these direct thought passages we see

---

[29] This scene is on page 239 of the *Tormento* galleys, which are stored in *caja* 19-3 at the Casa-Museo Pérez Galdós in Las Palmas de Gran Canaria.

the mental turmoil that Agustín undergoes as he balances his love for Amparo against the demands of conventional propriety. Agustín mentally engages in a direct confrontation with the elements of Spanish society he had hoped to embrace – *familia, Estado, Fe* – and concludes that they all exist on the rotten foundation of *engaño*. Through the arguments he presents to himself, we see him rejecting the artificial social values he adopted during his sojourn in Madrid in order to re-embrace the authentic personal values which he had developed over the course of his life. The lack of societal restraints in the New World had obliged him to form a personal code of honor based on fairness and integrity. By returning to this code, Agustín is able to judge Amparo according to his own yardstick of acceptability. Thus, he mentally vows to forgive her past actions based on her present remorse, and in addition, he declares his intention to do so in open defiance of societal norms: "Bruto, desgraciado salvaje, que no debías haber salido de tus bosques, júrate que si te dice la verdad la perdonarás... Sí que la perdonaré... Me da la gana de perdonarla, señora sociedad... Si es culpable y está arrepentida, la perdonaré, señora sociedad de mil demonios, y me la paso a usted por las narices" (ch. 36). By the end of the novel Agustín does indeed forgive Amparo, and he flaunts that forgiveness in front of everyone. As Agustín and Amparo unapologetically embark on their life together in full view their acquaintances, they blatantly reject what Bakhtin calls the secondhand, externalizing and finalizing definitions of others in order to create their own definition of themselves and their relationship.[30] Indeed, their arrangement does not conform to the typical pattern established between rich older men and poor young girls. Such affairs – like the one between Feijoo and Fortunata – are grudgingly condoned by Madrid society because they are covertly conducted. Agustín and Amparo are not like those secret lovers, but neither are they like the many polygamous couples found in Brownsville. Agustín and Amparo must absent themselves from both Madrid and the New World in order to develop their relationship on its own terms in the neutral territory of France. Though not legally sanctioned, their union is built on a solid foundation of mutual commitment, and furthermore, it is not

---

[30] Mikhail Bakhtin, *Problems of Dostoevsky's Poetics*, trans. and ed. Caryl Emerson, Theory and History of Literature 8 (Minneapolis: U of Minnesota P, 1984) 58-59.

hidden from the public eye. Rather, it insistently exhibits itself as a legitimate entity which others will simply have to accept, as evidenced in the invitation Agustín and Amparo extend to Rosalía and Francisco to join them in France the next summer. Having defined themselves in opposition to society's norms, Agustín and Amparo display an honesty in their "illicit" relationship which highlights the hypocrisy of "respectable" society they left behind.

Hypocrisy is also an issue in the development of Polo's character. Unlike Agustín, Polo engages in covert activities which place him squarely within the mainstream of Madrid's social hypocrisy. Yet, a similarity between Agustín and Polo has been pointed out by John Sinnigen, who views these men as undergoing a process of growth as they reject the falseness of society in order to reach the personal integrity that resides in them both.[31] Like Agustín, Polo struggles to find his authentic self behind the "yo falsificado" that his profession requires. But in Polo's case, none of that struggle is experienced by the reader directly. Agustín and Polo are presented quite differently in terms of discoursive technique. Agustín's portrayal is like that of Amparo; he rarely speaks but his thoughts are often shown to us. Conversely, Polo is highly articulate, but we seldom know what he is thinking. That is, Agustín's portrayal is largely interior and Polo's is overwhelmingly exterior. We know him either through what he says and does, or from what others say about him. Polo is given only one extended interior view. It occurs in chapter 17 of *Tormento* when he is daydreaming about the many alternative routes his life might have taken had he not gone into the priesthood. But even in this most intimate view, we are not granted direct access to his mind. Rather, his fantasies are told to us by the narrator though indirect thought. Thus, we remain one step removed from them, a position that allows us to retain our critical distance. We can understand his frustration at having to live a lie and even applaud his determination to follow his conscience instead of bowing to societal pressures. But our emotions are not so fully engaged that we excuse the violent behavior he later exhibits toward Amparo. When he locks her in his apartment and tries to coerce her into resuming their affair, our loyalties lie with Amparo, just as they did in *El doctor Centeno*. Yet, Polo's single interiorization in *Tor-*

---

[31] John H. Sinnigen, "Galdós's *Tormento*: Political Partnership/Literary Structures," *Anales Galdosianos* 15 (1980): 77-80.

mento does humanize him to a greater degree than in the previous novel, and consequently, we sympathize with him more in this second work than in the first.

The thoughts of all three main characters in *Tormento* are used to help cultivate a compassionate response in the reader toward them as they each face a difficult situation in the novel. Our greater exposure to the thoughts of Amparo and Agustín produce a stronger emotional bond with them than with Polo. Nevertheless, Pedro Polo's inner pain is revealed to us sufficiently to create a somewhat charitable attitude toward him as well. In contrast, Marcelina Polo is denied sympathetic interiorizations and is made to present herself entirely through spoken words and actions. When in chapter 30 Marcelina refuses to tend to the dying Celedonia by saying "Por mi parte, me gustaría mucho asistir enfermos, resolver llagados y variolosos, limpiar heridos..., pero no tengo estómago. Cuando lo he intentado, me he puesto mala. También se auxilia a los desgraciados rezando por ellos," we see the selfishness of her religiosity. Similarly, six chapters later when she dangles Amparo's incriminating letters in front of Agustín, we see the spite that hides behind her contention that "yo no comprometo la reputación de ninguna persona, buena o mala. . . Yo no hago mal a nadie, ni a mis mayores enemigos." Totally devoid of the Christian virtues of charity and forgiveness, this "mujer de madera" simply adheres to the outward trappings of Catholicism. Although Amparo can offer aid and comfort to Pedro Polo, his own sister can not. In every word and action Marcelina reveals her counterfeit piety. She embodies the concept of religious hypocrisy in the same way that Rosalía de Bringas personifies social hypocrisy. But, as we shall see, Rosalía's characterization moves beyond simple social satire as she develops over the course of the trilogy.

ROSALÍA DE BRINGAS

Although Rosalía figures prominently in both *Tormento* and *La de Bringas,* discussion of her character generally has been limited to her presence in the latter novel with surprisingly little attention being given to her evolution over the course of the two works. In addition, scholars exhibit a lack of uniformity in their opinion of Rosalía. Some critics find her to be an entirely evil character while others react somewhat sympathetically to her. What accounts for this discrepancy? A possible answer may be found in the different discoursive treatment that Rosalía receives as she moves from one novel to the next. In *Tormento* her presentation is almost entirely external, which results in an unflattering portrait bordering on caricature. In *La de Bringas*, however, she is developed primarily through interiorization devices which help to counterbalance the negative aspects of her behavior. Thus, although Rosalía exhibits the same undesirable personality traits as in *Tormento* and even adds to her repertoire of reprehensible behavior in *La de Bringas*, the potential for a certain amount of reader sympathy to be generated in her favor is inherent in the discourse of the later novel. Unlike Amparo – whose interiorizations in *Tormento* merely reinforce the positive impression she had made in *El doctor Centeno* – Rosalía needs sympathetic interior views to help mitigate her previously negative characterization.

Rosalía is introduced to the reader in *Tormento's* second chapter. We are told that her "manía nobiliaria" has led her to fabricate the high-sounding name of Rosalía Pipaón de la Barca from very scanty genealogical evidence. Her pronunciation of this affectatious title is usually accompanied by a swelling of her nostrils, a physical trait that typifies her arrogant nature. To reinforce this implicit criticism of her pretentiousness the narrator provides a list of her true lineage which, being composed entirely of minor palace servants, contradicts the aristocratic background she attempts to project. Subsequent references to her dilated nostrils and elaborate name extend the force of the irony throughout the text, thereby allowing the reader to laugh at Rosalía's ill-founded feelings of social superiority which give rise to her other negative traits. Following this initial implied commentary, the narrator becomes more openly judgmental of Rosalía for her firm conviction of the primacy of social connections over hard work and education – an opinion, we are told, common to Spanish society during the time of the story in 1867 and still prevalent in the narrator's day some sixteen years later. This generalization extends the critical commentary beyond the fictional world of the text into the existing world of Galdós's Spain, and consequently projects Rosalía's character into the realm of social satire. The parallel between Rosalía's false values and those of her society is also made explicit when the narrator comments on Rosalía's interest in the theater not as a cultural event but rather as a social situation where she and others like her go to be seen in all their finery "aunque como en el caso suyo estos alardes fueran esforzados disimulos de la vergonzante miseria de nuestras clases burocráticas" (ch. 7). This disparity between actual wealth and the mere appearance of wealth, the narrator notes, has grown even greater in his own time. Once again the narrator has made the comparison between story NOW (when the events take place) and discourse NOW (when the events are being recounted) as well as the implicit link between the text and the extra-textual world of the reader. This theater scene also provides an opportunity to ironize Rosalía's physical appearance. Although she was initially described as "una de esas hermosuras gordas," now the narrator undercuts the compliment by revealing that this look is achieved by confining her body, "ordinariamente flácido y de formas caídas," within the restraints of a tight corset in order to fit into the theater gown. In this way, her attractive appearance is shown to be as much an artificially constructed fabrication as her social position.[32] Overall, in his description of Rosalía in the opening chapters of the novel the narrator expresses a combination of implicit and overt censure of her values, which he then generalizes so as to render Rosalía little more than a satirical caricature of a social type.

Having first established Rosalía's basic character flaws through direct characterization by the narrator, the text next reinforces these traits through ironic portrait. Once again the presentation is external, relying on either narrative summary of her actions or direct speech records of her words to allow Rosalía to inadvertently reveal her own undesirable features. The full impact of this type of characterization is the result of an ongoing accumulation of negative data by the reader over the course of the novel. Early in *Tormento* Rosalía's words and actions are used to exemplify those negative values already outlined by the narrator. For example, her

---

[32] For a discussion of the corset as an unnaturally restrictive device which imprisons Rosalía's body and serves to illustrate female confinement in nineteenth-century society see two studies by Lisa P. Condé, "'El maldito corsé' in the Works of Pérez Galdós," *Romance Studies* 20 (1992): 13; and *Stages in the Development of a Feminist Consciousness in Pérez Galdós (1843-1920)* (Lampeter: Edwin Mellen, 1990) 121-25. For an opposing interpretation of the corset as a liberating device which gives Rosalía control over her body and her life see Akiko Tsuchiya, "The Construction of the Female Body in Galdós's *La de Bringas*," *Romance Quarterly* 40 (1993): 38-42.

sense of priorities, governed by her "manía nobiliaria," is underscored in her decision to place the queen's picture rather than that of Christ in the honored center position on the wall. Then dramatic monologue – a traditionally ironic technique – is used effectively to confirm Rosalía's pretentiousness as she shows Cándida the wonders of her new apartment. Finally, Rosalía's disdain for those she sees as inferiors is evident in her treatment of Amparo. Indeed, her first words spoken in the text are directed at Amparo and are critical in nature: "Amparo, pero ¿qué haces? Te tengo dicho que no empieces una cosa antes de acabar otra. Más fuerza, hija, más fuerza. Parece que no tienes alma... Vamos, vivo... Yo quisiera que todas tuvieran este genio mío... Pero ¿qué haces, criatura? ¿No tienes ojos?" (ch. 3). After constantly ordering Amparo about like a servant, Rosalía rewards the poor girl with such treats as half-rotten food and discarded scraps of clothing. In various early scenes we see her mistreat, bully, and embarrass Amparo. Rosalía exhibits her feelings of superiority over the girl in each word said to or about her. Thus, by the end of the seventh chapter Rosalía's character has been clearly defined and conveyed to the reader in a variety of exterior views.

However, the text as a whole occasionally departs from this discoursive pattern to provide fleeting inside views of Rosalía. For example, in two direct thought passages in chapter 6 she laments the fact that Agustín cannot be closely connected to their family through marriage since she herself is already married and her daughter is not yet of age. For Rosalía, Agustín's desirability as a marriage partner is based completely on his wealth, as evidenced by the terms she uses to refer to him – *salvaje, animal, monte de oro* – while mentally focusing on his yearly income of 30,000 *duros*. This pair of direct thought passages, amounting to a total of only 276 words, is Rosalía's longest interior view in *Tormento*. Yet through this very concentrated peek into Rosalía's consciousness, Galdós is able to establish the preoccupation that will dominate Rosalía's thoughts and actions throughout the remainder of the novel. Rosalía's idea of Agustín marrying into the Bringas family is echoed in two of her free indirect thought passages – one in the opening paragraph of chapter 10 ("¡Qué padrazo sería si se casara!") and the other in chapter 22 ("¡Ah! maldito Bringas, ¿por qué no nació Isabel cinco años antes!") – as well as in her direct thoughts later in chapter 22 ("Porque a mí, ¿qué me va ni me viene en esto?... Conmigo no se había de casar, porque soy casada; ni con Isabelita tampoco, porque es muy niña"). But by the end of that chapter Rosalía's anger over Agustín's engagement has risen to such a degree that she falsely projects vengeful feelings onto Amparo in a brief free indirect thought passage ("¡La muy pícara no había ido desde el sábado!... Estaba endiosada. Hacer quería ya papeles de humilladora, por venganza de haber sido tantas veces humillada"). Rosalía's final interior view ("Es nuestro – pensaba –, es nuestro"), found in chapter 37, reveals her joyful belief that her plans to sabotage the relationship between Agustín and Amparo had succeeded.

Throughout the forty-one chapter novel of *Tormento* these few paragraphs constitute Rosalía's entire interiorization. What function do these brief inside views have? We must remember that Booth speaks of the *sustained* use of *sympathetic* inside views to engender a compassionate response in the reader.[33] This is clearly not the case here since Rosalía's interior treatment in *Tormento* is extremely limited and does not depict a sympathy producing mental confusion but rather reveals a clear sighted ambition to exploit Agustín through an advantageous marriage. By dipping into Rosalía's mind on these few occasions, Galdós elicits additional disapproval from the reader who can see the hypocritical thoughts behind Rosalía's honeyed words to Agustín. Thus, these interior views serve to reinforce the ironic portrait of Rosalía being constructed by the reader. In addition, they inform us of the self-interested motive for her scheming actions against Agustín's engagement later in the novel. Overall, Rosalía's unsympathetic interior views work in conjunction with the various exteriorization techniques to create in the reader what Susan Feagin calls the antipathetic response of *Schadenfreude*: the "enjoyment of a character's pain or misfortune, as well as its opposite, displeasure in response to a character's joy or success."[34] It is this antipathetic response to Rosalía which carries the reader through the remainder of *Tormento*.

After her strong presence in the first seven chapters Rosalía virtually disappears from the text while the romance between Agustín

[33] Wayne C. Booth, *The Rhetoric of Fiction*, 2nd ed. (1961; Chicago: U of Chicago P, 1983) 239-49.

[34] Susan L. Feagin, *Reading with Feeling: The Aesthetics of Appreciation* (Ithaca: Cornell UP, 1996) 129.

and Amparo unfolds. During these developments Rosalía's character is limited to brief conversations with Amparo or Agustín in her home before leaving or upon returning. Indeed, it is her absence from both her home and the text that allows the plot progression to take place. Rosalía reemerges as an active character a full fifteen chapters later when she is informed of Agustín and Amparo's betrothal. While ostensibly treating Amparo as an honored guest, Rosalía secretly begins to amass evidence against the girl's suitability as a marriage partner in hopes of keeping Agustín a bachelor until her own daughter is old enough to become his bride. Having found the damaging facts she needed, Rosalía devises a plan for exposing Amparo's former association with Polo without herself appearing to have malicious intentions. This scheme is presented in a segment of the text characterized by a notable contrast in story order versus discourse order. The three days following Amparo's visit to Polo's home are first told with regard to Amparo's actions in chapters 32, 33, and 34 and then they are retold by focusing on Agustín's actions in chapters 35 and 36. It becomes the responsibility of the reader to construct the plot progression of the story from these separate discoursive sections presenting conflicting information. This results in a dramatic irony which reveals Rosalía's role in the organization and execution of her plan.

These chapters are filled with time references such as chiming clocks, dawn and dusk, and specific hours and days, thereby allowing the reader to ascertain the chronology of events. The story pertaining to Amparo contains the following elements: On *Monday* Amparo is informed by Rosalía that she is aware of Amparo's past and that certain letters confirming her guilt are in Marcelina's possession. Amparo is then left alone while Rosalía has a private meeting with Torres. When she returns, Rosalía tells Amparo to go home and to keep the affair a secret from Agustín. On *Tuesday* Amparo spends the entire day at home undisturbed by any visitors or messages. During this time she considers suicide and chooses poison as her method. On *Wednesday* Francisco calls on Amparo to tell her that Agustín had been told everything by Mompous, and that Rosalía denies having had anything to do with the matter. He then urges her to speak with Agustín before he has the opportunity to visit Marcelina. Upon arriving at Agustín's house and finding him already gone, Amparo attempts suicide. This version of the story is immediately followed by a retelling that features Agustín's movements during the same three days. On *Monday* Agustín goes to Rosalía's house after Mompous tells him about Amparo's past affair. Rosalía tells him not to go to Amparo's home since she would not be there, and that he should instead wait for her at his own apartment since she promised Rosalía that she would visit him soon to explain everything. On *Tuesday* Rosalía visits Agustín and tells him that she had tried to contact Amparo at her house but the girl was nowhere to be found. Pretending to console him, Rosalía reminds Agustín that Marcelina may be able to clear up any doubts he has concerning Amparo's past behavior. On *Wednesday* after his meeting with Marcelina, Agustín returns home to find Amparo unconscious.

The discrepancies in the two versions of the story are readily discernible, particularly in terms of the lies told to Agustín about Amparo's whereabouts. Crucial to the success of the plan is the necessity of keeping the couple apart long enough for Agustín to examine the letters. The lies Rosalía tells Agustín are designed to prevent just such a meeting from taking place. Rosalía's controlling hand over the entire operation is evident to the reader, but this is implied in the discourse order rather than openly stated. Indeed, the sole reference to Rosalía's involvement is an indirect allusion found in the narrator's preface to the second version of the events, where he states that no one knows exactly how Agustín learned of the matter, but that it is believed that Mompous told him after Torres had brought the story to him "desde la Costanilla," that is, from the street on which Rosalía lives. Torres's friend Mompous, we remember, has a daughter of marriageable age, and therefore Rosalía could count on him to use this damning information to break up Amparo's engagement to Madrid's most eligible bachelor. It is the textual evidence itself, then, that allows the reader to piece together Rosalía's important role as choreographer of the entire incident.

Seymour Chatman's concept of character – as a paradigm of traits which exist on the story level but are communicated through the discourse – finds no better example in Galdós's early contemporary novels than Rosalía de Bringas.[35] In *Tormento* various aspects of the discourse reveal the many character flaws that contribute toward our bad impression of her. This is done first through

---

[35] Chatman *Story and Discourse* 119-28.

the use of a reliable narrator who both satirizes Rosalía as a representative type and ironizes her as an individual character; then through the depiction of Rosalía primarily in external views accompanied by isolated instances of unsympathetic inside views; and finally through the ordering of the story events to expose Rosalía's deceit through dramatic irony. In order to cap off this negative portrayal, the novel closes with yet another unflattering exterior view of Rosalía. In chapter 38 the highly sympathetic Felipe Centeno complains to Ido about Rosalía's tendency to appropriate items from Agustín's apartment for her own use. Not only does this pilfering activity reflect badly on Rosalía in general, but Felipe's comment may also remind the reader of a similar conversation that passes between Ido and Felipe at the end of *El doctor Centeno* concerning the boy's thieving former landlady, who goes so far as to steal the frock coat off Miquis's dead body. Thus, an implicit parallel is made between Rosalía and the veteran swindler Cirila. Given all of these discursive cues in *Tormento*, it is no wonder that José F. Montesinos would call Rosalía "una mujer odiosa, la más odiosa que quizá inventara Galdós."[36] Neither is it surprising that Stephen Gilman would classify her as having the sickest of all the diseased minds found in the Centeno-Tormento-Bringas trilogy.[37]

In contrast, the discourse of *La de Bringas* employs distinctly different narrative voice features which, perhaps, accounts for the more sympathetic reception of Rosalía's character by such scholars as Julián Palley, Roberto Sánchez, Maurice Hemingway, Lou Charnon-Deutsch, Stephen Miller, Ricardo Gullón, and Jennifer Lowe, the last two of whom note that reader sympathy stems from our knowledge of Rosalía's motivations in *La de Bringas*.[38] How are

---

[36] Montesinos 2: 98.

[37] Stephen Gilman, *Galdós and the Art of the European Novel: 1867-1887* (Princeton: Princeton UP, 1981) 140.

[38] Palley says that Rosalía's characterization falls between satire and pathos, resulting in a mixture of irony and compassion toward her. Sánchez calls her a tragicomic character who is both a martyr and an object of ridicule. Hemingway says that the moral dimension of Rosalía's character is too ambiguous to be declared either good or bad. Both Charnon-Deutsch and Miller see *La de Bringas* as a *Bildungsroman* that chronicles Rosalía's attempts at self-determination in a male-dominated society. See Julián Palley, "Aspectos de *La de Bringas*," *Kentucky Romance Quarterly* 16 (1969): 348; Roberto G. Sánchez, "The Function of Dates and Deadlines in Galdós' *La de Bringas*," *Hispanic Review* 46 (1978): 311; Maurice Hemingway, "Narrative Ambiguity and Situational Ethics in *La de Bringas*," *Galdós' House of Fiction*, ed. A. H. Clarke and E. J. Rodgers (Llangrannog: Dolphin, 1991) 21-24;

these motivations communicated to the reader? Above all, this is achieved through the use of inside views. Unlike the externally oriented characterization of Rosalía employed in the preceding novel, the discourse of *La de Bringas* relies heavily on direct and free indirect thought to portray Rosalía. Diane Urey, in her insightful treatment of Rosalía in both works, notes that the most important difference between Rosalía's presentation in *Tormento* and in *La de Bringas* is based on the greater amount of distance created between her and the reader in the first novel than in the second.[39] Indeed, as Rosalía's mental world is gradually revealed to us, we draw closer to her. Consequently she ceases to be merely a caricature of a type and becomes a fuller character with human desires, fears, and weaknesses. Interior views, because of their empathetic quality, are particularly effective in reducing the vast emotional distance that normally exists between the reader and such an antipathetic character as Rosalía. In *La de Bringas* Rosalía's numerous interiorizations document her feelings as she reacts to the external pressures exerted upon her, thereby allowing us to travel with her though the novel and understand the reasons behind her actions. In the process, the reader's antipathetic response to Rosalía is lessened. Whereas we rejoice in Rosalía's failure to break up the relationship between Amparo and Agustín in *Tormento*, we take less pleasure in the misfortunes which befall Rosalía in *La de Bringas*.

Our intimate connection with Rosalía's consciousness first occurs in the tenth chapter after a brief reintroduction to her character. The occasion is a shopping spree with Milagros during which Rosalía tries on a beautiful but costly shawl, the seductive power of which gives her a physical sensation similar to sexual arousal. Clearly the desire to own the item is strong, and this temptation (coupled with Milagros's urgings) proves too much for Rosalía's willpower. In the chapter's last paragraph Rosalía's mental debate with her con-

---

Lou Charnon-Deutsch, "*La de Bringas* and the Politics of Domestic Power," *Anales Galdosianos* 20.1 (1985): 65-74, expanded as chapter 4 of *Gender and Representation: Women in Spanish Realist Fiction*, Purdue U Monographs in Romance Languages 32 (Amsterdam: John Benjamins, 1990); and Stephen Miller, "*La de Bringas* as *Bildungsroman*: A Feminist Reading," *Romance Quarterly* 34 (1987): 195-97; Ricardo Gullón, *Galdós novelista moderno* (Madrid: Taurus, 1960) 75-78; and Jennifer Lowe, "Galdós' Presentation of Rosalía in *La de Bringas*," *Hispanófila* 50.2 (1974): 63-65.

[39] Diane F. Urey, *Galdós and the Irony of Language* (Cambridge: Cambridge UP, 1982) 31.

science as to whether or not she should buy the shawl begins the long chain of free indirect thought passages which run through the novel and later join with direct thought passages to display her mind as she grapples with the far-reaching consequences of this purchase.[40]

These interior views help establish the reader's involvement in Rosalía's predicament as she emotionally interacts in three important relationships: with her husband Francisco, with Manuel Pez, and with Milagros. The mental panic Rosalía suffers when bills come due and the strategies involved in securing the needed money while hiding her clandestine financial dealings from Francisco are all related through her direct and free indirect thoughts.[41] More importantly, her feelings of deprivation due to her husband's extreme economical measures are documented by the same discoursive means. Francisco, who had been presented as a commendably frugal man in *Tormento,* now reveals his miserliness in several conversations with his wife, notably in chapters 22 and 26, where he attempts to control every household expenditure no matter how minor. Although he has hoarded a personal fortune, he continually chastises Rosalía for every small indulgence. In all, Francisco's parsimonious behavior now makes him the subject of his own unflattering ironic portrait. While it is true that Rosalía blatantly lies to her husband on various occasions,[42] it is also true that Rosalía's wish to be liberated from Francisco's economic extremism is not

---

[40] For a discussion of how ornamental goods such as this shawl traditionally are associated with the feminine and the marginal but become a central focus of this novel see Luisa Elena Delgado, "'Más estragos que las revoluciones': Detallando lo feminino en *La de Bringas,*" *Revista Hispánica Moderna* 48.1 (1995): 31-42.

[41] Although Catherine Jagoe views Rosalía as one of Galdós's spendthrift antiheroines who exemplifies the morally dangerous consumption of luxury goods by the female bourgeoisie, Aldaraca, Miller, and Charnon-Deutsch all stress that the motive behind Rosalía's purchases is less linked to her desire for clothes than to her desire for independence from her husband's tyranny over the family funds. In addition, Aldaraca points out that "Galdós breaks with the literary stereotype [of the consuming woman out of control], because Rosalía is capable, like a man, of regaining her lost self-control" (175). I also would add that when Jagoe uses the narrator's criticism of Rosalía to support her interpretation, she fails to take into consideration that the unreliable status of that narrator calls into question the validity of his opinions. See Jagoe, *Ambiguous Angels: Gender in the Novels of Galdós* (Berkeley: U of California P, 1994) 91-95.

[42] In "Rosalía and the Rhetoric of Dialogue in Galdós' *Tormento* and *La de Bringas,*" *Revista de Estudios Hispánicos* 12 (1978): 208, Robert M. Fedorchek states that deception is the hallmark of Rosalía's spoken dialogue.

unreasonable, and neither is her fear of his exaggerated response to her dilemma. It is in this atmosphere that the reader witnesses through interior views Rosalía's reaction to Francisco's offer – first given and later withdrawn – to hand over the financial reins of the household to her. Having believed his confidence in her judgment to be genuine, she acts on his offer only to later find herself in the position of needing to replace the money she lent to Milagros during her brief dominion over the family funds. With Milagros unable to repay the loan, Rosalía is forced to resort to progressively more extreme measures to acquire the money, including trading her sexual favors for it.

The shame she feels after the first of these extramarital liaisons is intensified by the knowledge that she has dishonored herself in vain. Her shock and disappointment from Pez's failure to fulfill his promised role as her benefactor is discursively rendered in the free direct thought passage filling the lengthy opening paragraph of the forty-fourth chapter. [43] Indeed, her response is understandable given the attraction she had felt for Pez and the esteem in which she had held him, also communicated to the reader through interior views. Her free direct thoughts early in chapter 17 and her free indirect thoughts which began chapter 29 both showed Rosalía reflecting on Pez's desirable social position and fashionable appearance. When she compared him to Francisco, Pez was deemed the more suitable marriage partner in Rosalía's estimation for a woman such as herself. The pride she felt from his advances and her belief in his offers of financial assistance, again captured in inside views, justify her sense of betrayal when his promises are not honored. Vanity repeatedly has been cited as the main flaw which leads to Rosalía's ruin. Nevertheless, an equally important contributing factor is her gullibility, which allows her to believe the false words and promises of others: Pez's flattery and his pledge of financial backing; Milagros's compliments on Rosalía's fashion sense and her assurances of repaying the borrowed money; and Francisco's confidence in her judgment and his offer to give her control over the family finances. Rosalía's reactions to each of these external forces are revealed in inside views, as is her mental confusion resulting

---

[43] This passage is mistakenly identified as indirect in my article, "The Narrative Voice Presentation of Rosalía de Bringas in Two Galdosian Novels," *Crítica Hispánica* 12 (1990): 83.

from her growing realization that she has been the victim of the vices of others – Pez's lechery, Francisco's avarice, and Milagros's extravagance. Rosalía must now come to terms with the situation by somehow rationalizing her behavior, including her infidelity. She does this by mentally formulating a philosophy wherein necessity justifies behavior. This coping mechanism sustains her through not only her humiliating experience with Refugio, but also through her subsequent entry into the world of elegant prostitution.

In the Rosalía-Refugio confrontation scene Rosalía is repaid in kind for her calculated cruelty toward Amparo in *Tormento*. [44] However, if her cruelty in the former novel earned her the reader's hatred, the cruelty she now experiences results in some measure of pity, especially since it is received at the hands of a character who has never engaged the reader's affection. The Refugio who sarcastically belittles Rosalía in *La de Bringas* is the same Refugio who had maliciously berated Amparo in *Tormento*. The nature of Rosalía's interior view in this scene differs from all others in the text. Free indirect thought – appearing alone or in combination with direct thought – usually dominates her interiorizations. Here, however, free indirect thought is completely absent. Instead, we find an ongoing record of Rosalía's direct thoughts, in which she uncharacteristically addresses someone else instead of herself. This other-directed but internally verbalized monologue constitutes a silent response to her adversary's sarcasm. When juxtaposed against her spoken words, these thoughts show the degree of self-control she must exhibit and the amount of self-pride she must swallow. It also underscores the degree of her self-delusion since in her mental comments Rosalía refuses to acknowledge that she and Refugio are now on the same moral footing and profess essentially the same philosophy of situational ethics. Clinging to her belief in social superiority, she can blindly continue to view Refugio as her inferior in all respects, including the moral. As long as Rosalía retains her social status, she can justify her behavior as necessary – and even ennoble it as the means of sustaining the family after the revolutionary upheaval –

---

[44] This scene has been analyzed from various points of departure. See William H. Shoemaker, "Galdós' Classical Scene in *La de Bringas*," *Hispanic Review* 27 (1959): 423-34, rpt. in Shoemaker, *Estudios sobre Galdós* (Madrid: Castalia, 1970) 145-58; Nimetz 80-84; and James H. Hoddie, "Galdós' *La de Bringas* in Light of Hegel's Views on Comedy," *Revista de Estudios Hispánicos* 17 (1983): 21-41.

without considering herself to be reduced to the moral level of the lower classes.

In addition to Rosalía's discoursive portrayal through interiorizations, a separate aspect of narrative voice – that of the narrator's persona – also contributes toward softening the reader's opinion of Rosalía in *La de Bringas*. The narrator of this second novel is decidedly different from the reliable narrator of *Tormento*. Although the narrator of *La de Bringas* professes values similar to those of his predecessor, he himself does not uphold those values. Rather, he exhibits the same unprincipled behavior which he condemns in others. The reader's confidence in his reliability is undermined early in the text when he shows his willingness to exploit his political connections. Through his friend Manuel Pez, who owes him a favor, he enlists Francisco's aid in settling a legal matter to his advantage, and he later repays Francisco with gifts from his estate. As Peter Bly observes, this "clearly shows that the narrator is a willing participant in the Isabelline system of deals, favours and personal recommendations at the expense of justice and probity . . . ensuring that his subsequent appearances and comments are not accepted totally without hesitation" by the reader. [45] Unlike the undramatized narrator of *Tormento,* the narrator of *La de Bringas* assumes an identity and plays a small but important role as he interacts with the other characters at three points in the text. In the opening chapter he engages in the aforementioned act of political favoritism. Midway through the text he appears at one of doña Tula's afternoon gatherings, thereby reminding the reader of his social ties to the monarchists. Finally, at the close of the novel he reveals that he is the revolutionary junta's administrator of palace property. The fact that he holds this post shows that he can opportunistically shift his loyalties to fit the political climate. In this capacity he is approached by Rosalía who offers him her sexual favors in return for certain monetary considerations. Having taken advantage of her invitation once, he decides against resuming the financially draining affair. Therefore, the narrator's unethical behavior at the beginning of the novel is matched by his immoral association at the end. Consequently, his censure of Rosalía's lifestyle must be judged in light of

---

[45] Peter A. Bly, *Pérez Galdós: La de Bringas*, Critical Guides to Spanish Texts 30 (Grant & Cutler, 1981) 90.

his own actions in the text. The criticism of Rosalía by *Tormento's* reliable narrator is sincere while that of *La de Bringas's* unreliable narrator is hypocritical. This difference accounts in part for the reader's stronger adverse reaction to Rosalía in the earlier work. Since we find the narrator of *La de Bringas* to be untrustworthy, we are less likely to accept his opinions about Rosalía. We must come to our own conclusions about her, and in the process of doing so, we rely on Rosalía's numerous interior views. Due to the private nature of her thoughts, we become drawn into a more personal relationship with Rosalía than we had with her in *Tormento*.

To intensify the empathetic effect of Rosalía's interior views, Galdós makes her thoughts the only ones we hear throughout virtually all of *La de Bringas*. There are only two exceptions, and both concern the *cenotafio*. Chapter 3 opens with a record of Francisco's direct thoughts as he calculates what the materials for the project will cost him. The intensity with which he tallies insignificant sums of money suggests the excessive pettiness in financial matters which he will exhibit later in the novel. A similarly revealing interiorization occurs in chapter 17 where we are made privy to Manuel Pez's direct thoughts as he examines the partially constructed hair picture: "Vaya una mamarrachada... Es como salida de esa cabeza de corcho. Sólo tú, grandísimo tonto, haces tales esperpentos, y sólo a mi mujer le gustan... Sois el uno para el otro." This single interiorization of Manuel Pez highlights his overall hypocrisy because it shows his real thoughts to be in direct conflict with the flattering words he had just showered on Francisco concerning the object: "Es una maravilla... ¡Qué manos! ¡Qué paciencia! Esta obra debiera ir a un Museo." This glimpse into Pez's mind warns the reader that he is a man whose spoken words are not to be trusted. Therefore we see Pez for the phony he is well before Rosalía realizes it. These two brief interior views of Pez and Francisco are the only moments that we enter the mind of any character other than Rosalía. Even during his blindness Francisco is denied any sympathetic interiorizations that might dilute our emotional attachment to Rosalía and cause us to side with Francisco instead of his wife. These isolated interiorizations of Pez and Francisco do not favorably dispose us toward these characters. Rather, they serve as thumbnail sketches to quickly establish the basic flaws that Pez and Francisco will confirm through their words and actions as the novel progresses.

At all other times in *La de Bringas* it is only Rosalía who receives an interior treatment. This has the effect of increasing our empathetic attachment to Rosalía while maintaining our emotional distance from the other characters. Direct and indirect speech, as well as narrative commentary are used to create the text's numerous external portrayals. But two characters – Pez and Milagros – also are presented through free indirect speech, a discursive technique which highlights their negative qualities. As was seen in *La desheredada* and *Fortunata y Jacinta*, the overall effect of this technique is mimicry, and as such it exaggerates the tone of the original. Therefore, it is an excellent vehicle for recording Milagros's most self-serving moments. For example, since Milagros's frequent requests for monetary assistance from Rosalía generally appear in free indirect speech, the reader can clearly hear the combination of flattery and persistence in Milagros's tone, which is delivered in a manner that feigns a close friendship between the two women. Similarly, Pez talks a great deal in this novel, but the majority of it is conveyed through the exaggerated medium of free indirect speech. Consequently, his martyred tone when complaining about his family life in chapter 13; his empty rhetoric when discussing politics in chapter 27; and his off-handed description of how he uses his connections to defraud the customs office in chapter 36 all are communicated to the reader more forcefully than if his words had been recorded in direct speech. By using free indirect speech with Pez, Galdós also is able to utilize the double-voicing inherent in that technique to show that the narrator's conceptual point of view does not differ at all from the one being expressed. The narrator and Pez are, as Hazel Gold puts it, kindred spirits.[46] The political and moral collusion between these two veteran exploiters of people and governments is discursively suggested through Pez's free indirect speeches, which carry with them the tacit approval of the narrator. The irony in this double-voicing is not the result of a disparity between the narrator's values and those of Pez, but rather, it arises from the implied author's censure of the hypocritical set of standards which both Pez and the narrator share.

---

[46] Gold 36; and "Francisco's Folly: Picturing Reality in Galdós' *La de Bringas*," *Hispanic Review* 54 (1986): 59. Also, Robert H. Russell, "Percepción, proporción y onomástica en *La de Bringas*," *Actas del Cuarto Congreso Internacional de Estudios Galdosianos (1990)* (Las Palmas: Cabildo Insular de Gran Canaria, 1993) 1: 821, calls the narrator "otra figura pisciforme."

Having examined the discoursive techniques used in each of the two novels featuring Rosalía de Bringas, we can now return to our original question as to the differing reactions to her character. Why do some critics refer to Rosalía in entirely negative terms, while others afford her varying degrees of sympathy? A possible answer lies in each individual critic's emphasis on certain textual aspects over others. As we have seen, in *Tormento* Rosalía's actions and personal faults are conveyed by the narrative voice in such a way as to render her a thoroughly despicable character. That is, both the story and the discourse combine to preclude any feelings of sympathy toward her on the part of the reader. Indeed, no critic has expressed a sympathetic response to the Rosalía de Bringas portrayed in *Tormento*. It is only within the context of the second novel that certain critics have been more generous in their assessment of Rosalía's character. Despite the fact that Rosalía continues to engage in unethical behavior in *La de Bringas*, this text displays a radical departure in the discoursive technique used to portray Rosalía, thereby allowing the reader a fuller understanding of her character and subsequently building an empathetic response to her plight. In this way the discoursive presentation lessens the impact of the story's events. Perhaps it can be said, then, that those critics who consider Rosalía to be a totally evil character are building on her negative portrayal in *Tormento* by giving prominence to the *story* level of *La de Bringas* in which the lying and hypocritical Rosalía now adds adultery to her list of sins. Here the focus is on Rosalía's traits and her actions within the plot. On the other hand, those critics who are less harsh with Rosalía may be responding more readily to the *discourse* of the second text which uses interior views (showing her mental distress while contending with the various external demands made upon her) to fill out Rosalía's character and to temper the overall effect produced by her behavior.

My own interpretation of Rosalía favors the more sympathetic view of her, not only because such an interpretation takes into consideration both the story level and the discourse level of her portrayal, as I have shown in my analysis above, but also because it recognizes a complexity in Rosalía's character that Galdós uses to convey a more subtle form of social criticism than would have been possible with a totally evil character. Rosalía's transformation from an antipathetic character in *Tormento* to a somewhat sympathetic one in *La de Bringas* makes the society around her seem all the

more corrupt and sordid. In *Tormento* Rosalía's deception and
hypocrisy merely serves as a foil to Agustin's and Amparo's sincerity
and honesty. But in *La de Bringas* Rosalía is surrounded by characters who are even more mendacious than she is. As Feagin has
noted, when antipathetic characters such as Rosalía are taken advantage of by others, the natural response in the reader is pleasure
because the character is seen as getting what he or she deserves
(130-31). But Galdós complicates the matter in Rosalía's case. By
generating empathy for Rosalía through interior views, Galdós
places the reader *with* Rosalía as she tries to survive in a world
where no one – not even the narrator – can be trusted. This encour-
ages the reader to look beyond Rosalía's personal hypocrisy to see
the corruption which permeates society as a whole. The reader's
empathetic understanding of the motives for Rosalía's behavior
does not translate into an uncritical acceptance of all her actions,
however. Among Galdosian scholars even Rosalía's most ardent
apologists have difficulty reconciling their admiration for Rosalía's
ability to assert her independence in a patriarchal society, with their
concern over Rosalía's final embrace of the corrupt practices required of her to succeed in that society.[47] In my view, this tension is
a result of the novel's interaction of story and discourse, and it is
used as a rhetorical strategy to extend the social criticism of the
novel into the real life of the flesh-and-blood reader. That is, the
empathetic effect of Rosalía's interior views creates a degree of
reader complicity with her manipulation of the sordid world she in-
habits, and it is the discomfort which the flesh-and-blood reader
feels at that complicity which leads to an examination of his or her
own extra-textual behavior and values. Rather than simply being allowed to feel morally superior to Rosalía, the flesh-and-blood reader is discoursively placed on Rosalía's level in the novel and is
obliged to question whether he or she also exists on that ethical
plane in the real world.

* * *

---

[47] See, for example, the following statement by Charnon-Deutsch: "This is not
to imply that Rosalía is a character of heroic proportions or that she transcends the
corrupt, pretentious society that is so prominently ridiculed in *La de Bringas*. Clearly she is portrayed as a woman who has succumbed to the pressures of the age in
which she lives. Yet she has learned and gained something from her lessons and has
transcended the domestic organization she once despised" (*Gender and Representation* 135).

Felipe, Amparo, and Rosalía are allowed to develop over the course of the Centeno-Tormento-Bringas trilogy into fully realized characters – each with a rich inner consciousness that is exposed to the reader's view. By shifting away from the initial exterior portrayal of each character, Galdós is able to draw the reader into a close personal relationship with Felipe (despite his youth), with Amparo (despite her sexual involvement with a priest), and with Rosalía (despite her vanity). In addition to granting interiorizations to these characters, Galdós facilitates our emotional connection to them through present tense narration and filtered descriptions for Felipe and Amparo (thereby mediating our experience of the events through their consciousnesses), and through the use of an unreliable narrator whose criticism of Rosalía seems hollow in light of his own indiscretions.

The third-person narratives discussed in this chapter and the previous one display the panoply of narrative devices which typify the discursive sophistication of Galdós's *segunda manera*. Direct, indirect, and free indirect forms of both speech and thought combine to convey the various perspectives of the characters. Through the interplay of interiorization and exteriorization techniques these texts influence how the reader responds affectively to the characters and the attitudes they hold. Varying degrees of narrator reliability add to the complexity of Galdós's narrative style and further contribute toward the reader's reception of the characters and the ideological issues raised in the texts.

The next chapter will concentrate on two first-person narratives: *El amigo Manso* and *Lo prohibido*. Galdós has less discursive flexibility in these texts than in the third-person narratives we have considered thus far because he must restrict his interior views to the protagonist-narrators. Nevertheless, I will show how Galdós overcomes the limitations inherent in first-person narration through structural innovations which also are part of his *segunda manera* approach to writing literature.

CHAPTER 3

FICTIONAL AUTOBIOGRAPHIES:
EL AMIGO MANSO AND *LO PROHIBIDO*

The protagonist-narrator format of *El amigo Manso* and *Lo prohibido* sets these novels apart from the ones surrounding them. This is an uncommon form of narration for Galdós, who rarely used it after completing the first series of *Episodios nacionales*. The comments he made in the epilogue to the first edition of *La batalla de los Arapiles* explain why:

> Ya que hablo de mis culpas, no ocultaré la principal en estos diez libros, fruto de dos años de incesante trabajo, y es que con mi habitual imprevisión adopté la forma autobiográfica la cual, si bien no carece de encanto, tiene grandísimos inconvenientes para una narración larga, y no puede de modo alguno sostenerse en el género novelesco-histórico, donde la acción y trama se construyen con multitud de sucesos que no debe alterar la fantasía, y con personajes de existencia real. Únanse a esto las escenas y tipos que el novelista tiene que sacar de sus propios talleres; establézcase la necesidad de que los acontecimientos históricos ocurridos en los palacios, en los campos de batalla, en las asambleas, en los clubs, en mil sitios diversos y de no libre elección para el autor, han de pasar ante los ojos de un *solo* personaje, narrador obligado e indispensable de tan diversos hechos en período de tiempo larguísimo y en diferentes ocasiones y lugares, y se comprenderá que la forma autobiográfica es un obstáculo constante en la libertad del novelista y a la puntualidad del historiador.[1]

[1] Alan E. Smith, "El epílogo a la primera edición de *La batalla de los Arapiles,*" *Anales Galdosianos* 17 (1982): 106-07. In the 1885 second prologue to the illustrat-

Indeed, since a protagonist-narrator must operate within the novel-istic world with the same limitations that actual people have in the real world, in order to acquire information such a narrator must either witness an event first hand or somehow learn about it from secondary sources. Consequently, for Gabriel Araceli to be able to relate the history of Spain from an autobiographical position in the first series of *Episodios nacionales*, Galdós needed to change his physical location on a regular basis and give him ready access to a wide variety of characters whose knowledge of events could supple-ment Gabriel's personal experience. Galdós provided Gabriel with occupations – servant and soldier – that granted him a large mea-sure of mobility. Gabriel's employers brought him into situations that normally would have been barred to him, such as the world of the theater and the court at El Escorial. Similarly, his service in sev-eral different fighting units took him to battle sites all over Spain. But even the most creative plotting strategy would not allow Gabriel to be present at events occurring simultaneously in differ-ent places. Therefore, he had to rely on other characters for infor-mation. Indeed, the lengthy eyewitness account of the siege of Gerona was told to Gabriel (and the reader) by an intradiegetic narrator, Andrés Marijuán, because Gabriel had been fighting in Zaragoza at that time. In this way Galdós was able to record both of these important military campaigns rather than having to choose between them. Throughout the series Gabriel's fellow characters served as his informants for events he missed because he had been absent, unconscious, or asleep. But when it was not plausible for a character to volunteer information willingly, Galdós resorted to such clichéd contrivances as having Gabriel hide behind curtains in order to overhear conversations without being detected. To further fill in missing details, Gabriel also availed himself of letters, news-papers, and other written sources of information.

Thanks to this constant scurrying about, Gabriel was able to abide by all of the rules of first-person autobiographical narration, not once overstepping the rigid boundaries that define the role of a protagonist-narrator. But Galdós understandably tired of the Her-culean efforts necessary to sustain this limited narrative stance over

---

ed edition of the *Episodios nacionales* Galdós presents essentially the same argu-ment for discontinuing the Gabriel de Araceli autobiographical pose beyond the first series.

the course of a ten novel series. Therefore, in the second series he adopted the pose of an omniscient narrator. Nevertheless, he did use individual protagonist-narrators for three of its novels: Juan Bragas de Pipaón in *Memorias de un cortesano de 1815* and *La segunda casaca*, and Genara de Baraona in *Los cien mil hijos de San Luis*. But in each case, the omniscient narrator of the second series intrudes on these personal accounts to provide information beyond the scope of the limited protagonist-narrators. In this way Galdós was able to combine what he called the "encanto" of first-person narration while recouping some of the "libertad" that such a format denied him in the first series. When Galdós next returned to the autobiographical format in *El amigo Manso* and *Lo prohibido*, he had devised new methods of freeing himself somewhat from the restrictions inherent in that form of narration. By examining these two contemporary novels in light of the protagonist-narrated *episodios* that preceded them, we can better appreciate the subtlety with which Galdós handles his narrators, Máximo Manso and José María Bueno de Guzmán, and the stories they tell.

* * *

El amigo Manso begins with Manso's open acknowledgment of himself as a fictional construct.[2] "Yo no existo," he declares, going on to explain that he is an artistic fabrication of human thought. He is an idea, which by the end of chapter 1 has been transformed into a literary entity by the author in a magical display of burnt paper and spilled ink. As a result, at the beginning of chapter 2 he declares, "Yo soy Máximo Manso," in an assertion of his new status:

---

[2] The autonomy from the author which Manso enjoys as a consequence of his fictional self-awareness has been the subject of a number of scholarly studies, most notably, John W. Kronik, "*El amigo Manso* and the Game of Fictive Autonomy," *Anales Galdosianos* 12 (1977): 71-94; Arnold M. Penuel, "Some Aesthetic Implications of Galdós' *El amigo Manso*," *Anales Galdosianos* 9 (1974): 145-48; and Ricardo Gullón, "'El amigo Manso' entre Galdós y Unamuno," *Mundo nuevo* 4 (1966): 36-39, rpt. in *Técnicas de Galdós* (Madrid: Taurus, 1980) 73-82. Kronik views Manso's autonomy as part of a larger experiment by Galdós concerning fictionality in general. Thus, Galdós uses *El amigo Manso* as a metanovel in order to expose the artifice behind realistic fiction. Penuel sees Manso's autonomy as Galdós's means of combating the tendency of his readers to search for real life models for his characters. Gullón considers *El amigo Manso* to be the first *nivola* because Unamuno simply adopted and continued techniques previously used by Galdós in his creation of an openly fictitious and autonomous character.

he is now the protagonist of his own story. At the end of the novel, when he has fulfilled his function, his character dies, and in the last chapter he is reinstated within his original realm of non-existence. In effect, the first and last chapters of this novel serve as a frame for the forty-eight chapter embedded story about Manso's friendships, family entanglements, and unrequited love. This frame is totally detachable from the story it contains, and without it the embedded story would have conformed completely to the conventions of autobiographical fiction. With the self-referential frame, however, the novel brings those conventions to the attention of the reader. The story within a story format exposes the conventional differences between omniscient and limited narration which the reader normally accepts without question but now must contend with in order to reconcile the two separate positions that Manso occupies in the text.

When Manso is in the frame, he enjoys the "godlike vantage point beyond time and place," which Friedman associates with editorial omniscience.[3] Although he speaks to the reader with the "yo" form of address, he is not subject to the limitations of first-person narration. He is able to enter the minds of his characters at will, and his privileged knowledge surpasses even that of the author who, as Harriet Turner has observed, "is hardly more than a scribe" recording the story Manso dictates to him.[4] Once Manso leaves the frame and enters the story, however, the situation drastically changes. As with all protagonist-narrators, Manso is both the teller of the story and one of the characters in it. As such, he is subject to all of the constraints of his fellow characters. His knowledge of events is derived completely from his personal experience and through the information that other characters give him. He can't be in more than one place at the same time. He has no powers beyond those of his five senses, and even they are subject to the normal physical boundaries. Finally, he cannot enter the minds of the other characters to read their thoughts and, therefore, he is only able to speculate on their motivations by piecing together evidence gathered from their words or actions. This last limitation is the single

[3] Norman Friedman, "Point of View in Fiction: The Development of a Critical Concept," *PMLA* 70 (1955): 1171.

[4] Harriet S. Turner, "The Control of Confusion and Clarity in *El amigo Manso*," *Anales Galdosianos* 15 (1980): 52.

most important feature which distinguishes first-person narration from omniscient narration. Galdós calls the reader's attention to this convention by juxtaposing the all-knowing Manso in the frame against the all too fallible Manso in the embedded story.

Manso's limitations while functioning within the embedded story have caused a great deal of critical confusion concerning his status vis à vis Wayne Booth's concept of narrator reliability. This is due to the common error of equating omniscient privilege with reliability, and a single point of view with unreliability, as seen in Kay Engler's insistence that "unreliability is inherent in the 'first-person' narrator, an inevitable consequence of the choice of that form of narration."[5] While it is true that some of Galdós's protagonist-narrators are unreliable, one needs only to cite Gabriel Araceli as an example to the contrary. Early in the series Gabriel develops an honor code grounded in such values as personal responsibility, tolerance and respect for others, honesty, and loyalty to both his country and his fellow man. His youth and inexperience at times cause him to lose sight of these concepts, but he always returns to them as the core of his value system. Because these values are in accord with those advocated by the implied author, by critical consensus Gabriel is considered to be the *portavoz* for the entire first series of *episodios*. A parallel situation occurs with the highly principled but socially inept Máximo Manso. Eamonn Rodgers classifies Manso as unreliable because "[f]or most of the narrative, he is ignorant of certain facts which affect him personally, and his assumptions about human nature are mistaken."[6] But once again these characteristics are merely the consequence of his status as a protagonist-narrator. The number of limitations under which a narrator must labor is *not* an issue in determining his reliability. Rather, it is a matter of the norms and values he upholds. This aspect of a narrator's persona cuts across the boundaries between homodiegetic and heterodiegetic narrators. Each individual narrator has the capacity for reliability or unreliability regardless of the narrative format chosen by the author. Booth is very clear on this point:

[5] Kay Engler, *The Structure of Realism: The Novelas Contemporáneas of Benito Pérez Galdós*, North Carolina Studies in the Romance Languages and Literatures 184 (Chapel Hill: North Carolina UP, 1977) 140-41.

[6] Eamonn Rodgers, *From Enlightenment to Realism: The Novels of Galdós 1870-1887* (Dublin: Jack Hade, 1987) 82.

If the reason for discussing point of view is to find how it relates to literary effects, then surely the moral and intellectual qualities of a narrator are more important to our judgment than whether he is referred to as "I" or "he," or whether he is privileged or limited. . . . For lack of better terms, I have called a narrator *reliable* when he speaks for or acts in accordance with the norms of the work (which is to say, the implied author's norms), *unreliable* when he does not.[7]

Booth goes on to state that reliable narrators are those "who, however human and limited and bewildered, earn our basic trust and approval" (274).

Thus, when Booth speaks of the norms and values of the text, he is not referring to the norms and values held by the characters within the novelistic world, but rather, he is speaking of the norms and values projected as desirable by the implied author. These norms and values represent the implied author's social, political, religious, and ethical attitudes and assumptions. The narrator who upholds the attitudes and assumptions of the implied author is reliable, the narrator who does not is unreliable. In the case of *El amigo Manso*, the implied author's high principles are in direct opposition to the shallow and self-serving values embraced by Restoration society. By condemning those characters who perpetuate the corruption and vanity of his society, Manso aligns himself with the implied author. Therefore, he is a reliable narrator. Nevertheless, this reliability only pertains to the ideological realm. It does not endow him with any privileges normally denied a protagonist-narrator. Manso still retains all of the limitations associated with first-person narration. Harriet Turner's statement that Manso "is reliable and unreliable at the same time" is an attempt to reconcile Manso's moral and ethical worthiness with the practical restrictions imposed upon him by his protagonist-narrator status.[8] Indeed, out of ignorance of the facts he jumps to wrong conclusions, is misled by appearances, and overlooks what is important while focusing on

---

[7] Wayne C. Booth, *The Rhetoric of Fiction*, 2nd ed. (1961; Chicago: U of Chicago P, 1983) 158-59.

[8] Harriet S. Turner, "Strategies in Narrative Point of View: On Meaning and Morality in the Galdós Novel," *Homenaje a Antonio Sánchez Barbudo: Ensayos de literatura española moderna*, ed. Benito Brancaforte, Edward R. Mulvihill, Roberto G. Sánchez (Madison: Wisconsin UP, 1981) 65.

the trivial. But these misinterpretations do not render him unreliable in Booth's sense of the term because they do not negate Manso's support of the implied author's social, political, religious, and ethical attitudes or assumptions. The reader can rely on Manso to be a trustworthy guide throughout the *ideological* world of the novel. But at the same time, we are aware that Manso is surrounded by characters who lead him to draw false conclusions because they keep secrets from him.

Manso's limited point of view as a protagonist-narrator within the embedded story forms the basis for the irony which permeates the novel. This irony has two layers. The first results from the interaction between the frame and the story it contains. The privileges which Manso enjoys within the frame are denied him in the interior tale. Consequently, Manso in the frame can look down upon his interior counterpart from a superior position. The entire novel is Manso's self-revealing and intentionally ironic portrait of himself – as both a character and as a limited narrator – given from the higher perspective of editorial omniscience. [9] This leads to the second layer of irony, which involves the relationship between the reader and Manso. Because we can view Manso as merely one of the many characters operating in the embedded story, we are able to take a global perspective of the situations in which he participates. Thus, we perceive interrelationships and patterns which Manso misses because of his limited perspective. The inferences we draw as a consequence allow us to decipher what is happening long before Manso does. Both these levels of irony work in conjunction to create not only a complex characterization of Manso but also an elaborately constructed method of conveying his fictional autobiography.

As a character within the story, Manso is restricted to a single point of view. [10] But that perspective has many dimensions: percep-

---

[9] In Genette's terminology, this is an intentionally ironic self-portrait of the intradiegetic narrator by the extradiegetic narrator.

[10] Manso's point of view within the story is also discussed by Nancy A. Newton and Ricardo Gullón, both of whom point to the different degrees of distance that Manso puts between himself and what he sees. When Manso dispassionately observes his surroundings, he is what Newton calls "object-centered." But when he gets involved with his surroundings, he becomes "subject-centered." To Gullón he is a "narrador-personaje" capable of objective observation but sometimes slipping into subjectivity. See Newton, "*El amigo Manso* and the Relativity of Reality," *Revista de Estudios Hispánicos* 7 (1973): 121-22; and Gullón, "'El amigo Manso', de Galdós," *Nuevo Mundo* 5 (1966): 60-61, rpt. in *Técnicas de Galdós* 85-89.

tual (through his physical senses); conceptual (through his attitudes/world view); and interested (through the personal stake he has in the situation). [11] His conceptual point of view is basically in agreement with the values of the implied author. He does, however, exhibit the same over reliance on logic and reason that typifies León Roch's characterization. Eamonn Rodgers has pointed out that "the Krausist emphasis on the discipline of reason could lead to an over-valuing of the intellect," thereby negating in practice what Krausism advocated in theory: "the harmonious balance between intellect, appetite, feeling, and imagination" (86). This is indeed what happens to Manso. He filters all of life through the prism of reason, but in the process he is unable to make the imaginative leaps that would tie together the data he collects. Furthermore, as Denah Lida has noted, Manso insists on defining his romantic feelings within the boundaries of logic, thereby ignoring Sanz's warnings that sentiments are not reducible to analysis. [12] Manso's conviction in the primacy of reason over all else is evident in chapter 2, where he says "Constantemente me congratulo de este mi carácter templado, de la condición subalterna de mi imaginación, de mi espíritu observador y práctico, que me permite tomar las cosas como son realmente, no equivocarme jamás respecto a su verdadero tamaño, medida y peso, y tener siempre bien tirantes las riendas de mí mismo" (ch. 2). This turns out to be the most ironic statement in the novel because Manso's blind adherence to reason and logic has a distorting rather than clarifying effect on both his perceptual and interest perspectives. Consequently, Manso is often unaware of the underlying importance of the events occurring around him.

His attempt to understand what in fact is happening under the surface of these events constitutes what John Rutherford calls the novel's enigma, which is solved though a series of questions concerning Irene that are posed by Manso and the reader throughout the course of the narration. As new evidence comes to light, certain questions are answered, and these have an impact on Manso's previous assumptions. [13] In Iserian terms, gaps occur in the text due to

---

[11] See Seymour Chatman, *Story and Discourse: Narrative Structure in Fiction and Film* (Ithaca: Cornell UP, 1978) 151-58.

[12] Denah Lida, "Sobre el 'krausismo' de Galdós," *Anales Galdosianos* 2 (1967): 17.

[13] John Rutherford, "Story, Character, Setting, and Narrative Mode in Galdós's *El amigo Manso,*" *Style and Structure in Literature: Essays in the New Stylistics*, ed. Roger Fowler (Ithaca: Cornell UP, 1975) 200-08.

the secrecy of Irene, Manolo, José María, and doña Cándida. In order to fill those gaps, Manso (and the reader) must undergo an inferential process of connecting existing information in a meaningful way. Because of Manso's status as a character within the story, his ability to pull together the various pieces of this novelistic puzzle is more restricted than that of the reader. Consequently, we realize aspects of the enigma before Manso does. More importantly, however, we also are able to see how Manso's efforts are hampered by his love for Irene. In effect, his perceptual perspective (what he sees and hears) is filtered through his interest perspective (focused upon Irene as the object of his affections), causing him to evaluate all of Irene's actions as if they were directly related to himself. This situation is further compounded by Manso's conceptual perspective – dominated by reason – which in turn serves as the filter for his interest perspective. An example will help clarify this process.

Manso is a 35 year old bachelor who has never had a romantic relationship. Suddenly he finds himself smitten by Irene, a young woman of 19. Why? First, it is because she is beautiful, and Manso's mind recently has been filled with "ideas sobre lo bello" since he is in the process of writing a prologue to Hegel's *Sistema de Bellas Artes* in Spanish translation. Second, Irene's quiet demeanor and job as a governess has led Manso to assume that she is as captivated by learning and as uninterested in high society as he is. Therefore, he endows her with all of the virtues he desires in a woman and dubs her a "mujer-razón." That is, his interest perspective has been influenced by his conceptual perspective. Once this interest perspective has been thus engaged, it in turn begins to affect Manso's perceptual perspective. At the height of his infatuation with Irene, he has two conversations with her where he simply does not listen to what she is saying. But the reader does, and this contributes to the dramatic irony that characterizes the relationship between Manso and the reader. In chapter 16, while discussing her duties as a governess to José María's young children, Irene tells Manso that she is tired of "dando lecciones de lo que no entiendo bien." Manso is not taken aback by this confession indicating Irene's inability to grasp simple elementary school material. Rather, he interprets her dissatisfaction as stemming from boredom due to being *overqualified* for her position: "Usted se aburre, ¿no es verdad? Usted es demasiado inteligente, demasiado bella, para vivir asalariada." This response indicates Manso's conceptual perspective's preoccupation with beauty and intelligence, which obscures his perceptual perspective's processing of Irene's words. Similarly, in chapter 18 Manso is surprised to find Irene still up during one of José María's late night parties. When he tells doña Jesusa that such behavior "es contrario a sus costumbres," the old woman tells him that, on the contrary, "[a]lgunos ratos se va al corredor a ver un poquito de la sala." When Manso and doña Jesusa are joined by Irene moments later, "[s]u fisonomía revelaba gozo y estaba menos pálida. Parecía agitada, con mucho brillo en los ojos y algo de ardor en las mejillas." She sums up her impression of the party by saying: "¡Qué lujo, qué trajes! Es cosa que deslumbra..." Despite all this evidence indicating Irene's facination with the glamour and glitter of Madrid's social set, Manso insists on forcing what he hears and sees into the confines of his conceptual view of Irene, saying to her: "ni a usted ni a mí nos agrada esto. Por fortuna, estamos conformados de manera que no echamos de menos estos ruidosos y brillantes placeres, y preferimos los goces tranquilos de la vida doméstica, el modesto pan de cada día con su natural mixtura de pena y felicidad, siempre dentro del inalterable círculo del orden." Doña Jesusa is so impressed with Manso's rhetorical ability that she praises him profusely, with Irene shaking her head in agreement. But, as the text notes, Irene just gives her "aprobación a los elogios" that Jesusa showers on Manso. In no way does she indicate her agreement with the *ideas* he expressed. Her silence is taken by Manso as tacit approval, but the reader suspects otherwise.

Indeed, when we look back through the text for earlier conversations between Manso and Irene in order to see if our suspicions are valid, we find that very little of what they have said to each other is reproduced in dialogue form. Rather, their conversations are described to us by Manso. In chapter 14 we are told that Irene agreed with Manso's opinions concerning topics as varied as education, religion, bullfighting, and home decorating. And in chapter 15 he tells us how Irene's opinion matched his own with regard to theatrical performances with religious themes. Since their conversations are not recorded in direct speech, the reader wonders if Manso's recollections are entirely accurate. Perhaps, like the conversation at José María's party, Irene remains politely silent while Manso does all the talking. Indeed, in chapter 16 we see that Manso's tendency to read Irene's silence in his favor can lead him to ungrounded assumptions. In that chapter Manso asks Irene why the light in her room had been on so late the night before. When she avoids answering him, Manso comes to the preposterous conclusion that this vital young woman had been secretly studying some of the long, dry, philosophical books that he had written! Clearly such a supposition is merely the fruit of Manso's conceptual and interest perspectives distorting his perceptual perspective. Consequently, when we re-read Manso's assertion that in Irene he has found the "mayor consonancia y parentesco entre su alma y la mía," we suspect that he simply is projecting his own conceptual and interest perspectives onto her.

As the narrative progresses, our suspicions are born out. It is important to note, however, that the clouding of Manso's vision due to his conceptual and interest perspectives is only partly responsible for Manso's lack of understanding about what is occurring around him. Also to blame are his fellow characters who deliberately conceal information from him. As the secrets which have been hidden by Irene, Manolo, José María, and doña Cándida gradually are revealed to Manso, he is fully capable of readjusting his opinion of Irene. He finally realizes that Irene is merely what he calls a "mujer-mujer" instead of a "mujer-razón," but he still continues to love her despite the imperfections he sees in her. That is, his interest perspective is still engaged, but it now has been liberated from the influence of his conceptual perspective. Since he no longer has to view Irene through his reason-centered conceptual perspective, he can simply love her for what she is: "una persona de esas que llamaríamos de distinción vulgar, una dama de tantas, hecha por el patrón corriente, formada según el modelo de mediocridad en el gusto y hasta en la honradez, que constituye el relleno de la Sociedad actual" (ch. 42). Seven chapters later he again returns to this idea: "era como todas. Los tiempos, la raza, el ambiente, no se desmentía en ella." Here Galdós uses Manso to introduce the formula of "race, milieu, et moment," as one which is just as valid for middle- and upper-class society as it is for the urban or rural poor so favored by naturalistic writers. Manso's *desengaño* concerning Irene allows him to place her, and his erstwhile student Manolo, within the larger context of Madrid during the Restoration. In the process, he realizes that his educational efforts are no match for the power exerted over the general populace by society. Debra Castillo has noted that the primary goal of Krausist pedagogy was to bring a student "to a refined sense of moral and ethical considerations." [14] But such a goal is not fully realizable within a shallow, selfish, vain, opportunistic society that rewards oratorical flourish over well-reasoned arguments. As Carlos Blanco Aguinaga remarks, Manso's tutoring of Manolo has done little more than provide the veneer of sophistication that will allow him to rise within the social hierarchy. [15] Charles Steele sees *El amigo Manso* as Galdós's critique of the Krausist school system which failed to take into consideration society at large when putting into practice its theories. [16] G. A. Davies agrees that Galdós is negatively commenting on the conflict between Krausist theory and practice, but he sees society as sharing some of the blame because educational reform can only work if individuals in society are willing to accept it. [17] Indeed, the indifference of Manso's students to his lessons is graphically displayed at the end of the novel after Manso has returned to the frame. He dips into the minds of his former pupils – including Manolo – and finds precious little of what he taught them buried under the more recent layers of life experience. Manolo's real school is the Congreso, where moral and ethical considerations are of little importance. Similarly, Irene's formal schooling is wasted in her role as a society wife so occupied with fashion and parties that she never thinks to open a book. [18]

Manso's inability to win over his students to a more moral and ethical way of life does not negate the validity of the value system governing his own behavior, however. Striving for higher ideals is admirable whether or not they ultimately are attained, and Manso's worthy attempt constitutes his superiority over those around him who merely pursue self-interested goals. Manso is an exaggerated version of León Roch, and like his predecessor, his single-minded

[14] Debra A. Castillo, "The Problematics of Teaching in *El amigo Manso*," *Revista de Estudios Hispánicos* 19.2 (1985): 46.

[15] Carlos Blanco Aguinaga, "*El amigo Manso* y el 'ciclo céntrico de la sociedad'," *Nueva Revista de Filología Hispánica* 24: 428-31.

[16] Charles W. Steele, "The Krausist Educator as Depicted by Galdós," *Kentucky Foreign Language Quarterly* 5 (1958): 138-40.

[17] G. A. Davies, "Galdós' *El amigo Manso*: An Experiment in Didactic Method," *Bulletin of Hispanic Studies* 39 (1962): 29.

[18] Although, as Catherine Jagoe, *Ambiguous Angels: Gender in the Novels of Galdós* (Berkeley: U of California P, 1994) points out, Krausists viewed the education of women merely as a "means to the real end of educating the future men of Spain, since mothers were inevitably the first educators of children" 100.

reliance on theoretical concepts blinds him to the truths around him and leads to his disillusionment. Manso in the frame can look down on the embedded story with a bemused comprehension of the human frailties that affect all the characters, including Manso. But of all the characters Manso is by far the least culpable because his shortsightedness comes from an excess of qualities that are good. He never acts in a mean-spirited or inconsiderate manner. Although he is blatantly deceived by Irene, he does not respond in kind. Rather, he selflessly works toward securing her future happiness. Manso stands with the implied author against the pettiness and triviality exhibited by the other characters. His honesty and generosity serve as a counterpoint to their "pasión exaltada, debilidad de espíritu y elasticidad de consciencia" (ch. 42). Harriet Turner likens him to a "médico que diagnostica los males de la sociedad, como lo fue Augusto Miquis de *La desheredada*." [19] Indeed, the similarity between these two characters is underscored by Augusto's brief appearance in chapter 33, where he helps Manso to find a wet-nurse for Lica's baby. Counted among Manso's friends are men like himself – Augusto Miquis and León Roch – while he avoids the company of doña Cándida, Federico Cimarra, the marqués de Tellería, and Ramón María Pez. Manso's reliability is thus reaffirmed through his personal relationships with characters from previous Galdosian novels. As Martha Krow-Lucal has noted, Galdós's practice of using recurring characters enriches the reading experience because of the numerous associations that the reader can bring from past novels to the one at hand. [20] His friendships serve as a form of shorthand to align Manso with other Galdosian characters who are critical of the shallow values prevalent in society at the time. But those readers of *El amigo Manso* who are unfamiliar with Galdós's previous work are not at a disadvantage because Galdós clearly establishes the traits of all characters who are essential to the plot, whether or not they have appeared elsewhere before.

As we have seen in *La desheredada*, *Fortunata y Jacinta*, and the Centeno-Tormento-Bringas trilogy, this characterization is usually

---

[19] Harriet S. Turner, "¿Es Manso un pobre hombre?," *Actas del Segundo Congreso Internacional de Estudios Galdosianos* (Las Palmas: Cabildo Insular, 1980) 2: 388.

[20] Martha G. Krow-Lucal, "El personaje recurrente en la obra de Galdós," *Textos y Contextos de Galdós*, ed. John W. Kronik and Harriet Turner (Madrid: Castalia, 1994) 160.

accomplished in Galdós's third-person narratives through direct commentary coupled with more subtle means of developing character, such as the granting or withholding of interior views. In first-person narratives, however, only the protagonist-narrator is permitted interior views. Consequently, in *El amigo Manso*, all characters other than Manso automatically receive an exterior treatment. In addition to what the narrator says about them, they reveal themselves through their words and actions. Although direct speech, in the form of dialogues, is the most common way of communicating the characters' words to the reader, other ways can be employed for their connotative effects. In *El amigo Manso*, Galdós frequently uses free indirect speech with doña Cándida and Lica. As we have seen in Galdós's other novels, the overall effect of this technique is mimicry, and as such it exaggerates the tone of the original. Therefore, doña Cándida's pretentiousness and Lica's flightiness become more apparent when what they say is rendered in speech that is free and indirect rather than tagged and direct. Of course, the free indirect aspect of this technique also carries with it the double-voicing that is so effective for ironic purposes. In protagonist-narrated texts such as this one, the double-voicing is particularly powerful because the narrator is also a character, and therefore has a more easily identifiable persona than the typical heterodiegetic chronicler-narrator. In *El amigo Manso* the solid, no-nonsense, logical approach that Manso applies to life contrasts sharply with the way doña Cándida and Lica deal with the world. Consequently, when free indirect speech is used to capture these characters' spoken words, Manso's implicit reaction to what they say is also present.

Throughout the novel Manso's silent censure of doña Cándida's numerous untruths is conveyed in this way. A particularly effective use of free indirect speech with this character is found in the second and third paragraphs of chapter 48, where doña Cándida is lamenting to Lica the loss of Irene's company due to her upcoming marriage to Manolo. Like Manso, we know the truth about her relationship with Irene and about her counterfeit wealth. Therefore, we join Manso in appreciating the irony in doña Cándida's self-sacrificing tone and feigned concern for Irene's welfare:

> ¿Qué sería de ella ya, a su edad, privada de la dulce compañía de su queridísima sobrina..., única persona que de los García Grande quedaba ya en el mundo? Pero el Señor sabía lo que se

hacía al quitarle aquel gusto, aquel apoyo moral... Nacemos para padecer, y padeciendo morimos... Por supuesto, ella sabía dominar su pena y aun atenuarla, considerando la buena suerte de la chica. ¡Oh!, sí, lo principal era que Irene se casara bien, aunque su tía se muriera de dolor al perder la compañía...

and in her mock indignation at being linked to a socially inferior family:

> ¡ay!, la carne, la carne... Irene se casaba con uno de los tres enemigos del alma. No se puede una acostumbrar a ciertas cosas, por más que hablen de las luces del siglo, de la igualdad y de la aristocracia del talento... Ella transigía con el chico; pero con la mamá... ¡imposible! ¡Si al menos no fuera tan ordinaria...!

and in the specious generosity of sharing her possessions with the couple:

> ¿Para qué quería nada ella ya?... Maravillas tenía aun en sus cofres, que harían gran papel en la casa de los jóvenes esposos... Y el sobrante de sus rentas..., también para ellos.

The falsehood and hypocrisy of each of doña Cándida's statements is intensified because the reader is in agreement with the disdainful double-voicing provided by Manso in this free indirect speech passage. Throughout the novel this narrative device is used to implicitly reinforce the explicit condemnation of doña Cándida which Manso expresses in his narrative commentary.

But not all free indirect speech is critical in nature. For example, Galdós uses this technique to place Lica's chatty, colloquial manner of expressing herself in contrast to Manso's formal language and careful delivery. Thus, by juxtaposing Lica's emotional outbursts against Manso's more reasoned and cautious reactions, this technique points out the different temperaments of these two characters. A good example is found in chapter 21, where Lica is complaining to Manso about the bad habits José María has acquired due to his association with Federico Cimarra and those of his ilk:

> Ya no le valía quejarse y llorar, porque él no hacía maldito caso de sus quejas ni de sus lágrimas. Se había vuelto *muy guachinan-*

go, muy pillo, y siempre encontraba palabras para escaparse y aun para probar que no rompía un plato. Tenía olvidada a su mujer, olvidados a sus hijos: todo el santo día se lo pasaba en la calle, y, por la noche, salía después de la reunión y ya no se le veía hasta el día siguiente a la hora de almorzar. Marido y mujer sólo cambiaban algunas palabras tocante a la invitación, al té, a la comida, y pare usted de contar...

Esto podría pasar si no hubiera otras cosas peores, faltas graves. José María estaba echado a perder; la compañía y el trato de Cimarra le habían *enciguatado*; se había corrompido como la fruta sana al contacto de la podrida... Ya no le quedaba duda a la pobrecita de la atroz infidelidad de su esposo. Ella se sentía tan afrentada, que sólo de pensarlo se le salían los colores a la cara, y no encontraba palabras para contarlo... Pero a mí podría decírmelo todo. Sí; revolviendo una mañana los bolsillos de la ropa de José María, había encontrado una carta de una *sinvergüenza*... ¡Una carta pidiéndole dinero!... Se volvía loca pensando que la plata de sus hijos iba a manos de una...

Pero a la infeliz esposa no le importaba la plata, sino la *sinvergüencería* ... ¡Ay! Estaba bramando. Con ser ella una persona decente, si cogiera delante a la bribona que le robaba a su marido, le había de dar una buena soba y un par de galletas bien dadas. ¡Ay qué Madrid, qué Madrid éste! Vale más andar en comisión por el monte, vivir en un bohío, comer vianda, jutía y naranjas cajeles, que peinar a la moda, arrastrar cola, hablar fino y comer con ministros... Mejor estaba ella en su bendita tierra que en Madrid. Allí era reina y señora del pueblo; aquí no le hacían caso más que los que venían a comerle los codos, y después de vivir a su costa se burlaban de ella. Luego esta vida, Señor, esta vida en que todo es forzarse una, fingir y ponerse en tormento para hacer todo a la moda de acá, y tener que olvidar las palabras cubanas para saber otras, y aprender a saludar, a recibir, a mil tontadas y boberías... No, no; esto no iba con ella. Si José no se enmendaba, ella se plantaba de un salto en su tierra, llevándose a sus hijos.

Lica's free indirect speech continues through the end of the chapter. She is so upset that her sentences tumble over each other without being completed, and Manso finds himself in the position of having to calm her down even though he suspects that her anger is justified. Although Lica is disorganized, flighty, and capricious at times, she is not a bad character. She has what Manso describes as an "alma bondadosa," and he genuinely likes her, especially since she shares Manso's scorn for the empty values of high society. Therefore, the content of Lica's conversation is not criticized. Rather, it is her speaking style that is highlighted for comic effect. In this, and all of Lica's free indirect speech passages, double-voicing is used to mildly poke fun at Lica's effusiveness while also registering Manso's exasperation over having to deal with Lica's spontaneous intrusions into his orderly life.

A type of double-voicing also exists between the two Manso's in the text – his frame persona and his story persona – due to the novel's self-referential premise. In the novel's first chapter the author asks the omniscient Manso in the frame to tell his story. He complies, but in the telling, his limited story persona takes over. Manso's story persona speaks, but the presence of his frame persona is still felt. In effect, all of Manso's narration within the story functions as if it were a first-person variation of free indirect speech. Consequently, it all carries with it the double-voicing that combines the story persona's words with the frame persona's implied commentary. From his privileged position in the frame, Manso can look down upon his limited self in the story with an indulgent superiority, watching himself become enmeshed in petty intrigues that he doesn't fully understand, and seeing his vain attempts to reconcile his reason-centered philosophy of life with his love for Irene and his feelings of jealousy toward José María and Manolo. What Manso in the frame presents to the author (and the reader) is an intentionally ironic self-portrait of his limited self, as seen from his privileged position of editorial omniscience.

The protagonist-narrator within the story presents the events from his point of view as they occurred. This is a standard convention of autobiographical fiction which, despite its retrospective nature, does not require the narrator to reveal the outcome of events until the end of the narrative. Manso in the embedded story knows that he will lose Irene to Manolo, but he withholds that information because to do otherwise would ruin the suspense for the reader. As the protagonist-narrator he controls the order of the narrative, but Manso in the frame still retains his editorial function and briefly intrudes three times on that narrative. These more or less evenly spaced interruptions remind the reader of his hidden presence behind the protagonist-narrator's words. Two of these interruptions merely point to the then/now difference in the times of reference between the story persona and the frame persona: the declaration in chapter 15 that "aun hoy" he recalls the strong smell of coffee that always permeated José María's house; and the assertion in chapter 39 that "aun hoy" he finds it unusual that his appetite was not adversely affected by the news of Irene's love for Manolo. The intrusion of Manso's frame persona at the opening of chapter 14 is different, however, because it seems to indicate a lack of omniscience on his part. He asks if his "propósito" (i.e. marriage to Irene) "¿Nació del sentimiento o de la razón? Hoy mismo no lo sé, aunque trato de sondear el problema, ayudado de la serenidad de espíritu de que disfruto en este momento." But how can Manso's frame persona not know the answer to this question, especially in light of the *desengaño* his story persona eventually undergoes? Here Manso is simply resorting to the temporary suspension of privilege common to editorial omniscience. Like the typical Galdosian chronicler-narrator, Manso feigns ignorance as a ruse to make himself appear more objective about the facts he does divulge. [21] Despite his pretense of limitation, his omniscient privileges remain in tact, allowing him to end the novel with a catalog summarizing the thoughts of the story's characters. His superiority vis-à-vis his story persona is blatantly stated in the concluding paragraph of the novel where he likens himself to an adult who looks with disdain upon the toys he cherished in childhood.

In *El amigo Manso* Galdós used an innovative structuring device to liberate himself to some degree from the constraints associated with autobiographical fiction. He created a dual-layered narrative in which the limited protagonist-narrator (standard to the genre) must operate within a frame narrated through editorial omniscience. The resulting irony stems from the conventional restrictions imposed upon Manso's story persona. His total misreading of various situations within the story is due to his status as a character, who like all characters, is bound by a single point of view and vulnerable to misperceptions. All protagonist-narrators are burdened by such limitations. Manso just displays them to a greater degree, and in the process, underscores the conventional underpinnings of

---

[21] It is interesting to note, however, that Manso's question juxtaposes "sentimiento" with "razón" but does not choose between them, thereby indicating that Manso's conceptual and interest perspectives were so enmeshed at that point in the story that it was impossible to separate them.

this form of narration. In this novel Galdós bends the rules without entirely breaking them. Although in the frame Manso oversteps the limitations normally assigned to a narrator of autobiographical fiction, Manso in the story conforms completely to the conventions of that genre. This bit of anti-realistic experimentation exists at the periphery of the text, never once invading the basic story. Yet, the ironic possibilities resulting from the nested structure allowed Galdós to create a richer novel than had he written it completely within the typical protagonist-narrator format seen in the early *Episodios nacionales*.

* * *

In his next protagonist-narrated novel, *Lo prohibido*, Galdós once again takes liberties with the conventional autobiographical format, thereby expanding the creative possibilities of that genre. The text supposedly consists of the memoirs of the wealthy José María Bueno de Guzmán, covering the period of September 1880 through November 1884 – from his early retirement at the age of 36 until his death. They document his romantic entanglements with his three married cousins: Eloísa, his spendthrift mistress; Camila, who steadfastly resists his advances; and María Juana, whose openness to seduction is never pursued fully. The memoirs originally began as a pleasant way for José María to spend a two week period in San Sebastián while waiting for Camila and her husband to meet him there on vacation, and his stated purpose for writing the memoirs was to help him clarify his thoughts and to provide a guide for other men of the world who may find themselves in the similar position of having to juggle various women. This premise, however, is not explained until the fourth chapter of the second volume – over half the way through the lengthy novel – when the chronology of the story reaches the day on which José María begins his writing. Robert Ricard has commented on the rigidly chronological progression of the events of the novel, which he sees as the salient feature of *Lo prohibido*. [22] However, this uninterrupted linear progression only applies to the order of the story, not to the order of the discourse recording those events. The memoirs are not presented as

[22] Robert Ricard, *Galdós et ses romans* (Paris: Center de Recherches de l'Institut d'Etudes Hispaniques, 1961) 75-80.

José María's on-going project, but rather, they are reserved for his isolated periods of free time. This results in four distinct segments which are written during separate time periods and which do not correspond to the formal chapter divisions:

1st SEGMENT:

narrator's NOW:

Summer 1883

story NOW:

1880 – Spring 1883

2nd SEGMENT:

narrator's NOW:

Semana Santa 1884

story NOW:

Spring 1883 – Semana Santa 1884

3rd SEGMENT (Ido del Sagrario as amanuensis):

narrator's NOW:

July & August 1884

story NOW:

Semana Santa – August 1884

4th SEGMENT:

narrator's NOW:

November 1884

story NOW:

August-November 1884

The disparity between the time of the writing and the time of the events serves to underscore the dual function of the protagonist-narrator: José María's role as a character within the story, and his status as the narrator of the discourse. Moreover, as we shall see, the focus on José María's act of writing the memoirs in stages not concurrent with the action of the story establishes the illusion that he is also the actual author of the text.

In the first segment, written in the summer of 1883, José María tells us that he had intended to relate the events starting in 1880 through his present. However, his writing is interrupted by the arrival of Camila and her husband in mid-August, and he is only able to cover the material through the Spring of 1883 – up to the death of Eloísa's husband but not including José María's falling out with Eloísa nor his infatuation with Camila. That is, the story NOW (the present of the events of the story) does not reach the narrator's NOW (the narrator's present at the time of writing). José María's time-frame as a character is explicitly shown to be different from

his time-frame as a narrator. Furthermore, he continues to participate in events even though he has not yet recorded them in his narrative. Thus, José María appears to have an existence separate from
the narration itself; that is, he seems to have a life in the real world
which he will eventually get around to narrating in the text.

This illusion is reinforced by the mention of José María's subsequent writing periods. In volume 2, chapter 8, section 1 José María
tells the reader that he resumed his writing during the *Semana Santa*
of 1884, and that during a period of some four or five days he man-
aged to bring the memoirs up to date, relating the events between
Eloísa's husband's death and Eloísa's disfiguring illness. He says:
"Aquí di punto, esperando los nuevos sucesos para calcarlos en el
papel en cuanto ellos salieran de las nieblas del tiempo." That is,
the story NOW has finally caught up to the narrator's NOW, and
consequently, José María had to wait for more adventures so as to
have more material to narrate. This strongly suggests that he has a
life in the outside world and that his interaction with other real
people constitutes the experiences from which he draws to write his
memoirs.

The next addition to the memoirs occurs in July and August of
1884 and relates the events leading up to and including José María's
accident and financial ruin. Due to his illness, José María uses a recurring Galdosian character, Ido del Sagrario, as his amanuensis.
José María's impaired verbal ability forces him to rely on Ido to
read his thoughts and fill in the narrative from sketchy details, an
arrangement which works out well since José María tells us that
"con sólo mirarme adivinábame los pensamientos. Tal traza al fin se
daba, que contándole yo un caso en dos docenas de palabras, lo
ponía en escritura con tanta propiedad, exactitud y colorido, que
no lo hiciera mejor yo mismo, narrador y agente al propio tiempo
de los sucesos" (vol. 2, ch. 11, sec. 1). Ido's previous appearance in
El doctor Centeno and *Tormento,* however, immediately causes the
reader to associate this character with the type of writing found in
the popular serialized novel. The reader suspects that Ido will in-
corporate folletinesque elements – melodrama, suspense, formulaic
plotlines, romanticized characters – into the portion of the memoirs
he writes. In response to our worries, José María assures us that he
has held a tight reign on Ido's literary imagination, thereby curtail-
ing Ido's inclination to fabricate scenes. José María's power of veto
makes him appear to be the ultimate authority for what was or was

not included in the memoirs. Thus, the illusion that José María is the author of his own autobiography is further solidified since the events contained in the text are presented as ones which actually occurred, as opposed to those which Ido wanted to invent. Though a fictional narrative, Lo prohibido takes on the guise of narrated fact; the fictional narrator, José María, is projected into the role of an actual author; and the fictional characters appear to populate the real world in which José María lives.

In the fourth and final segment José María adds information concerning the period between August and November 1884: the recouping of José María's finances and the birth of Camila's twins.[23] More importantly, José looks over the memoirs to make sure that Ido did not falsify aspects of his life and to see that the names have been sufficiently disguised so as to be unrecognizable. Stating that the names have been changed reinforces the illusion that the characters are real people whose identity needs to be hidden in order to protect their privacy. Also, rechecking the content of the manuscript for Ido's untruths gives additional credence to José María's contention that the events narrated are facts documenting actual occurrences. The novel closes with an explicit reference to José María's manuscript being under consideration by a publisher who not only recognizes José María's claim to authorship but also promises to honor his request that it not be printed until after he

---

[23] In "Creative Asynchrony: The Moral Dynamism of Lo prohibido," Crítica Hispánica 13 (1991): 47-48; and "The Unfinished Anagnorisis: the Illness and Death of José María Bueno de Guzmán in Galdós' Lo prohibido," Galdós' House of Fiction, ed. A. H. Clarke and Eamonn Rodgers (Llangrannog: Dolphin, 1991) 129-30, Eamonn Rodgers describes José María's manuscript as having only three phases of composition. To do this, Rodgers collapses the fourth segment of the manuscript into the third. However, volume 2, chapter 11, section 1 of Lo prohibido clearly states that José María spent July and August of 1884 dictating to Ido his "prosaicas aventuras en Madrid desde el otoño de 80 al verano del 84." Since the events of the story continued until November of 1884, they could only have been added when José María returned to his manuscript soon after the birth of Camila's baby. José María was fully capable of writing, as he himself admits when speaking of his decision to hire Ido as his amanuensis for the third segment: "No me era difícil escribir, pues mi mano derecha conservábase expedita; pero se cansaba pronto y los trazos no eran muy correctos." Ido simply served as an expedient method of recording the large volume of material covered in the third segment. Since José María did not suffer a relapse between August and November of 1884, we can assume that his writing ability had not worsened. Therefore, he easily could have written the extremely brief fourth section of his manuscript, covering only two major events during a three month period.

dies. His status as author fully secured, he can leave his manuscript in the hands of his publisher and calmly await his own death.

Unlike Máximo Manso, who achieves authorial independence by recognizing his fictionality, José María Bueno de Guzmán gains autonomy by establishing himself as a nonfictional person who physically wrote a book about his life which was published posthumously and which the flesh-and-blood reader is holding in his or her hands. Both Manso and José María are aware of their roles as narrators and focus reader attention on the conventions associated with first-person narration. But whereas Manso revels in his fictional status, José María rejects it entirely. José María's authorial autonomy, though illusory, gains credibility through the segmented memoir format of the text which seems to endow him with a life outside the narration as well as within it.

José María also differs from Máximo Manso in terms of his reliability as a narrator. In *Lo prohibido* Galdós once again exposes the morally decadent lifestyle of Restoration high society, but this time he does so through the unreliable narration of one of its proponents rather than the reliable narration of one of its detractors. José María belongs to Spain's *nouveau riche* upper middle class eager to take on the material trappings of the declining aristocracy. Affectation and social climbing are its hallmarks, and its members abide by a code of ethics which José Montesinos calls an elastic morality based on a relativistic justification of reprehensible behavior. [24] For José María money and sexual conquest – usually presented in tandem – define his world and color each of his personal relationships. He describes the daily life of a segment of society that holds values which in the main are even more decadent than his own, yet he generally accepts the validity of that way of life and restricts his criticism to the extreme manifestations that it produces, such as Eloísa's chronically extravagant spending. He not only condones but perpetuates the shallow and immoral behavior of his social circle by participating in its financial indulgences and adulterous activities. When he measures his own worth against the depravity and corruption of his peers, he hypocritically finds himself to be somewhat culpable but on the whole more decent than they. Indeed, the memoirs represent his rationalization of a lifestyle that the implied author condemns for its waste of human potential.

---

[24] José F. Montesinos, Introducción, *Lo prohibido*, by Benito Pérez Galdós (Madrid: Castalia, 1971) 21.

Why does Galdós use an unreliable narrator in *Lo prohibido?* What effects are achieved through unreliable narration that could not be derived from reliable narration? The answer to these questions rests on the relationship that exists between the narrator, the narratee, the implied author, and the implied reader. Reliable narrators serve as advocates for the implied author's social, political, religious, or ethical attitudes and assumptions. Since the narrator is the reader's primary link to the story, reliable narration is a highly effective manner of influencing the reader's response in favor of the implied author's norms and values. Nevertheless, when prudently used, unreliable narration can produce an even stronger impression on the reader. Rather than propose attitudes for the reader to accept, unreliable narration offers ones that must be violently rejected. Unreliable narrators are powerful tools for censuring entire value systems because the reader is asked to disagree with the narrator's total outlook on life. This process actively engages us in the moral and ideological world of the text as we endeavor to reconstruct the social, political, religious, or ethical attitudes indirectly proposed by the implied author. This is an ironic form of narration because the reader must call into question the narrator's world view based on a secret communication between the implied reader and the implied author.

Seymour Chatman uses the following chart to represent this process, with the broken line indicating the secret ironic message about the narrator's unreliability:[25]

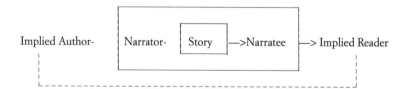

The narratee is the fictional entity to whom the narrator speaks. As Gerald Prince has noted, both narrators and narratees can possess specific traits and adhere to specific ideological positions.[26] In the

      [25] Seymour Chatman, *Coming to Terms: The Rhetoric of Narrative in Fiction and Film* (Ithaca: Cornell UP, 1990) 151.
      [26] Gerald Prince, "Introduction to the Study of the Narratee," *Reader-Response Criticism: From Formalism to Post-Structuralism*, ed. Jane P. Tompkins (Baltimore: Johns Hopkins UP, 1980) 7-25.

narrative transaction cited by Chatman above, the narrator and the narratee share a set of norms and values which are at odds with the norms and values of the implied author. Thus, while the narrator tells the story to the narratee, the implied reader can stand with the implied author in judgment of the attitudes or assumptions expressed by the narrator and accepted by the narratee. Since neither the narrator nor the narratee is aware of being assessed in this manner, the situation is inherently ironic and the narrator is being ironized in the act of narrating.

This process is clearly seen in Galdós's first example of unreliable narration: Juan Bragas's autobiographical account in *Memorias de un cortesano de 1815* and *La segunda casaca*. In these *episodios* Galdós levels biting criticism at the corruption of Fernando VII's government by documenting Juan Bragas's rise to power through political opportunism. Since Galdós had never before created a narrator whose values were in direct opposition to those of the implied author, he took care to firmly establish Bragas's unreliability for the reader. He did this by making our initial introduction to Bragas occur in the *episodio* immediately preceding *Memorias de un cortesano de 1815*. As a minor character in *El equipaje del Rey José*, Bragas displays cynical and self-serving behavior in clear contrast to the sincerity, loyalty, and honor exhibited by the protagonist of the second series, Salvador Monsalud. By delineating Bragas's negative traits in this way, Galdós warned the reader to distrust the opinions put forth by Bragas as the protagonist-narrator of the next two *episodios*. Galdós further solidified Bragas's status as an unreliable narrator by creating a confrontation scene between Bragas and Gabriel Araceli in chapter 22 of *Memorias de un cortesano de 1815*. Having proved his reliability in the first series, Gabriel can authoritatively speak against "la bajeza, la adulación, la falsedad, la doblez, la vil codicia, la envidia, la crueldad" which are hallmarks of the corrupt reign that Bragas glorifies. The reader thus becomes aligned with Gabriel (and the implied author) against Bragas and all he stands for. As Bragas speaks to his narratee, all of his statements become subject to our censure. Since Bragas views Fernando VII's return to power as the end of a godless liberal tyranny and the re-establishment of the legitimate absolute monarchy, the terminology he uses to describe events arouses the reader's indignation and creates a more violent reaction than would have been possible had a reliable narrator related the same events in a tone critical to the crown. Also, by presupposing that the narratee will condone his un-scrupulous behavior, Bragas is revealing the depth of the political corruption and its all-pervasive quality in a way that a sermonizing reliable narrator could not achieve. The freedom which Bragas feels in expressing his opinions to his like-minded narratee is ironically overturned by the undetected presence of the implied reader. Bragas assumes that his opinions will go unchallenged, and it is this wrong assumption that is responsible for the impact of his unreli-able narration. All of his judgments undergo an inversion by the reader, who knows that everything lauded is to be condemned and everything criticized is to be praised.

José María Bueno de Guzmán similarly writes for a narratee who shares his overall value system. Indeed, he often comments on how typical of his socio-economic class he is, and how helpful his memoirs may be for other men dealing with the same problems and complications he has lived through. From the very onset of the novel, the implied reader begins to question, evaluate, and reject the value system that José María holds. How does the reader come to realize José María's unreliability? He had not appeared in any previous novels, so he cannot be immediately identified as an un-trustworthy character. Neither is there a scene where a reliable nar-rator from a previous novel – such as Manso – explicitly reproaches José María for his unethical lifestyle. These tactics from Galdós's first unreliable narrative are no longer necessary in *Lo prohibido* be-cause Galdós's literary reputation had become so well established by 1884 that the reader soon recognizes José María as a member of the decadent and morally impoverished high society that had so often been criticized before. Galdós merely needed to provide a list of José María's friends and business acquaintances – Jacinto Villa-longa, el marqués de Fúcar, Federico Cimarra, Gonzalo Torres, Gustavo Tellería – to reassure us that our negative assessment of José María is valid. Because we are quick to perceive José María's lack of reliability, we are able to judge the inappropriateness of his attitudes on a continuous basis throughout the novel. This results in what Wayne Booth calls a secret collusion between the reader and the implied author, working together to agree on the standard of values by which the narrator is found to be sorely deficient (304). Due to this partnership between the implied reader and the implied author, the narrator soon becomes the butt of an ironic portrait as he reveals his biases and justifies his faults in his own words.

So evident is José María's unreliability that no scholar has declared that this narrator is a spokesman for the implied author. Nevertheless, Arthur Terry has noted that José María's reliability does increase toward the end of the novel.[27] How is this shift possible? Again, it is necessary to keep in mind the narrative premise of the text. During the entire first volume José María conforms to the standard expectations of a fictional protagonist-narrator. Since the text is presented as his memoirs, the reader assumes that they are being written from the globally retrospective point of view associated with that genre. Suddenly in the second volume – hundreds of pages into the novel – this narrative convention is subverted. We learn that the text was composed in various stages, and therefore that it combines elements of both a diary and a memoir. Generally the narrator of a memoir is in command of all the facts, and consequently is aware of how the events interrelate and how the various situations eventually were resolved. José María does not have the benefit of such global hindsight. Because his memoirs are a collection of four separately written segments, certain portions were penned before he knew the final outcome of the events. Like a diary, the text is a collection of discrete units; however, the time span covered in each unit is greater than normally found in diary notations. The overall format, then, allows José María more retrospective knowledge than a daily diary, but less than a true memoir. If we examine the individually written segments in terms of narrator reliability, we find that in the first two segments José María clearly holds values contrary to those of the implied author, while in the last two segments his materialism and hedonism abate. Thus, the narrator displays an abrupt shift toward greater reliability between the second and third segments. This phenomenon is made possible by the hybrid quality of the text which incorporates aspects of both the diary and the memoir genres. If the text were just a daily diary, it would show a gradual movement away from unreliability as José María slowly comes to realizations affecting his ongoing conceptual outlook. If the text were a true memoir, José María's reliability would remain constant since he would be writing from a single conceptual perspective. It is the segmentation of the text into individually written parts which permits this sudden change in his

[27] Anthony Terry, "*Lo prohibido:* Unreliable Narrator and Untruthful Narrative," *Galdós Studies*, ed. J. E. Varey (London: Tamesis, 1970) 67-68 and 86.

reliability status since José María's world view is altered by the events occurring during the several months between the writing of the second and third segments. This period is one of personal crisis affecting all aspects of his life – monetary, social, and physical. He is financially ruined, Camila and Constantino withdraw their valued friendship, and he is partially paralyzed due to an accident. It is well within the bounds of verisimilitude for José María to indulge in introspective examination during his convalescence, with the resulting insights bringing about a degree of character growth that would narrow the gap somewhat between his values and those of the implied author. The third and fourth segments, comprising the last three chapters of the novel, reflect this alteration in José María's conceptual perspective.

The segmented nature of the memoirs also permits the introduction of a further complication which has a bearing on José María's reliability – Ido del Sagrario as the amanuensis of the third segment. Since Ido must divine José María's thoughts and all details of the events from the very broad outline dictated to him, he goes beyond the passive role of scribe and becomes a collaborative narrator of the third segment. Despite José María's repeated assurances that he has held Ido's imagination in check and that he allowed no falsification of the facts, the reader is reluctant to discount Ido's contribution to the text. After all, this segment represents Ido's interpretation of events as conveyed to him "en dos docenas de palabras." José María did not actually think or say the words recorded in the text, but rather, he merely approved them as written. Given Ido's tendency to romanticize situations, the reader wonders to what degree Ido embellished the truth. Even if we accept José María's contention that Ido did not alter the content of the memoirs, we cannot ignore that he left his mark on their style. In addition to the numerous literary, classical, historical, and Biblical allusions noted by Kay Engler (166), Ido's influence is discernible in the subtle shift in narrative voice techniques in this segment. Above all, there is a decided increase in the number and length of interior views. During the first two segments José María's direct thoughts are brief, infrequent, and merely reaffirm his negative characterization because they record his adulterous intentions and the schemes he devises to achieve his sexual conquests. In the third segment, however, José María's direct thoughts occur more often, are more extensive, and take on a new tone as he questions the validity of his long-held values and recognizes the desirability of the pure and innocent love between Camila and Constantino. [28] Free indirect thoughts, absent in the other segments, are introduced here to further convey José María's inner turmoil. His interiorizations somewhat temper the previous negative portrayal of him and elicit a certain amount of reader sympathy and compassion for his plight. This effect is largely attributable to Ido's rendering of José María's story content in a more intimate style. As Booth has observed, the sustained use of a sympathetic inside view is one of the most successful devices for inducing a parallel response in the reader, and as such it is a particularly effective means of reducing the emotional distance between the reader and a morally deficient character (243-49). Although the reader is only receiving Ido's version of José María's thoughts, the stylistic presentation gives us the impression that we have direct access to José María's consciousness. Thanks to the many direct and free indirect thought passages, we feel that we are experiencing José María's moral transformation first hand. But despite the first person reference, this material is mediated through Ido. The difference in the discursive devices employed here is acceptable and plausible due to the segmentation of the memoirs into discretely written units, with Ido in control of the third one. The brief fourth section, in which José María again takes charge of the narration, returns to the discursive orientation found in the first two segments, relying heavily on dialogue and direct narrative commentary.

Ido's considerable role in the production of the third segment calls into question the depth of José María's moral conversion. Though it is fully possible that José María did in fact learn the error of his ways, the reader is somewhat uneasy with his embrace of the implied author's values at the close of the novel – a reversal more suited to the *folletín* so favored by Ido del Sagrario. That this change occurs at the very point where Ido takes charge of the nar-

---

[28] Galdós's use of Camila and Constantino to project positive values in contrast to the false values of Restoration society has been studied by various critics: Alda Blanco, "Dinero, relaciones sociales y significación en *Lo prohibido*," *Anales Galdosianos* 18 (1983): 61-73; Geraldine M. Scanlon, "Heroism in an Unheroic Society," *Modern Language Review* 79 (1984): 831-45; and Bridget A. Aldaraca, *El Ángel del Hogar: Galdós and the Ideology of Domesticity in Spain*, North Carolina Studies in the Romance Languages and Literatures 239 (Chapel Hill: U of North Carolina P, 1991) 218-30.

rative is further disquieting. As Michael Nimetz states, "one has the nagging sensation that these so-called 'prosáicas aventuras' are in some way a product of Ido del Sagrario's fecund imagination. . . . *Apparently,* José María's document is true; *in reality,* it might well be romanticized."[29] In this segment Ido fleshes out the insights that José María achieved through crisis-caused introspection, and he conveys them to us in imaginary interior views. That is, not only are we reading Ido's interpretation of José María's feelings, but we are reading them in a stylistic medium that typically is used to evoke an empathetic response in the audience. Since José María affirms the validity of the content of the segment, we can accept that he did experience some change in his world view. However, the extent of his repentance may have been exaggerated.[30] Whereas the segmented nature of the narrative permits an altered world view to appear suddenly in the third section, Ido's dominion over that portion of the memoirs casts into doubt the degree to which José María actually has aligned himself with the implied author's values. In short, a change may well have taken place, but was it as spectacular as presented? Once again Ido has been used by Galdós – albeit in a more subtle way – to make the reader aware of the conventions of popular fiction. In addition to the criticism of the *novela por entregas* implied in José María's rejection of Ido's fanciful and romantic episodes for the memoirs, Galdós introduces an element of doubt that José María's efforts to control Ido's literary inclinations were completely successful. These clashes between Ido and José María ask the reader to mentally juxtapose the conventions of the serialized "novela de impresiones y movimiento" against those of the realistic novel, thereby making it clear that these two forms of literature are philosophically at odds with each other.[31]

---

[29] Michael Nimetz, *Humor in Galdós: A Study of the Novelas contemporáneas* (Yale UP, 1968) 92-93.

[30] James Whiston and Eamonn Rodgers both cite José María's treatment of Eloísa at the close of the novel as evidence that his moral conversion was not complete. See James Whiston, "Ironía y psicología en *Lo prohibido* de Galdós," *Romance Quarterly* 37 (1990): 203-04; and Rodgers, "Creative Asynchrony" 53-54; "Unfinished Anagnorisis" 139-40.

[31] Galdós uses the term "novela de impresiones y movimiento" in his 1870 essay "Observaciones sobre la novela contemporánea en España," to refer to the kind of non-realistic literature written by Ido. Galdós criticizes these novels for failing to represent contemporary Spanish middle-class society. He also comments on the serialization process itself, stating that it is an excellent way to reach readers of

In summary, *Lo prohibido* is stated as being composed of memoirs written in segments during four separate time periods. This narrative premise grants the protagonist-narrator a degree of flexibility normally denied him. By allowing discrepancies between the story order of the events and the discourse order of the segments, and by focusing reader attention on the act of writing, the narrator is able to assert his independence from the narrative and attain the illusion of authorship. In addition, the time which elapses between the writing of the segments accounts for the seemingly abrupt change in the narrator's reliability in the last chapters of the novel. Finally, Galdós capitalizes on the reader's expectations of Ido del Sagrario in order to reinforce the illusion of José María's autonomy as well as to undermine the impact of his moral conversion at the end of the novel, resulting in the reader's renewed awareness of the differences between the realistic novel and popular fiction.

* * *

In *El amigo Manso* and *Lo prohibido* Galdós used his protagonist-narrators to comment upon the superficiality, depravity, hypocrisy, and self-interest that permeated the middle and upper levels of Restoration society. In the first of these novels, however, the social atmosphere serves merely as a backdrop for Manso's personal story. Consequently, Galdós could employ a reliable narrator to periodically express overt criticism of the corruption and selfishness around him, while primarily exemplifying the values of the implied author through his virtuous conduct. Such a narrator might have appeared overly preachy, however, in a novel entirely dedicated to exposing the baseness of Restoration society. Therefore, for *Lo prohibido* Galdós turned to a form of narration that allowed him to fuse the novel's content with its style. As the novel's unreliable narrator, José María personifies all that is wrong with the world in which he lives. The reader's rejection of him, and all that he stands for, is achieved without the use of sermons or speeches by a *portavoz* of the implied author. With a reliable narrator, *Lo prohibido*

---

all social classes. But he laments that editors are using this highly efficient method to distribute non-realistic literature. See *Ensayos de crítica literaria*, ed. Laureano Bonet (Barcelona: Península, 1990) 108-09.

could have fallen into the mold of a thesis novel. Instead, it is a masterfully sustained piece of social satire.

Both these novels also display Galdós's versatility and imagination when dealing with narrative conventions. Rather that simply abandoning the autobiographical format because of its inherent limitations, Galdós chose to revitalize it by exploring its structural possibilities. By creating Máximo Manso's nested narratives and José María Bueno de Guzmán's segmented narrative, Galdós dynamically altered a conventionally static genre style. Furthermore, by tapping into the ironic potential of protagonist-narration, he fully engaged the reader's inferential abilities within these structural modifications. As a result, both *El amigo Manso* and *Lo prohibido* display a complexity that belies their roots in autobiographical fiction.

CONCLUSION

Despite R. A. Cardwell's article stressing the continuity between Galdós's novels before and after 1881,[1] there is general critical agreement that the *primera época* and *segunda manera* novels represent distinct phases of Galdós's writing. For many critics, beginning with Clarín, the major factor which distinguishes the *segunda manera* from Galdós's previous work is the presence of naturalistic elements. But with few exceptions,[2] scholars do not consider Galdós's naturalism to be deterministic. Although heredity and environment can strongly influence behavior in Galdós's novels, the individual character is viewed as being ultimately in control of his or her destiny through the exercise of free will. Furthermore, many scholars have suggested additional factors which mitigated the influence of naturalism on Galdós. Among these are Krausism, the Cervantine and picaresque traditions, and Spanish medical theories. Overall, it is believed that Galdosian naturalism does not imitate that of Zola.

---

[1] R. A. Cardwell, "Galdós' Early Novels and the *Segunda Manera*: A Case for a Total View," *Renaissance and Modern Studies* 15 (1971): 44-62.

[2] Vernon Chamberlin sees hereditary and environmental influences predetermining behavior in the novels from *La desheredada* through *Fortunata y Jacinta* and H. L. Boudreau states that the "premise of *Torquemada* is that the bedrock of human nature is predetermined (inherited) and invariable, while social conditions (environment) result only in superficial and inauthentic accretions" (114). See Chamberlin's two articles: "Changing Patterns of Mechanistic Imagery in Galdós's Naturalistic and Postnaturalistic Novels," *Anales Galdosianos* 24 (1989): 61-68 and "'Vamos a ver las fieras': Animal Imagery and the Protagonist in *La desheredada* and *Lo prohibido*," *Anales Galdosianos* 23 (1988): 27-33. Also see Boudreau's "The Salvation of Torquemada: Determinism and Indeterminacy in the Later Novels of Galdós," *Anales Galdosianos* 15 (1980): 113-28.

Rather, it finds its own particular course within the urban milieu of the *segunda manera* novels.[3]

But naturalism is not the only thing that differentiates the *segunda manera* novels from their predecessors. Scholars frequently mention that the focus on political or religious issues in Galdós's early historical and thesis novels became less pronounced in his novels beginning with *La desheredada*. I would suggest that the narratological differences between the *primera época* and *segunda manera* novels are rooted in this shift of emphasis. The historical and thesis novels of the *primera época* have overtly political agendas, and Galdós's uses discoursively effective means of carrying out those agendas. Typically, the competing ideologies within these *primera época* texts are voiced through confrontational dialogues between the characters. In these scenes, direct speech is used to present arguments in favor of the individual ideological positions. Explanato-

---

[3] See three studies by Eamonn Rodgers, "Galdós' *La desheredada* and Naturalism," *Bulletin of Hispanic Studies* 45 (1968): 285-98, *From Enlightenment to Realism: The Novels of Galdós 1870-1887* (Dublin: Jack Hade, 1987) 63-77, and "The Reception of Naturalism in Spain," *Naturalism in the European Novel: New Critical Perspectives*, ed. Brian Nelson (Oxford: Berg, 1992) 120-34; two studies by Enrique Miralles, introducción, *La desheredada*, by Benito Pérez Galdós (Barcelona: Planeta, 1992) and "Galdós y el naturalismo," *Insula* 514 (1989): 15-16; two studies by Walter T. Pattison, *El naturalismo: Historia externa de un movimiento literario*, *Benito Pérez Galdós* (Boston: Twayne, 1975) and *Benito Pérez Galdós*, TWAS 341 (Boston: Twayne, 1975) 63-67; two studies by James Whiston, "Determinism and freedom in *Fortunata y Jacinta*," *Bulletin of Hispanic Studies* 57 (1980): 113-127 and "The Struggle for Life in 'Fortunata y Jacinta'," *The Modern Language Review* 79.1 (1984): 77-87; two studies by Martha G. Krow-Lucal, "Balzac, Galdós and Phrenology," *Anales Galdosianos* 18 (1983): 7-14 and "The Evolution of Encarnación Guillén in *La desheredada*," *Anales Galdosianos* 12 (1977): 21-28; and two studies by M. Gordon, "The Medical Background to Galdós' *La desheredada*" *Anales Galdosianos* 7 (1972): 67-77 and "'Lo que le falta a un enfermo le sobra a otro': Galdós' Conception of Humanity in *La desheredada*," *Anales Galdosianos* 12 (1977): 29-37. Also see Mariano López Sanz, *Naturalismo y espiritualismo en la novelística de Galdós y Pardo Bazán* (Madrid: Pliegos, 1985) 13-83; Carmen Bravo Villasante, "El naturalismo de Galdós y el mundo de *La desheredada*," *Cuadernos Hispanoamericanos* 230 (1969): 479-86; Brian J. Dendle, "On the Supposed 'Naturalism' of Galdós: *La desheredada*," *Papers on Romance Literary Relations Discussed by the Romance Literary Relations Group, MLA, New York, Dec. 1978*, ed. Hugh H. Chapman, Jr. (University Park: Penn. State UP, 1980) 12-28; José F. Montesinos, *Galdós* (Madrid: Castalia, 1980) 2: ix-xix; Sherman H. Eoff, *The Novels of Pérez Galdós: The Concept of Life as Dynamic Process* (St. Louis: Washington UP, 1954) 32-40; Ricardo Gullón, *Galdós, novelista moderno* (Madrid: Gredos, 1966) 130; Robert H. Russell, "The Structure of *La desheredada*," *Modern Language Notes* 76 (1961): 794-800; and Michael A. Schnepf, "The Naturalistic Content of the *La desheredada* Manuscript," *Anales Galdosianos* 24 (1989): 53-59.

ry or judgmental pronouncements by the narrator also enter into this airing of ideological issues. Thus, what Susan Suleiman calls the "doctrinal intertexts" of each novel are overtly presented though statements by either the characters or the narrator.[4] In *El audaz* and *La Fontana de Oro*, these doctrinal intertexts pertain to politics, in *Marianela* they are philosophical, while in *Doña Perfecta*, *Gloria*, and *La familia de León Roch* they deal with religion. Of course, these doctrinal interexts represent only the core theme of each novel. Other beliefs, values, and assumptions are also present, but they are not given the explicit treatment afforded the political or religious themes.[5] By making extensive use of both narrative commentary and direct speech records of the characters in the *primera época* novels, Galdós is able to place the fine points of each doctrinal argument in front of the reader for his or her assessment. Through these discursive devices Galdós overtly engages the reader in the clash of conflicting ideologies which forms the basis of each text.

This does not occur in Galdós's *segunda manera* novels. Rather, the social, political, religious, and ethical concerns of these texts are indirectly revealed to the reader through an interplay of the story and the discourse. Since blatant discussions of doctrinal interexts are absent, the reader must engage in a continual process of evaluation and reassessment of all textual evidence. In particular, the reader must draw inferences about the ideological attitudes and assumptions of the characters based on their actions, general conversations, and thoughts. These characters are less overtly motivated by ideology than the characters in the thesis and historical novels. However, they still are "ideologically demarcated," as Bakhtin would say, by what they do, say, and think.[6] Thus, in the *segunda manera* novels, the ideological dimension of the characters remains, but the presentation of that ideology is implicit rather than explicit. Through the interaction of the characters' perspectives within these

---

[4] Susan Rubin Suleiman, *Authoritarian Fictions: The Ideological Novel as a Literary Genre* (New York: Columbia UP, 1983) 56.
[5] Indeed, the purpose of resisting reading is to bring to light the covert beliefs, values, and assumptions present in a text. See for example Catherine Jagoe's discussion of Galdós's equivocal approach to gender ideology in *Gloria* and *La familia de León Roch*. *Ambiguous Angels: Gender and the Novels of Galdós* (Berkeley: U of California P, 1994) 59-84.
[6] M. M. Bakhtin, *The Dialogic Imagination*, trans. Michael Holquist, ed. Caryl Emerson and Michael Holquist (Austin: U of Texas P, 1981) 335.

novels, Galdós presents an interaction of ideas and values as well. In order to convey these perspectives to the reader, Galdós adds variety to his discoursive style, particularly with regard to his interiorization devices. In keeping with the more covert form of presentation in his *segunda manera* novels, Galdós also minimizes the presence of the narrator. The less intrusive narrator now becomes just one more voice within the interplay of perspectives, which allows Galdós the freedom to experiment with the narrator's role, both in terms of structural limitations and in terms of reliability. In general, the *segunda manera* novels display an overall tendency toward self-revelation by the characters rather than through the narrative summary or commentary so prevalent in the *primera época* novels. Indeed, the narrator's less prominent position in the novels beginning with *La desheredada* marks the single most important narratological difference between Galdós's *primera época* and his *segunda manera*.

In my discussion of Galdós's early *segunda manera* novels, I have shown that the perspectives of the characters are communicated to the reader through a wider range and more extensive use of interiorization devices than in the *primera época* novels. Through the use of free thought in both its direct and indirect forms, for example, Galdós is able to seamlessly insert the consciousness of his characters into the discourse of the *segunda época* novels without formally declaring that he has switched from the voice of the narrator to that of one of the characters. This technique, combined with the non-contextualized and/or presuppositional content of the thoughts, gives the *segunda manera* novels the appearance of spontaneity and naturalness in their expression of the characters' minds. Techniques such as filtered description and present tense narration, though not officially interiorization devices, further contribute toward the character-orientation of the *segunda manera* novels by focalizing segments of the narrative from the point of view of an individual character rather than that of the narrator. The polyphonic structure of Galdós's *segunda manera* is in a large part achieved through discoursive representations of the characters' perspectives. In particular, interiorization devices realize Bakhtin's ideal of self-consciousness as the artistic dominant in the construction of the hero's image.[7] Galdós's *segunda manera* heroes interact with their

---

[7] Mikhail Bakhtin, *Problems of Dostoevsky's Poetics*, trans. and ed. Caryl Emerson, Theory and History of Literature 8 (Minneapolis: U of Minnesota P, 1984) 51.

fellow characters and with the narrator, and in the process, their thoughts display their struggles to overthrow the finalizing definitions of others. The overall effect of the discourse in the *segunda manera* novels is to focus reader attention on the characters rather than on political, social, or religious issues. That is not to say that issues are not raised in these novels. On the contrary, much social criticism is conveyed to the reader. But the agency for that transmission is the reader's relationship with the characters. Through his use of discoursive devices Galdós influences how the reader affectively responds to the various characters, and consequently, that response disposes the reader in favor of certain attitudes and values. Galdós also varies the effects of his discoursive techniques from one novel to another by altering the narrative situation. Reliable, semi-reliable, and unreliable narration each require a different type of reader involvement in the text. First- and third-person narration each provide a separate set of operating principles for the author as well as the reader. By experimenting with both the discoursive techniques and the situational possibilities of his novels, Galdós was able to devise a complex array of rhetorical strategies built upon the basic concept of granted and withheld inside views.

When we look beyond *Fortunata y Jacinta* to the novels which follow it, we see that the discoursive techniques which Galdós's developed from 1881 through 1887 continued to be employed in essentially the same manner throughout the remainder of his *novelas contemporáneas*: direct and free indirect thought are used to provide a less mediated expression of the characters' minds than tagged indirect thought; filtered description and present-tense narration serve as empathetic vehicles to the characters' points of view; and free indirect style supplies opportunities for both ironic and sympathetic effects. Galdós's experiments with narrative structure also continue in his post-*Fortunata y Jacinta* texts. Of particular note are his innovative approaches to first-person narration and the evolution of his *sistema dialogal*. Both of these are represented in the companion texts *La incógnita* and *Realidad*.

In *La incógnita* Galdós further explores the concept of first-person narration through a novelistic genre known for capitalizing on the inherent limitations of a single point of view. In general, the epistolary novel joins an individual perspective (in the form of letters in the first-person) with other individual perspectives (in similarly constructed letters) in order to achieve a multiplicity of perspectives which the reader can discern but which remains hidden from those engaged in the correspondence. That is, multiple points of view and multiple versions of reality are presented to the reader through the interplay of letters between various senders and receivers. What Janet Gurkin Altman calls "patterns of implication" are created which allow the reader to pull together those perspectives in ways that the individuals involved cannot.[8] In *La incógnita* Galdós uses the epistolary format, but he does not allow the patterns of implication to form. In this novel two friends, Infante and Equis, carry on a spirited correspondence during the novelistic time-frame of three and a half months, but the only letters that are included in the text, with a sole exception, are those written by Infante. Each of these characters is a sender and a receiver, but the only evidence of that exchange consists of Infante's allusions to Equis's letters. Thus, Galdós has converted the dual-perspective format of his epistolary novel into a single-perspective account by simply eliminating the letters of one of the correspondents. Manolo Infante is, in essence, a protagonist-narrator whose incomplete knowledge of events is the consequence of his limited point of view. In this way, Galdós once again foregrounds the fundamental drawback of first-person narration. Meanwhile, the reader, restricted to Infante's single perspective, cannot realize the task of filling in the gaps – las incógnitas – which normally emerge in an epistolary novel. Due to the limitations of first-person narration, neither Infante nor the reader have the necessary information to resolve either the detective story plotline (about Federico's death) or the romantic plotline (concerning Augusta's fidelity). But at the end of *La incógnita* Galdós satisfies both Infante and the reader by recasting the novelistic material in a different form.[9] In the penultimate letter of the novel Infante thanks Equis for the present he has just received: the manuscript of a dialogue novel, entitled *Realidad*, which answers all of Infante's questions concerning Federico and Augusta. In speaking of *La incógnita* and *Realidad*, Infante calls the former "la cara exterior," "la superficie," and "la verdad aparente," whereas the latter is "la cara interna," "la descripción interior del asun-

[8] Janet Gurkin Altman, *Epistolarity: Approaches to a Form* (Columbus: Ohio State P, 1982) 182.

[9] For a discussion of the metafictionality of *La incógnita*'s ending see my article, "Turning *La incógnita* into *Realidad*: Galdós's Metafictional Magic Trick," *MLN* 105: 385-91.

to," and "la verdad profunda." The terminology used in this comparison is important because it points to the fundamental difference in narrative presentation between these two novels. *La incógnita* can only present the outward appearance of things because of the limited first-person perspective of the narrator. In contrast, the omniscient orientation of *Realidad* allows it to reveal the characters' inner thoughts and feelings concealed behind what is visible. The end of *La incógnita* explicitly refers the reader to its omniscient counterpart which completes the story by resolving the problems of limited narration.

Realidad, in turn, becomes the next step in the development of Galdós's *sistema dialogal*. The theatrical formatting used for individual scenes in *La desheredada, El doctor Centeno, Tormento*, and *La de Bringas* now extends throughout the entire text of *Realidad*. Galdós explains the value of his *sistema dialogal* in terms of its impact on the reader: "Con la virtud misteriosa del diálogo parece que vemos y oímos, sin mediación extraña, el suceso y sus actores, y nos olvidamos más fácilmente del artista oculto que nos ofrece una ingeniosa imitación." [10] In *Realidad* we have access to everything that the characters say and think through their direct speech and thoughts, and consequently, the narrator's presence is restricted to the stage directions and *acotaciones*. The narrator's lack of prominence can cause us to forget his existence entirely, but he does remain an omniscient presence in the text. Indeed, it is due to the narrator's omniscience that the reader comes to know the inner world of the characters. In *El abuelo* and *Casandra*, as well as *Realidad*, the narrator's *acotaciones* tell us the characters' feelings, while the *apartes* and *para sí* segments provided by the narrator allow us to read the characters' minds. Despite their designation as *novelas dialogadas*, these texts do not eliminate the narrator in favor of pure dialogue. In the prologue to *Casandra* Galdós speaks of the dialogue novel as a "subgénero, producto del cruzamiento de la novela y el teatro," a pairing of two related genres to create a new and revitalized art form. [11] Here we have a synthesis of the narrator's strong presence in narrative fiction and his absence in theatrical produc-

[10] Benito Pérez Galdós, prólogo, *El abuelo, Obras completas: Novelas*, ed. Federico Carlos Sainz de Robles (Madrid: Aguilar, 1970) 3: 800-01.
[11] Benito Pérez Galdós, prólogo, *Casandra, Obras completas: Novelas*, ed. Federico Carlos Sainz de Robles (Madrid: Aguilar, 1970) 3: 906.

tion. In these novels Galdós allows his characters to reveal their qualities and motivations through an essentially exterior manner of presentation: dialogue. This relies heavily on the reader's inferential ability to reconstruct the characters from the implied evidence, as in a stage play. Unlike an audience watching a dramatized production, however, the reader of a dialogue novel does not have the physical presence of actors visibly communicating non-verbal information (such as emotional states) to help in the interpretive process. Thus, the narrator's descriptive *acotaciones* flesh out the dialogue-oriented framework of the text. Similarly, narrative *acotaciones* allow the dialogue novel to achieve what is not possible on the stage. For example, emotional states or information that one character purposely hides from another can be indicated parenthetically by the narrator, whereas a live performance would require an additional scene revealing what was hidden. These theatrically formatted works, which are novels to be read rather than plays to be enacted, continue Galdós's ongoing process of using discoursive devices to develop character in a progressively less intrusive manner, but without losing the narrator's voice entirely.

* * *

The early contemporary novels discussed in this book show the development of a new mode of writing for Galdós which would carry him through the remainder of his literary career. For it was in the novels beginning with *La desheredada* and continuing through *Fortunata y Jacinta* that Galdós discovered his mature narrative voice. The two major trends of his *segunda manera* are character-oriented presentation and narrative innovation. Both are realized through an intricate combination of discoursive devices which influence our response to the characters by controlling our access to their thoughts, feelings, words, and actions. *What* occurs in these novels is experienced by the reader through the discoursive presentation. Reactions to that content, therefore, are influenced by *how* it is conveyed. Story and discourse both contribute toward the reader's appreciation of the novel.

My approach to Galdós's *segunda manera* novels has employed narratological terminology for various purposes: to examine the narrative transaction between the author, the text, and the reader; to explore the connection between affective response, discoursive devices, ideological issues, and rhetorical strategies; and to consider the relationship between discursive technique and polyphony. In so doing, I have combined narratological practices with the theoretical concepts of reader response and rhetorical criticism, as well as with the ideological and stylistic concerns of Bakhtinian analysis. As such, my approach is typical of the applied form of "critical narratology" currently being practiced in conjunction with poststructuralist and postmodern theories of narrative.[12] Critical narratology is an extremely flexible method of inquiry because it is by definition a pluralistic endeavor which joins narratological terminology with any number of other theoretical programs. My own combination of critical concepts is merely one among many possibilities. Indeed, recent scholarship on English-language literature has shown how easily narratological concepts can be used to ground explorations of race, class, and gender from various critical orientations.[13] It is my hope that this study of Galdós's *segunda manera* has demonstrated that narratology, with its attention to narrative levels and the expression of perspective, can serve as a point of departure for other Galdosian scholars investigating socio-cultural aspects of literary representation.

---

[12] See Ingeborg Hoesterey, introduction, *Neverending Stories: Toward a Critical Narratology*, eds. Ann Fehn, Ingeborg Hoesterey, and Maria Tatar (Princeton: Princeton UP, 1992) 3-14.

[13] For example, see Susan S. Lanser, "Sexing the Narrative: Propriety, Desire, and the Engendering of Narratology," *Narrative* 3 (1995): 85-94; Robyn R. Warhol, "'Reader, Can You Imagine? No, You Cannot': The Narratee as Other in Harriet Jacobs's Text," *Narrative* 3 (1995): 57-72; Shlomith Rimmon-Kenan, "Narration, Doubt, Retrieval: Toni Morrison's *Beloved*," *Narrative* 4 (1996): 109-23; James Phelan, "Present Tense Narration, Mimesis, the Narrative Norm, and the Positioning of the Reader in *Waiting for the Barbarians*," *Understanding Narrative*, ed. James Phelan and Peter J. Rabinowitz (Columbus: Ohio State UP, 1994) 222-45; James Phelan, *Narrative as Rhetoric: Technique, Audiences, Ethics, Ideology* (Columbus: Ohio State UP, 1996); and various articles in Kathy Mezei, ed., *Ambiguous Discourse: Feminist Narratology and British Women Writers* (Chapel Hill: U of North Carolina P, 1996).

WORKS CITED

Alas, Leopoldo [Clarín]. *Galdós*. Madrid: Renacimiento, 1912. Vol. 1 of *Obras completas*. 4 vols.

Aldaraca, Bridget A. *El Ángel del Hogar: Galdós and the Ideology of Domesticity in Spain*. North Carolina Studies in the Romance Languages and Literatures 239. Chapel Hill: U of North Carolina P, 1991.

———. "The Revolution of 1868 and the Rebellion of Rosalía Bringas." *Anales Galdosianos* 18 (1983): 49-60.

Altman, Janet Gurkin. *Epistolarity: Approaches to a Form*. Columbus: Ohio State UP, 1982.

Andreu, Alicia G. "*La Cruz del Olivar* por Faustina Saez de Melgar: Un modelo literario en la vida de Isidora Rufete." *Anales Galdosianos* Anejo (1980).

———. *Galdós y la literatura popular*. Madrid: Sociedad General Española de Librería, 1982.

———. *Modelos diológicos en Galdós*. Purdue U Monographs in Romance Languages 27. Amsterdam: John Benjamins, 1989.

———. "*Tormento*: Un Discurso de Amantes." *Hispania* 72 (1989): 226-32.

Bahamonde, Ángel, and Jesús A. Martínez. *Historia de España: Siglo XIX*. Madrid: Cátedra, 1994.

Bakhtin, Mikhail. *The Dialogic Imagination*. Trans. Michael Holquist. Ed. Caryl Emerson and Michael Holquist. Austin: U of Texas P, 1981. Trans. of *Voprosy literatury i estetiki*. 1975.

———. *Problems of Dostoevsky's Poetics*. Trans. and ed. Caryl Emerson. Theory and History of Literature 8. Minneapolis: U of Minnesota P, 1984.

Bal, Mieke. *Narratology: Introduction to the Theory of Narrative*. Trans. Christine van Boheemen. Toronto: U of Toronto P, 1985.

Bally, Charles. "Le style indirect libre en français moderne." *Germanisch-Romanisch Monsatsschrift* 4 (1912): 549-56 and 597-606.

Banfield, Ann. *Unspeakable sentences: Narration and representation in the language of fiction*. Boston: Routledge and Kegan Paul, 1982.

Blanco, Alda. "Dinero, relaciones sociales y significación en *Lo prohibido*." *Anales Galdosianos* 18 (1983): 61-73.

Blanco Aguinaga, Carlos. "*El amigo Manso* y el 'ciclo céntrico de la sociedad'." *Nueva Revista de Filología Hispánica* 24: 419-37.

Bly, Peter A. "From Disorder to Order: The Pattern of *Arreglar* References in Galdós' *Tormento* and *La de Bringas*." *Neophilologus* 62 (1978): 392-405.

———. *Galdós's Novel of Historical Imagination: A Study of the Contemporary Novels*. Liverpool: Francis Cairns, 1983.

Bly, Peter A. *Pérez Galdós: La de Bringas.* Critical Guides to Spanish Texts 30. Grant & Cutler, 1981.

―――. *Vision and the Visual Arts in Galdós: A Study of the Novels and Newspaper Articles.* Liverpool: Francis Cairns, 1986.

Booth, Wayne C. *The Rhetoric of Fiction.* 2nd ed. Chicago: U of Chicago P, 1983.

Boudreau, H. L. "The Salvation of Torquemada: Determinism and Salvation in the Later Novels of Galdós." *Anales Galdosianos* 15 (1980): 113-28.

Braun, Lucille V. "The Novelistic Function of Mauricia la Dura in Galdós' *Fortunata y Jacinta.*" *Symposium* 31 (1977): 277-89.

Bravo Villasante, Carmen. "El naturalismo de Galdós y el mundo de *La desheredada.*" *Cuadernos Hispanoamericanos* 230 (1969): 479-86.

Brooks, J. L. "The Character of Doña Guillermina Pacheco in Galdós' Novel, *Fortunata y Jacinta.*" *Bulletin of Hispanic Studies* 38 (1961): 86-94.

Cardona, Rodolfo. "Nuevos enfoques críticos con referencia a la obra de Galdós." *Cuadernos Hispanoamericanos* 250-52 (1970-71): 58-72.

Cardwell, R. A. "Galdós' Early Novels and the *Segunda Manera*: A Case for a Total View." *Renaissance and Modern Studies* 15 (1971): 44-62.

Castillo, Debra A. "The Problematics of Teaching in *El amigo Manso.*" *Revista de Estudios Hispánicos* 19.2 (1985): 37-55.

Caudet, Francisco. "*El doctor Centeno*: La «educación sentimental» de Galdós." *Studies in Honor of Bruce W. Wardropper.* Ed. Dian Fox, et al. Newark DE: Juan de la Cuesta, 1989. 41-66.

Chamberlin, Vernon A. "Changing Patterns of Mechanistic Imagery in Galdós's Naturalistic and Postnaturalistic Novels." *Anales Galdosianos* 24 (1989): 61-67.

―――. "'Vamos a ver las fieras': Animal Imagery and the Protagonist in *La desheredada* and *Lo prohibido.*" *Anales Galdosianos* 23 (1988): 27-33.

Charnon-Deutsch, Lou. *Gender and Representation: Women in Spanish Realist Fiction.* Purdue U Monographs in Romance Languages 32. Amsterdam: John Benjamins, 1990.

―――. "Inhabited Space in Galdós' *Tormento.*" *Anales Galdosianos* 10 (1975): 35-43.

―――. "*La de Bringas* and the Politics of Domestic Power." *Anales Galdosianos* 20.1 (1985): 65-74.

Chatman, Seymour. *Coming to Terms: The Rhetoric of Narrative in Fiction and Film.* Ithaca: Cornell UP, 1990.

―――. "Narratological Empowerment." *Narrative* 1 (1993): 59-65.

―――. *Story and Discourse: Narrative Structure in Fiction and Film.* Ithaca: Cornell UP, 1978.

Clarke, A. H., and Eamonn Rodgers, ed. *Galdós' House of Fiction.* Llangrannog: Dolphin, 1991.

Cohn, Dorrit. *Transparent Minds: Narrative Modes for Presenting Consciousness in Fiction.* Princeton: Princeton UP, 1978.

Condé, Lisa P. "'El maldito corsé' in the Works of Pérez Galdós." *Romance Studies* 20 (1992): 7-20.

―――. *Stages in the Development of a Feminist Consciousness in Pérez Galdós (1843-1920).* Lampeter: Edwin Mellen, 1990.

Correa, Gustavo. "Pérez Galdós y la tradición calderoniana." *Cuadernos Hispanoamericanos* 250-52 (1970-71): 221-41.

―――. *El simbolismo religioso en las novelas de Pérez Galdós.* Madrid: Gredos, 1962.

Cossío, Manuel Bartolomé. "In Memorium: Galdós y Giner: Una carta de Galdós." *Boletín de la Institución Libre de Enseñanza* 44 (1920): 60-62.

Cuff, David. "The Structure and Meaning of Galdós' *Tormento.*" *Reflexión* 2 3-4 (1974-75): 159-67.

Culler, Jonathan. *Structuralist Poetics: Structuralism, Linguistics, and the Study of Literature*. Ithaca: Cornell UP, 1975.

Davies, G. A. "Galdós' *El amigo Manso*: An Experiment in Didactic Method." *Bulletin of Hispanic Studies* 39 (1962): 16-30.

Delgado, Luisa Elena. "'Más estragos que las revoluciones': Detallando lo feminino en *La de Bringas*." *Revista Hispánica Moderna* 48.1 (1995): 31-42.

Dendle, Brian J. "Isidora, the *mantillas blancas*, and the Attempted Assassination of Alfonso XII." *Anales Galdosianos* 17 (1982): 51-54.

————. "On the Supposed 'Naturalism' of Galdós: *La desheredada*." *Papers on Romance Literary Relations Discussed by the Romance Literary Relations Group, MLA, New York, Dec. 1978*. Ed. Hugh H. Chapman, Jr. University Park: Penn. State UP, 1980. 12-28.

Engler, Kay. *The Structure of Realism: The Novelas Contemporáneas of Benito Pérez Galdós*. North Carolina Studies in the Romance Languages and Literatures 184. Chapel Hill: North Carolina UP, 1977.

Eoff, Sherman H. *The Novels of Pérez Galdós: The Concept of Life as a Dynamic Process*. Saint Louis: Washington UP, 1954.

Feagin, Susan L. *Reading with Feeling: The Aesthetics of Appreciation*. Ithaca: Cornell UP, 1996.

Fedorchek, Robert M. "Rosalía and the Rhetoric of Dialogue in Galdós' *Tormento* and *La de Bringas*." *Revista de Estudios Hispánicos* 12 (1978): 199-216.

Fetterley, Judith. *The Resisting Reader: A Feminist Approach to American Fiction*. Bloomington: Indiana UP, 1978.

Franz, Thomas R. "Galdós the Pharmacist: Drugs and the Samaniego Pharmacy in *Fortunata y Jacinta*." *Anales Galdosianos* 22 (1987): 33-46.

Friedman, Norman. "Point of View in Fiction: The Development of a Critical Concept." *PMLA* 70 (1955): 1160-84.

Garma, Ángel. "Jacqueca, seudo-oligofrenia y delirio en un personaje de Galdós." *Ficción* (1958): 84-102.

Genette, Gérard. *Narrative Discourse: An Essay in Method*. Ithaca: Cornell UP, 1980.

————. *Narrative Discourse Revisited*. Ithaca: Cornell UP, 1988.

Gilman, Stephen. *Galdós and the Art of the European Novel: 1867-1887*. Princeton: Princeton UP, 1981.

————. "Narrative Presentation in «Fortunata y Jacinta»." *Revista Hispánica Moderna* 34 (1968): 288-301.

Gold, Hazel. "Francisco's Folly: Picturing Reality in Galdós' *La de Bringas*." *Hispanic Review* 54 (1986): 47-66.

————. *The Reframing of Realism: Galdós and the Discourses of the Nineteenth-Century Spanish Novel*. Durham: Duke UP, 1993.

Goldman, Peter B. "Juanito's *chuletas*: Realism and Worldly Philosophy in Galdós's *Fortunata y Jacinta*." *The Journal of the Midwest Modern Language Association* 18.1 (1985): 82-101.

Goldman, Peter B., and Andrés Villagrá. "Personajes y transformaciones en *Fortunata y Jacinta*." *Romance Quarterly* 39 (1992): 61-70.

Gordon, M. "'Lo que le falta a un enfermo le sobra a otro': Galdós' Conception of Humanity in *La desheredada*." *Anales Galdosianos* 12 (1977): 29-37.

————. "The Medical Background to Galdós' *La desheredada*." *Anales Galdosianos* 7 (1972): 67-77.

Gullón, Germán. *El narrador en la novela del siglo XIX*. Madrid: Taurus, 1976.

————. "Originalidad y sentido de *La desheredada*." *Anales Galdosianos* 17 (1982): 39-50.

————. "Unidad de «El doctor Centeno»." *Cuadernos Hispanoamericanos* 250-52 (1970-71): 579-85.

192   GALDÓS'S *SEGUNDA MANERA*

Gullón, Ricardo. "'El amigo Manso', de Galdós." *Mundo nuevo* 4 (1966): 59-65. Rpt. in *Técnicas de Galdós* 85-89.

———. "'El amigo Manso' entre Galdós y Unamuno." *Mundo nuevo* 4 (1966): 32-39. Rpt. in *Técnicas de Galdós*. 73-82.

———. *Galdós novelista moderno*. Madrid: Taurus, 1960. Madrid: Gredos, 1966.

———. *Técnicas de Galdós*. Madrid: Taurus, 1980.

Hemingway, Maurice. "Narrative Ambiguity and Situational Ethics in *La de Bringas*." Clarke and Rodgers, *Galdós' House of Fiction* 15-27.

Hernadi, Paul. "Dual Perspective: Free Indirect Discourse and Related Techniques." *Comparative Literature* 24 (1972): 32-43.

Hoddie, James H. "Galdós' *La de Bringas* in Light of Hegel's Views on Comedy." *Revista de Estudios Hispánicos* 17 (1983): 21-41.

Hoesterey, Ingeborg. Introduction. *Neverending Stories: Toward a Critical Narratology*. Eds. Ann Fehn, Ingeborg Hoesterey, and Maria Tatar. Princeton: Princeton UP, 1992.

Hough, Graham. "Narrative and Dialog in Jane Austen." *The Critical Quarterly* 12 (1970): 201-29.

Iser, Wolfgang. *The Act of Reading: A Theory of Aesthetic Response*. Baltimore: Johns Hopkins UP, 1978.

———. *The Implied Reader: Patterns of Communication in Prose Fiction from Bunyan to Beckett*. Baltimore: Johns Hopkins UP, 1974.

———. *Prospecting: From Reader Response to Literary Anthropology*. Baltimore: Johns Hopkins UP, 1989.

Jagoe, Catherine. *Ambiguous Angels: Gender in the Novels of Galdós*. Berkeley: U of California P, 1994.

———. "Disinheriting the Feminine: Galdós and the Rise of the Realist Novel in Spain." *Revista de Estudios Hispánicos* 27 (1993): 225-48.

Jahn, Manfred. "Windows of Focalization: Deconstructing and Reconstructing a Narratological Concept." *Style* 30 (1996): 241-67.

Kronik, John W. "*El amigo Manso* and the Game of Fictive Autonomy." *Anales Galdosianos* 12 (1977): 71-94.

———. "Narraciones interiores en *Fortunata y Jacinta*." *Homenaje a Juan López Morillas: De Cadalso a Aleixandre: Estudios sobre literatura e historia intelectual españolas*. Ed. José Amor y Vázquez, David Kossof. Madrid: Castalia, 1982. 275-91.

Krow-Lucal, Martha G. "Balzac, Galdós and Phrenology." *Anales Galdosianos* 18 (1983): 7-14.

———. "The Evolution of Encarnación Guillén in *La desheredada*." *Anales Galdosianos* 12 (1977): 21-28.

———. "El personaje recurrente en la obra de Galdós." *Textos y Contextos de Galdós*. Ed. John W. Kronik and Harriet Turner. Madrid: Castalia, 1994. 157-61.

Labanyi, J. M. "The political Significance of *La desheredada*." *Anales Galdosianos* 14 (1979): 51-58.

Lanser, Susan S. "Sexing the Narrative: Propriety, Desire, and the Engendering of Narratology." *Narrative* 3 (1995): 85-94.

Lida, Denah. "Sobre el 'krausismo' de Galdós." *Anales Galdosianos* 2 (1967): 1-27.

López, Ignacio-Javier. *Realismo y Ficción: La desheredada de Galdós y la novela de su tiempo*. Barcelona, PPU, 1989.

López-Baralt, Mercedes. "Sueños de mujeres: La voz de *anima* en *Fortunata y Jacinta*." *Hispanic Review* 55 (1987): 491-512.

López Muñoz, José Luis. "Felipe Centeno, un héroe oscuro e inédito." *Papeles de Son Armadans* 73. 219 (1979): 249-58.

López Sanz, Mariano. *Naturalismo y espiritualismo en la novelística de Galdós y Pardo Bazán*. Madrid: Pliegos, 1985.

Lowe, Jennifer. "Galdós' Presentation of Rosalía in *La de Bringas*." *Hispanófila* 50.2 (1974): 49-65.

———. "Spoken and unspoken: Soliloquy, Monologue, and Aside in some of Galdós' 'Novelas contemporáneas'." *Revista Canadiense de Estudios Hispánicos* 8 (1983): 110-20.

MacKay, Carol Hanbery. *Soliloquy in Nineteenth-Century Fiction*. Houndmills, Basingstoke, Hampshire: MacMillan P, 1987.

Meyers, Jeffrey. *Disease and the Novel, 1880-1960*. New York: St. Martin's Press, 1985.

Mezei, Kathy, ed. *Ambiguous Discourse: Feminist Narratology and British Women Writers*. Chapel Hill: U of North Carolina P, 1996.

Miller, Stephen. "*La de Bringas* as *Bildungsroman*: A Feminist Reading." *Romance Quarterly* 34 (1987): 189-99.

Miralles, Enrique. Introducción. *La desheredada*. By Benito Pérez Galdós. Barcelona: Planeta, 1992. IX-LXXXI.

———. "Galdós y el naturalismo." *Insula* 514 (1989): 15-16.

Montesinos, José F. Introducción. *Lo prohibido*. By Benito Pérez Galdós. Madrid: Castalia, 1971. 7-41.

———. *Galdós*. Madrid: Castalia, 1980. 3 vols. 1968-73.

Moreno Castillo, Gloria. "La unidad de tema en «El doctor Centeno»" *Actas del Primer Congreso Internacional de Estudios Galdosianos*. Madrid: Cabildo Insular de Gran Canaria, 1977. 382-96.

Nelles, William. "Getting Focalization into Focus." *Poetics Today* 11 (1990): 365-82.

Neumann, Anne Waldron. "Characterization and Comment in *Pride and Prejudice*: Free Indirect Discourse and the 'Double-voiced' Verbs of Speaking, Thinking, and Feeling." *Style* 20 (1986): 364-94.

Newton, Nancy A. "*El amigo Manso* and the Relativity of Reality." *Revista de Estudios Hispánicos* 7 (1973): 113-25.

Nimetz, Michael. *Humor in Galdós: A Study of the Novelas Contemporáneas*. New Haven: Yale UP, 1968.

Palley, Julián. "Aspectos de *La de Bringas*." *Kentucky Romance Quarterly* 16 (1969): 339-48.

Pascal, Roy. *The Dual Voice*. Manchester: Manchester UP, 1977.

Pattison, Walter T. *Benito Pérez Galdós*. TWAS 341. Boston: Twayne, 1975.

———. *El naturalismo: Historia externa de un movimiento literario, Benito Pérez Galdós*. Boston: Twayne, 1975.

Penuel, Arnold M. "Some Aesthetic Implications of Galdós' *El amigo Manso*." *Anales Galdosianos* 9 (1974): 145-48.

Percival, Anthony. "Melodramatic Metafiction in *Tormento*." *Kentucky Romance Quarterly* 31 (1984): 151-60.

Pérez Galdós, Benito. Prólogo. *El abuelo*. By Pérez Galdós. *Obras completas: Novelas*. Vol. 3. Ed. Federico Carlos Sainz de Robles. Madrid: Aguilar, 1970. 800-01.

———. Prólogo. *Casandra*. By Pérez Galdós. *Obras completas: Novelas*. Vol. 3. Ed. Federico Carlos Sainz de Robles. Madrid: Aguilar, 1970. 906-07.

———. Prólogo. *Los condenados*. By Pérez Galdós. *Obras completas: Novelas, Teatro, Miscelánea*. Vol. 6. Ed. Federico Carlos Sainz de Robles. Madrid: Aguilar, 1961. 695-704.

———. *La desheredada*. Ed. Enrique Miralles. Barcelona: Planeta, 1992.

———. *Obras completas: Novelas*. Ed. Federico Carlos Sainz de Robles. 3 vols. Madrid: Aguilar, 1970.

Pérez Galdós, Benito. "Observaciones sobre la novela contemporánea en España." *Ensayos de crítica literaria*. Ed. Laureano Bonet. Barcelona: Península, 1990. 105-20.

Phelan, James. *Narrative as Rhetoric: Technique, Audiences, Ethics, Ideology*. Columbus: Ohio State UP, 1996.

———. "Narrative Discourse, Literary Character, and Ideology." *Reading Narrative*. Ed. James Phelan. Columbus: Ohio State UP, 1989. 132-46.

———. "Present Tense Narration, Mimesis, the Narrative Norm, and the Positioning of the Reader in *Waiting for the Barbarians*." *Understanding Narrative*. Ed. James Phelan and Peter J. Rabinowitz. Columbus: Ohio State UP, 1994. 222-45.

———. "*Self-Help* for Narratee and Narrative Audience: How 'I' – and 'You'? – Read 'How'." *Style* 28 (1994): 350-65.

Preston, Elizabeth. "Implying Authors in *The Great Gatsby*." *Narrative* 5 (1997): 143-64.

Prince, Gerald. "Introduction to the Study of the Narratee." *Reader-Response Criticism: From Formalism to Post-Structuralism*. Ed. J. Tompkins. Baltimore: Johns Hopkins UP, 1980. 7-25.

Rabinowitz, Peter J. *Before Reading: Narrative Conventions and the Politics of Interpretation*. Ithaca: Cornell UP, 1987.

Randolph, E. Dale A. "A Source for Maxi Rubín in *Fortunata y Jacinta*." *Hispania* 51 (1968): 49-56.

Ribbans, Geoffrey. "'Amparando/Desamparando a Amparo': Some reflections on *El doctor Centeno* and *Tormento*." *Revista Canadiense de Estudios Hispánicos* 17 (1993): 495-524.

———. "Dos paseos de Fortunata por Madrid y su integración dentro de la estructura de la novela." *Hispania* 70 (1987): 740-45.

———. "Notes on the Narrator in *Fortunata y Jacinta*." Willem, *Sesquicentennial Tribute* 88-104.

———. *Pérez Galdós: Fortunata y Jacinta*. Critical Guides to Spanish Texts 21. London: Grant & Cutler, 1977.

———. "Social Document or Narrative Discourse? Some Comments on Recent Aspects of Galdós Criticism." Clarke and Rodgers, *Galdós' House of Fiction* 55-83.

Ricard, Robert. *Galdós et ses romans*. Paris: Center de Recherches de l'Institut d'Etudes Hispaniques, 1961.

Rimmon-Kenan, Shlomith. "Narration, Doubt, Retrieval: Toni Morrison's *Beloved*." *Narrative* 4 (1996): 109-23.

Rodgers, Eamonn. "The Appearance-Reality Contrast in Galdós' *Tormento*." *Forum for Modern Language Studies* 6 (1970): 382-98.

———. "Creative Asynchrony: The Moral Dynamism of *Lo prohibido*." *Crítica Hispánica* 13 (1991): 45-56.

———. *From Enlightenment to Realism: The Novels of Galdós 1870-1887*. Dublin: Jack Hade, 1987.

———. "Galdós' *La desheredada* and Naturalism." *Bulletin of Hispanic Studies* 45 (1968): 285-98.

———. "The Reception of Naturalism in Spain." *Naturalism in the European Novel: New Critical Perspectives*. Ed. Brian Nelson. Oxford: Berg, 1992. 120-34.

———. "The Unfinished Anagnorisis: the Illness and Death of José María Bueno de Guzmán in Galdós' *Lo prohibido*." Clarke and Rodgers, *Galdós' House of Fiction* 127-41.

Rodríguez, Rodney T. "Las máscaras del engaño en *Tormento*." *Actas del VIII Congreso de la Asociación Internacional de Hispanistas*. Vol. 2. Madrid: Ediciones Istmo, 1986. 517-24.

Rodríguez, Rodney T. "The Reader's Role in *Tormento:* A Reconstruction of the Pedro Polo Affair." *Anales Galdosianos* 24 (1989): 69-78.

——— "La unidad orgánica de la trilogía *Centeno-Tormento-Bringas.*" *Actas del Tercer Congreso Internacional de Estudios Galdosianos.* Vol. 2. Las Palmas: Cabildo Insular de Gran Canaria, 1989. 179-85.

Rogers, Douglass M. "Amparo, o la metamorfosis de la heroína galdosiana." *Selected Proceedings of the Mid-America Conference on Hispanic Literature.* Ed. Luis T. González-del-Valle and Catherine Nickel. Lincoln: SSSAS, 1986. 137-46.

Romero Pérez, Francisco. "The Grandeur of Galdós' Mauricia la Dura." *Hispanic Journal* 3.1 (1981): 107-14.

Rueda, Germán. *Historia de España: El reinado de Isabel II.* Madrid: Temas de Hoy, 1996.

Russell, Robert H. "Percepción, proporción y onomástica en *La de Bringas.*" *Actas del Cuarto Congreso Internacional de Estudios Galdosianos (1990).* Vol. 1. Las Palmas: Cabildo Insular de Gran Canaria, 1993. 817-22.

———. "The Structure of *La desheredada.*" *Modern Language Notes* 76 (1961): 794-800.

Rutherford, John. "Story, Character, Setting, and Narrative Mode in Galdós's *El amigo Manso.*" *Style and Structure in Literature: Essays in the New Stylistics.* Ed. Roger Fowler. Ithaca: Cornell UP, 1975. 177-212.

Sánchez, Roberto G. "The Function of Dates and Deadlines in Galdós' *La de Bringas.*" *Hispanic Review* 46 (1978): 299-311.

———. "«El sistema dialogal» en algunas novelas de Galdós." *Cuadernos Hispanoamericanos* 235 (1969): 155-67.

Scanlon, Geraldine M. "*El doctor Centeno*: a study in obsolescent values." *Bulletin of Hispanic Studies* 55 (1978): 245-53.

———. "Heroism in an Unheroic Society." *Modern Language Review* 79 (1984): 831-45.

Schimmel, René. "Algunos aspectos de la técnica de Galdós en la creación de Fortunata." *Archivum* 7 (1958): 77-100.

Schnepf, Michael A. "*El doctor Centeno* Manuscript: Pedro Polo and Other Curiosities." *Romance Quarterly* 41 (1994): 36-42.

———. "Galdós's *La desheredada* Manuscript: Isidora in the Prado Museum." *Romance Quarterly* 37 (1990): 321-29.

———. "The Manuscript of Galdós's *Tormento.*" *Anales Galdosianos* 26 (1991): 43-49.

———. "The Naturalistic Content of the *La desheredada* Manuscript." *Anales Galdosianos* 24 (1989): 53-59.

Shoemaker, William H. "Galdós' Classical Scene in *La de Bringas.*" *Hispanic Review* 27 (1959): 423-34. Rpt. in *Estudios sobre Galdós.* Madrid: Castalia, 1970. 145-58.

———. *The Novelistic Art of Galdós.* Vol. 2. Valencia: Albatros, 1980. 3 vols. 1980-82.

Sieburth, Stephanie. "The Dialectic of Modernity in *La desheredada.*" Willem, *Sesquicentennial Tribute* 27-40.

———. *Inventing High and Low: Literature, Mass Culture, and Uneven Modernity in Spain.* Durham: Duke UP, 1994.

Sinnigen, John H. "Galdós's *Tormento*: Political Partnership/Literary Structures." *Anales Galdosianos* 15 (1980): 73-82.

———. "Individual, Class, and Society in *Fortunata y Jacinta.*" Ed. Robert J. Weber. London: Tamesis, 1974. 49-68.

Smith, Alan E. "El epílogo a la primera edición de *La batalla de los Arapiles.*" *Anales Galdosianos* 17 (1982): 105-08.

Sobejano, Gonzalo. "Muerte del solitario: (Benito Pérez Galdós: *Fortunata y Jacinta*, 4.ª, II, 6)." *El comentario de textos, 3: La novela realista.* Madrid: Castalia, 1982. 201-54. Rpt. in *Fortunata y Jacinta de Benito Pérez Galdós.* Ed. Germán Gullón. Madrid: Taurus, 1986. 313-53.

Sontag, Susan. *Illness as Metaphor.* New York: Farrar, Straus, and Giroux, 1977.

Steele, Charles W. "The Krausist Educator as Depicted by Galdós." *Kentucky Foreign Language Quarterly* 5 (1958): 136-42.

Suleiman, Susan Rubin. *Authoritarian Fictions: The Ideological Novel as a Literary Genre.* New York: Columbia UP, 1983.

Terry, Anthony. "*Lo prohibido:* Unreliable Narrator and Untruthful Narrative." *Galdós Studies.* Ed. J. E. Varey. London: Tamesis, 1970. 62-89.

Tsuchiya, Akiko. "The Construction of the Female Body in Galdós's *La de Bringas.*" *Romance Quarterly* 40 (1993): 35-47.

———. *Images of the Sign: Semiotic Consciousness in the Novels of Benito Pérez Galdós.* Columbia: U of Missouri P, 1990.

Turner, Harriet S. "The Control of Confusion and Clarity in *El amigo Manso.*" *Anales Galdosianos* 15 (1980): 45-61.

———. "¿Es Manso un pobre hombre?" *Actas del Segundo Congreso Internacional de Estudios Galdosianos.* Vol. 2. Las Palmas: Cabildo Insular, 1980. 383-99.

———. "Strategies in Narrative Point of View: On Meaning and Morality in the Galdós Novel." *Homenaje a Antonio Sánchez Barbudo: Ensayos de literatura española moderna.* Ed. Benito Brancaforte, Edward R. Mulvihill, Roberto G. Sánchez. Madison: Wisconsin UP, 1981.

Ullman, Joan Connelly, and George H. Allison. "Galdós as Psychiatrist in *Fortunata y Jacinta.*" *Anales Galdosianos* 9 (1974): 7-36.

Ullmann, Stephen. *Style in the French Novel.* New York: Barnes & Noble, 1964.

Urey, Diane F. *Galdós and the irony of language.* Cambridge: Cambridge UP, 1982.

———. "Repetition, Discontinuity and Silence in Galdós's *Tormento.*" *Anales Galdosianos* 20.1 (1985): 47-63.

Van Ess-Dykema, Carol Joy. "The Historical Present in Oral Spanish Narratives." Diss. Georgetown U, 1984.

Warhol, Robyn R. "'Reader, Can You Imagine? No, You Cannot': The Narratee as Other in Harriet Jacobs's Text." *Narrative* 3 (1995): 57-72.

Whiston, James. "Determinism and freedom in *Fortunata y Jacinta.*" *Bulletin of Hispanic Studies* 57 (1980): 113-27.

———. "Ironía y psicología en *Lo prohibido* de Galdós." *Romance Quarterly* 37 (1990): 199-208.

———. "The Materialism of Life: Religion in *Fortunata y Jacinta.*" *Anales Galdosianos* 14 (1979): 65-81.

———. "The struggle for Life in 'Fortunata y Jacinta'." *The Modern Language Review* 79.1 (1984): 77-87.

Willem, Linda M. "Moreno-Isla's Unpublished Scene from the *Fortunata y Jacinta* Galleys." *Anales Galdosianos* 27-28 (1992-93): 179-83.

———. "The Narrative Premise of Galdós's *Lo prohibido.*" *Romance Quarterly* 38 (1991): 189-96.

———. "The Narrative Voice Presentation of Rosalía de Bringas in Two Galdosian Novels." *Crítica Hispánica* 12 (1990): 75-87.

———, ed. *A Sesquicentennial Tribute to Galdós 1843-1993.* Newark DE: Juan de la Cuesta, 1993.

———. "Turning *La incógnita* into *Realidad*: Galdós's Metafictional Magic Trick." *MLN* 105: 385-91.

Wolfson, Nessa. "The Conversational Historical Present Altercation." *Language* 55 (1979): 168-82.

INDEX

Discoursive devices. *See* Narrative voice
Dostoevsky, Feodor, 32, 92
Double-voicing. *See* Point of view
Dramatic monologue. *See* Narrative voice,
    direct speech

Engler, Kay, 34-35, 77n36, 151, 174
Eoff, Sherman H., 180n3

Feagin, Susan L., 19-20, 133, 145
Fedorchek, Robert M., 35, 138n42
Fetterley, Judith, 26
Flaubert, Gustave, 16, 42, 52
Franz, Thomas R., 89n46
Friedman, Norman, 17-18, 150

Garma, Ángel, 89n46
Genette, Gérard, 14nn5-6, 16, 17n13,
    103n6, 153n9
Gilman, Stephen, 52, 75, 136
Gold, Hazel, 100-01, 113n16, 143
Goldman, Peter B., 72n30, 92n48
Gordon, M., 61n21, 180n3
Gullón, Germán, 68, 100n2, 103,
    124n28
Gullón, Ricardo, 45-46, 79, 92n48, 92-
    93, 136, 149n2, 153n10, 180n3

Hemingway, Maurice, 136
Hernadi, Paul, 17
Hoddie, James H., 140n44
Hoesterey, Ingeborg, 13, 187n12
Hough, Graham, 16

Irony, 37, 52-53, 55-58, 67-68, 77, 97,
    106, 118-19, 130-34, 136, 138, 143,
    153-55, 153n9, 160, 163-65, 170-72,
    178, 183
Iser, Wolfgang, 11, 21-27, 33, 75, 115,
    154

Jagoe, Catherine, 26-27, 29n28, 30-31,
    83, 138n41, 158n18, 181n5
Jahn, Manfred, 14n5
Joyce, James, 43-46

Krausism, 154, 157-58, 179
Kronik, John W., 92n47, 149n2
Krow-Lucal, Martha G., 159, 180n3

Labanyi, J. M., 60
Lanser, Susan S., 187n13
Lazarillo de Tormes, 112

Lida, Denah, 106n10, 154
López, Ignacio-Javier, 55n13
López-Baralt, Mercedes, 84n41
López Muñoz, José Luis, 106
López Sanz, Mariano, 180n3
Lowe, Jennifer, 35, 46, 136

MacKay, Carol Hanbery, 20, 119-20
Martínez, Jesús A., 28n26, 70n28
Meyers, Jeffrey, 111n15
Mezei, Kathy, 187n13
Miller, Stephen, 136, 138n41
Miralles, Enrique, 63n24, 180n3
Montesinos, José F., 100, 115, 136, 169,
    180n3
Moreno Castillo, Gloria, 101n4

Narrative techniques
    character-narration, 66, 91-94, 92n47,
        97
    filtered description, 37, 87-89, 97,
        103-05, 104n8, 123, 146, 182-83
    present tense narration, 37, 61-63,
        84-85, 106-11, 125-26, 146, 182-83,
        187n13
    presupposition, 44-45, 44n5, 47, 86,
        95, 182
    theatrical formatting (*sistema dia-
        logal*), 37, 61, 63-65, 97, 183-86
Narrative voice (discoursive devices)
    direct speech, tagged and free (di-
        alogue/dramatic monologue), 15-16,
        65-66, 76-78, 83-84, 89-90, 93-94,
        101-02, 109, 112, 120-21, 123, 129,
        131-32, 142-43, 146, 156, 160, 175,
        180-81, 185-86
    direct thought, tagged and free, 15-
        17, 20, 37, 42-49, 51, 57-61, 65, 76,
        78, 80-83, 88-90, 93-96, 101, 105-07,
        109, 111, 116, 121, 124-27, 132-33,
        137-40, 142, 146, 174-75, 182-83, 185
    free indirect speech, 15-17, 34-35, 37,
        76-78, 77n35, 97, 105, 118, 122-23,
        143, 146, 160-63
    free indirect style, 16-17, 34, 42, 52,
        55, 77, 87, 97, 118, 183. *See also* free in-
        direct speech; free indirect thought
    free indirect thought, 15-17, 20, 34,
        37, 49-53, 55-58, 61-62, 65, 76-83,
        89, 93, 96-97, 101, 105-08, 110-11,
        118-21, 124-26, 132-33, 137-40, 146,
        175, 182-83
    indirect speech, 15-16, 143, 146

NORTH CAROLINA STUDIES IN THE ROMANCE LANGUAGES AND LITERATURES

I.S.B.N. Prefix 0-8078-

Recent Titles

"EL ÁNGEL DEL HOGAR". GALDÓS AND THE IDEOLOGY OF DOMESTICITY IN SPAIN, by Bridget A. Aldaraca. 1991. (No. 239). *-9243-2.*

IN THE PRESENCE OF MYSTERY: MODERNIST FICTION AND THE OCCULT, by Howard M. Fraser. 1992. (No. 240). *-9244-0.*

THE NOBLE MERCHANT: PROBLEMS OF GENRE AND LINEAGE IN "HERVIS DE MES", by Catherine M. Jones. 1993. (No. 241). *-9245-9.*

JORGE LUIS BORGES AND HIS PREDECESSORS OR NOTES TOWARDS A MATERIALIST HISTORY OF LINGUISTIC IDEALISM, by Malcolm K. Read. 1993. (No. 242). *-9246-7.*

DISCOVERING THE COMIC IN "DON QUIXOTE", by Laura J. Gorfkle. 1993. (No. 243). *-9247-5.*

THE ARCHITECTURE OF IMAGERY IN ALBERTO MORAVIA'S FICTION, by Janice M. Kozma. 1993. (No. 244). *-9248-3.*

THE "LIBRO DE ALEXANDRE". MEDIEVAL EPIC AND SILVER LATIN, by Charles F. Fraker. 1993. (No. 245). *-9249-1.*

THE ROMANTIC IMAGINATION IN THE WORKS OF GUSTAVO ADOLFO BÉCQUER, by B. Brant Bynum. 1993. (No. 246). *-9250-5.*

MYSTIFICATION ET CRÉATIVITÉ DANS L'OEUVRE ROMANESQUE DE MARGUERITE YOURCENAR, par Beatrice Ness. 1994. (No. 247). *-9251-3.*

TEXT AS TOPOS IN RELIGIOUS LITERATURE OF THE SPANISH GOLDEN AGE, by M. Louise Salstad. 1995. (No. 248). *-9252-1.*

CALISTO'S DREAM AND THE CELESTINESQUE TRADITION: A REREADING OF *CELESTINA*, by Ricardo Castells. 1995. (No. 249). *-9253-X.*

THE ALLEGORICAL IMPULSE IN THE WORKS OF JULIEN GRACQ: HISTORY AS RHETORICAL ENACTMENT IN *LE RIVAGE DES SYRTES* AND *UN BALCON EN FORÊT*, by Carol J. Murphy. 1995. (No. 250). *-9254-8.*

VOID AND VOICE: QUESTIONING NARRATIVE CONVENTIONS IN ANDRÉ GIDE'S MAJOR FIRST-PERSON NARRATIVES, by Charles O'Keefe. 1996. (No. 251). *-9255-6.*

EL CÍRCULO Y LA FLECHA: PRINCIPIO Y FIN, TRIUNFO Y FRACASO DEL *PERSILES*, por Julio Baena. 1996. (No. 252). *-9256-4.*

EL TIEMPO Y LOS MÁRGENES. EUROPA COMO UTOPÍA Y COMO AMENAZA EN LA LITERATURA ESPAÑOLA, por Jesús Torrecilla. 1996. (No. 253). *-9257-2.*

THE AESTHETICS OF ARTIFICE: VILLIERS'S *L'EVE FUTURE*, by Marie Lathers. 1996. (No. 254). *-9254-8.*

DISLOCATIONS OF DESIRE: GENDER, IDENTITY, AND STRATEGY IN *LA REGENTA*, by Alison Sinclair. 1998. (No. 255). *-9259-9.*

THE POETICS OF INCONSTANCY, ETIENNE DURAND AND THE END OF RENAISSANCE VERSE, by Hoyt Rogers. 1998. (No. 256). *-9260-2.*

RONSARD'S CONTENTIOUS SISTERS: THE PARAGONE BETWEEN POETRY AND PAINTING IN THE WORKS OF PIERRE DE RONSARD, by Roberto E. Campo. 1998. (No. 257). *-9261-0.*

THE RAVISHMENT OF PERSEPHONE: EPISTOLARY LYRIC IN THE *SIÈCLE DES LUMIÈRES,* by Julia K. De Pree. 1998. (No. 258). *-9262-9.*

CONVERTING FICTION: COUNTER REFORMATIONAL CLOSURE IN THE SECULAR LITERATURE OF GOLDEN AGE SPAIN, by David H. Darst. 1998. (No. 259). *-9263-7.*

GALDÓS'S *SEGUNDA MANERA*: RHETORICAL STRATEGIES AND AFFECTIVE RESPONSE, by Linda M. Willem. 1998. (No. 260) *-9264-5.*

A MEDIEVAL PILGRIM'S COMPANION. REASSESSING *EL LIBRO DE LOS HUÉSPEDES* (ESCORIAL MS. h.I.13), by Thomas D. Spaccarelli. 1998. (No. 261) *-9265-3.*

When ordering please cite the *ISBN Prefix* plus the last four digits for each title.

Send orders to: University of North Carolina Press
                   P.O. Box 2288
                   CB# 6215
                   Chapel Hill, NC 27515-2288
                   U.S.A.